KENT AT WAR

The Unconquered County

1939 — 1945

by Bob Ogley

This illustrated history of the second world war relives the drama, the heroism and the horrors as they unfolded in Kent — a county in which many people were nearer to occupied Europe than they were to their own capital city. All the great events are here: mobilisation, the evacuation, the phoney war, Dunkirk, the Battle of Britain, the Blitz, the fighter sweeps from Kent airfields, D-Day, the flying bombs and rockets and VE Day in May 1945. This is not just a story of countless fighting men and women but of the ordinary people of the front line county, from the misery of ration queues and austerity clothing to the delights of Vera Lynn and the flicks. Most of the photographs come from the archives of the Kent Messenger and they cannot fail to stir powerful emotions as they bring back memories of the most dramatic years in the county's history.

Froglets Publications in association with Kent Messenger Group Newspapers

Froglets Publications Ltd

Brasted Chart,
Westerham, Kent TN16 1LY.

Tel: 01959 562972
Fax: 01959 565365

© Bob Ogley   Photographs Kent Messenger (unless otherwise stated).

ISBN 1 872337 82 1 (paperback) ISBN 1 872337 49 X (hardback)

Back cover illustration: Canterbury Cathedral sandbagged

This book was originated by Froglets Publications Ltd, printed and bound by Staples Printers Rochester Ltd, Neptune Close, Medway City Estate, Rochester, Kent ME2 4LT.

Jacket design by Alison Stammers

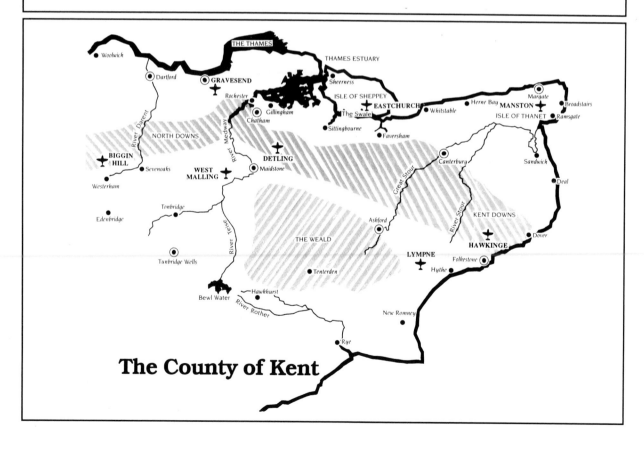

The County of Kent

Invicta — the unconquered county

THIS photographic history of the war years in Kent is a hybrid of journalism and history and contains pictures and stories of all the momentous events as they unfolded in the county. The inclusion of more than 200 photographs — most of them from the *Kent Messenger's* extraordinary archives — will not only make the book more appealing but stir powerful emotions. Those showing bomb damage, crashed aircraft and lost pilots may shock and upset but many will be humbled by the photographs of courage and resilience displayed by so many "ordinary people".

It is appropriate to pay tribute to the cameramen who saw, through their journalistic training, history as it was being made and recorded it for future generations (such as ours) to see. They knew at the time that Kent was the bastion of Britain and defender of London; a county that was experiencing all the vicissitudes of war except conquest. With the enemy in sight, threatened every day by bombs, incendiaries, rockets, shells, shrapnell — and invasion— they continued to do their job quite brilliantly. Ted Jeffries and brothers, Don and Stan Gullivan were the more permanent of the photographic staff between 1939 and 1945. To them and colleagues who came and went, we dedicate this book.

The former editor and proprietor of the *Kent Messenger*, the late Henry Roy Pratt Boorman published a photographic book of the war years in 1951. It was called Kent Unconquered. The quality of the pictures in that book inspired this publication and I am grateful to the Boorman family for their efforts in preserving much of the heritage of Kent.

The appetite for news in wartime was almost insatiable and a glance at the newspaper files confirms the obvious desire of the editor to report as much as possible. But so much at the time was secret, so much propaganda and so much confusion in the "fog of war" that truth was rather elusive. Added to that was the policy of censorship. No locations could be given, apart from the rather inadequate "somewhere in the south of England".

In this book we have reported what actually happened rather than what was said. We have tracked down locations, given the exact date and, in many cases, named the people involved. In this way we believe we have captured the drama and immediacy of the war years in Kent.

It includes, not only the most famous events such as Dunkirk, the Battle of Britain and D Day, but material about German activities, the county's secret army, the heroism of the soldier overseas, the great deception and much more.

Special features include all those from Kent who won the Victoria and George Cross, a list of casualty figures and every V2 rocket which fell in the county. We have a special section on the Maids of Kent, and the Kentish Maids, who left their homes and offices for the Land Army, the voluntary services or to be nurses or skilled mechanics. We have described the connection with the county of people such as William Joyce (Lord Haw Haw), William Penney, the physicist, General Sikorski, the Polish PM in exile and a few of the greatest aviators.

Those who played a leading part at the time will not forget the battle zones or the home front. They will recall the ration queues and austerity clothing. They will remember Vera Lynn and Glenn Miller, the twice weekly trip to the flicks and the spirit of camaraderie in the shelters and tunnels within the cliffs. Every Kent town had a British Restaurant, a rest centre and exchange store; and every Kent town contributed towards a squadron of Spitfires.

That Squadron was called Invicta. Invicta is the emblem of the county and the *Kent Messenger*. It simply means unconquered.

Acknowledgements

THIS book would not have been possible without the co-operation of many people and I would like to thank those who responded to my appeal for anecdotes and reminiscences and to those individuals who sent photographs. Practical help came from many quarters including The British Library, David Parry at the Imperial War Museum, the Kent County Records Office, the Public Records Office, English Heritage and museum staff through the county. I would particularly like to thank those in the local history departments of Folkestone, Bromley, Canterbury, Dover, Gravesend, Dartford, Ramsgate, Margate, Ashford, Sittingbourne, Bexley and Maidstone Leisure Centre, where I spent many hours looking through the bound copies of old newspapers. Great assistance came from John Iveson, curator of Dover Museum, Tom White of Kent Fire Brigade, Gordon McElwee, Peter Osborne, Hazel Pelling, Gordon Anckorn, Frank Chapman, Elizabeth Whittingham. Finally, I would like to thank William Dorrell, managing director of *Kent Messenger Group Newspapers* for his confidence in the project, Barry Hollis, picture editor and the staff of the KM for their support. The preparation of this book has been, in happiest manner, a combined operation among the staff of Froglets Publications. Jill Goldsworthy, Avril Oswald and Sarah Perkins helped with research, typesetting and the reading of proofs. Fern Flynn was involved with the production at all stages and without her optimistic and trusting support this book would have taken many more months to produce.

1939
The countdown to war

February: Jewish refugees, fleeing Germany, Austria and Czechoslovakia, were billeted at Richborough Camp, near Sandwich. Total grew to more than 3,500 as the year progressed.

March: Britain promised to support Poland in the event of a German invasion. Kent's anti-aircraft batteries, including all the territorial units, were strengthened.

April: Military conscription was introduced.

May: Italy and Germany signed the "Pact of Steel". Germany signed a non-aggression pact with Denmark.

June: Hundreds of Jews were deported from Germany to Poland. The RAF were said to be producing 750 aircraft a month.

July: Kent was one of 15 counties chosen to take part in a test black-out during July 8th-9th. Churchill proposed a military alliance with Russia.

August: British negotiations with Russia broke down and the German Foreign Minister was invited to Moscow, followed by the signing of the Nazi-

Kent was teetering on the brink of war but the sense of humour which was to prevail throughout is clearly reflected by this placard on the back of the car. The driver, from Maidstone, was determined that his family's seaside holiday was not going to be spoilt.

Soviet pact. The British Government announced that it stood by its promise to Poland. On August 24th military reservists were called up and ARP services warned to stand ready. More than 2,000 of Kent's refugees volunteered for National Service. Many become part of the Royal Pioneer Corps. All place names visible from the air were ordered to be obliterated. Special attention was given to gasholders which contained the name of the town in which they were situated.

September: German troops invaded Poland on September 1st. Black-out began in Kent on same day. Thousands of children, mothers, teachers and disabled from Medway towns moved to reception centres to prepare for evacuation.

September 3rd: Kent's first war baby, a boy, was born to Mrs A.F.Prentice at Holly Mount, Platt, 20 minutes after war was declared. Two hours later, Mrs Reginald Copper of Shipbourne Road, Tonbridge gave birth to a son.

September 4th: An appeal for blood donors was made throughout Kent. At Maidstone five doctors, three nurses, six VAD nurses and four scientists were dealing with 200 volunteers a day. They had sufficient cold storage for 2,000 bottles of blood.

October: First reported death of Kent person during the war was Engine Room Artificer, Herbert Smith, aged 30, of Chartham who died when HMS Kittiwake was struck by a mine.

November: In an Armistice Day broadcast, the Queen appealed to all women to show fortitude.

Kent didn't want to go to war, for memories of the bloody slaughter of 1914-18 were too fresh in the mind. But the county was ready for it and in the pubs and clubs people spoke about the possibility of air bombardment and, even worse, a gas attack. A handbook produced by the government explained how the poisonous gases used in the trenches in 1917 were likely to be a feature of this modern conflict. Gas masks were issued to all men, women and children and the order was given to organise mock gas attacks. At Beltring hop farm in the late summer of 1939, the hop pickers practised working with their gas masks on. The box that contained the mask was seen everywhere — in schools, in offices, at football matches — for to be without one was a punishable offence.

Late summer 1939. Three children, carrying the boxes that contain their gas mask, watch the harvesting at Westerham. War seems a long way off.

The storm breaks...

THERE was confusion in the summer of 1939 and, as confrontation became inevitable, there was fear. Appeasement, as the attempt by Britain and France to placate the dictators was known, was not going to work, but the brief respite won at Munich gave Britain the opportunity to prepare for war — and for the defence of the civilian population. While aircraft production trebled, urgent preparations were made for the evacuation of children from major cities, the provision of air raid shelters and gas masks and the welding of voluntary organisations into a vast national service.

Hitler's ranting broadcasts chilled the soul. While the British Prime Minister, Neville Chamberlain, clung to the hope that Europe might be heading for a period of tranquillity, the Führer was ready to pounce. In March 1939 he seized the rest of Czechoslavakia gaining an enormous strategic coup in eliminating at a stroke the efficiency of the Czech army and acquiring the great Skoda arms works. He then began to menace Poland, knowing that Britain and France had guaranteed to go to her aid in the event of an invasion.

As the deepening crisis began to intrude on everyday life, the people of Kent knew that all the main pieces were in place for the conflict to come. The only question was when. ARP services had already been mobilised and cellars and basements requisitioned for air raid shelters. Dover was fitting out the tunnels under the White Cliffs, Chislehurst was preparing its vast underground network of caves and Swanscombe had re-opened its extensive lime pits. Air raid exercises had been held in most towns, decontamination centres opened and volunteers were being trained in methods of gas proofing rooms.

In April, military conscription was introduced. In June, an appeal for blood donors brought 5,000 offers to the Centre in Maidstone. In July, a test black-out was held in every district in the county. In August, priceless stained glass windows were removed from Canterbury Cathedral. On September 1st, German troops invaded Poland.

Identical British and French warnings were delivered to Berlin telling Hitler to withdraw his troops and warning him what the consequences would be. The ultimatum was timed to expire at 11am on Sunday September 3rd.

The Hurricanes of 32 Squadron — scrambled on the morning of September 3rd.

...and the wailing begins

THAT fateful Sunday dawned brightly and many tensions were relieved by the sunshine — but not for long. At 11 o'clock, in clear, resonant tones and not without traces of emotion, came the Prime Minister's historic announcement. "....I have to tell you that no such undertaking has been received and that consequently this country is at war with Germany....".

Among those listening to their wireless sets were the pilots of RAF Biggin Hill where three fighter squadrons were billeted. The Hurricanes of 32 and 79 and the Blenheims of 601 stood, fuelled, armed and ready for instant take-off. In the Sector Operations room controllers and operators listened to the words of Neville Chamberlain. "Now may God bless you all. May He defend the right...."

His words had hardly died away before there was a wail of air-raid sirens. An aeroplane had been flying across the Channel towards the Thames Estuary and a tell-tale blip in the coastal radio-location stations gave warning of its approach. Nearer land it was picked up by the vigilant men of the Observer Corps. The defence network sprang into life. For Biggin Hill the war had begun and 32 Squadron was quickly in action. "Blue Section", shouted the Controller over the station tannoy, "patrol Gravesend, 5,000 feet. Scramble."

A few minutes later the Hurricanes were recalled. The suspect had landed at Croydon. It was a French transport bringing a party of Staff officers to London!

The people of Kent heard the air-raid warning and responded calmly. There was no panic. They made hurried tracks for the shelters and waited for the All Clear. There was one exception. A milkman delivering to a home in Tonbridge was invited to come in but declined. "I've got my round to do", he told Bill Williams, a *Courier* reporter. He went off down the road in his milk float!

500 (County of Kent) Auxiliary Squadron had been stationed at Detling Airfield since September 1938 where they were equipped with Anson Is for Coastal Command. A few weeks before war was declared 500 Squadron was transferred to Warmwell in Dorset for two weeks, before returning to Detling where the airmen were to remain until May 1941. Here they are at Maidstone Barracks Station, waiting for the train to take them to Dorset on August 1st, 1939.

SEPTEMBER 1939: THE RAF IN KENT

THIRTEEN RAF Squadrons were based on the Kent airfields — Biggin Hill, Manston, Hawkinge, Lympne, Detling and Gravesend — at the outbreak of war. Fighter Command controlled seven, Coastal Command, three, Bomber Command, one and Fleet Air Arm, two. One Squadron was attached to the air component of the Army. In addition there were two elementary and reserve flying schools. Eastchurch, on the Isle of Sheppey, was a care and maintenance base until the arrival of the Polish Air Force in December, 1939. The order of battle was as follows:

2 Squadron were at Hawkinge, flying Hector 1s. They converted to Lysander 1s and, on September 6th, joined the Air Component of the BEF based at Abbeville-Drucat.

3 Squadron were briefly at Manston having converted from Gladiators to Hurricanes. They moved to Croydon but left a detachment at Hawkinge for two months. In February 1940 the whole squadron flew out to Merville, France.

21 Squadron had a detachment at Detling for anti-submarine duties in the Channel. Later in 1939 they converted to Beauforts.

25 Squadron flew Blenheims from Hawkinge.

32 Squadron were at Biggin Hill. They converted to Hurricanes and moved to Gravesend in March 1940.

48 Squadron flew on coastal duties operating Anson Is. As war was declared they were transferred to Thorney Island but left a detachment at Detling.

79 Squadron was based at Biggin Hill flying Hurricanes. In November, 1939 they moved to Manston.

235 and 253 Squadrons were both formed on November 30th at Manston, one flying the single engine Fairey Battles and the other Hurricanes.

500 Squadron flew Anson Is from Detling.

601 Squadron was partly mobilised with Hurricanes and flew from Biggin Hill with 79 and 32 Squadrons.

Two Fleet Air Arms' Squadrons (816 and 818) were formed at Manston and the two training units were at Rochester.

Bye-bye mum, see you when the war is over

BY the evening of Sunday September 3rd, the mass evacuation of children from London and the Medway towns to reception areas considered safe from air attack, was almost complete. Thousands were received by families in Kent towns and villages. Each child was labelled with name, address and school number and carried a gas mask and the necessary clothing. They were marshalled at railway stations and issued with blank tickets, but no destinations were given.

In Sevenoaks, the London evacuees were placed in cattle pens at Sevenoaks Market where they waited until being transferred to local homes. They all wore warm coats for the cold weather, but it was hot and dusty.

People who had volunteered to have children in their care claimed those who most appealed to them. It was a humiliating experience for some. Others found homes immediately and settled down quickly to a strange life in the country.

One little boy, living on a farm in Aylesford, wrote to his mother in Penge after a few days: "Do come and see me mummy, but bring your gas mask because the pigs smell".

Boys from Rochester wave farewell.

Ready for the great evacuation, the children from Snodland thought it was a wonderful adventure. Below: Scholars from Ordnance Place, Chatham leave for the station. Country areas in Kent were at that time "reception areas". The object was to sprinkle the children of the Medway Towns all over England. North Kent was widely expected to be bombed immediately.

Boys from King's School, Rochester were evacuated to Scotney Castle where they are seen with the owners Mr and Mrs Hussey. Others went to Bayham Abbey and to the WRNS Warren School in the Ashdown Forest. Part of the Billingsgate fish market was evacuated to Maidstone where the fish porters set up shop in a garage. They remained there for a year and only moved when the Battle of Britain turned Maidstone into a high-risk area.

Meanwhile, London children were arriving in Kent towns. At the Agricultural Hall, Maidstone they were given a cup of tea before being taken to their new homes. Maidstone was a reception area and so, incredibly, was Dover!

Churchill entertains the former French Prime Minister, Leon Blum at Chartwell in May 1939. With them are Clementine (with fox cub) and Richard Law (son of former Conservative Prime Minister, Andrew Bonar Law), a Conservative MP who had, like Churchill, opposed the Munich agreement. M. Blum was in England to discuss the question of conscription.

He's back: Churchill joins War Cabinet

FOR many years Winston Churchill had been warning against Neville Chamberlain's policy of appeasement, telling the House of Commons that Britain was making terms for herself at the expense of small nations. After the Munich agreement had been signed and Czechoslovakia had been forced to give up some of its territory, Churchill said: "What I find unendurable is the sense of our country falling into the power, into the orbit and influence of Nazi Germany". He also spoke against the persecution of the Jews. "It is a horrible thing", he said, "that a race of people should be attempted to be blotted out of the society in which they have been born."

During this period he lived mostly at Chartwell,

Westerham, painting, writing and preparing speeches. The Press began to call, with increasing force, for his return to the Cabinet but the Government still rejected his advice and individual members continued to belittle his judgement. But his years in the wilderness were almost over.

On the day that war was declared, Winston Churchill joined the War Cabinet as First Lord of the Admiralty, the job that had been his between 1911 and 1915. Three months later he reached his 65th birthday, for many men the age of retirement. His energy, however, seemed unbounded and his determination to see Hitler defeated, despite the enormous German superiority, was obvious.

Offensive action may now begin — Hitler

THIS was the directive issued by Adolf Hitler on September 3rd, 1939: "Offensive action may now begin. In carrying out the war against merchant shipping, submarines also, for the time being, will observe prize regulations. Intensified measures leading to the declaration of danger zones will be prepared. I shall decide when these measures shall become effective. Attacks upon English naval forces at naval bases or on the high seas and on definitely identified troop transports will only be made in the event of English air attacks on similar targets and where there are particularly good prospects of success. This applies also to action by the Kustenfliegergruppen. I reserve to myself the decision about attacks on the English homeland and on merchant shipping".

Torpedoed by a German U-Boat

BY September 3rd, 80 per cent of Germany's ocean-going submarines had already been deployed around Britain and, as war was declared, the signal was radioed to open hostilities. The commander of one V30 German U-Boat identifying what he thought was a British armed merchantman, south of Rockall, fired two torpedoes and hit his target. It turned out to be the 13,500-ton Donaldson liner *Athenia*, sailing from Glasgow to Montreal with 1,418 people on board. 112 passengers and crew died. They were the first casualties of the war and the incident was a blunder which embarrassed the Nazis.

Among those who helped to rescue others was a young American, Jim Goodson, destined to become one of the most famous squadron commanders in the Eighth Air Force, credited with 32 aircraft destroyed, and a man who was to live in retirement in East Kent, hard by the airfields where he used to land his Spitfires, and Thunderbolts.

Jim Goodson remembered the powerful explosion which opened up a gaping hole in the hull of the *SS Athenia*. "I gazed down at a sort of Dante's Inferno", he later wrote. "At the bottom was a churning mass of water on which floated broken bits of stairway, flooring and furniture. Terrified people were clinging to this flotsam. Others were floundering in the water. Many were screaming that they couldn't swim and some were already close to drowning."

The American plunged into the water and, one by one, dragged the bodies to the foot of the broken companionway and left them to clamber up to other rescuers. He then went into the water, first to the children, and swam to the foot of the dangling steps. The Scots crew shouted encouragement — 'bloody guid, mon, keep 'em coming'. The ship listed but Goodson continued with his rescue job until there were no more to save.

By then the ship's lifeboats had been launched and Jim Goodson had no option but to jump into the water and strike out in the direction of a boat. It was full of passengers — Jewish, English, Polish and American — and no more were wanted. Goodson said: "I expected helping hands to lift me into the boat but instead a young man, screaming in a foreign language put his hand to my face to push me away. A frantic middle-aged woman was prising my fingers off the side of the boat. I heard the voices of the seaman in charge telling them to stop".

The American finally clambered on his lifeboat and was rescued by the crew of a Norwegian tanker. With this traumatic early experience, he decided not to wait for America to enter the war. Goodson joined the RAF and made his mark as an Eagle Squadron volunteer before transferring to the US Army Air Force in September 1942 and flying from most of Kent's airfields.

House-to-house delivery of gas masks in Bexley.

The Polish aces who came to Kent

POLAND stood no chance when her more powerful neighbour attacked. The German forces, in the wake of heavy aerial bombardments, proved conclusively that fast-moving armoured forces in combination with war planes could overcome trench warfare. Three weeks after the Reich crossed the frontier, the German High Command was able to claim that the Polish campaign was over.

"In a series of battles of extermination", read the German communiqué, "of which the greatest and most decisive was in the Vistula curve, the Polish army numbering a million men has been defeated, taken prisoner or scattered. Not a single Polish active or reserve division, not a single independent brigade, has escaped this fate. Only fractions of single bands escaped immediate annihilation by fleeing into marshy territory in East Poland."

Striking south from East Prussia and from Germany, the Wehrmacht had covered over 140 miles to reach the gates of Warsaw by September 8th. Warsaw then endured two weeks of bombardment in which the city was devastated. On September 17th the Red Army also invaded and by the end of the month the partition of Poland was agreed in Moscow. It was estimated that 60,000 Poles had been killed and 200,000 taken prisoner. Many escaped to Rumania, only to be interned.

Here the Polish Air Force regrouped. They had no intention of sitting passively behind barbed wire fences until the end of the war. Using all kinds of tricks and the most elaborate methods for escaping, they slipped out like eels between guards, policemen and gendarmes. Equipped with fictitious passports, dressed in second-hand civilian clothing they made their way to France where General Sikorski was reconstructing the Polish Armed Forces, including the Air Force.

One man to escape was Henryk Szczesny. In the fighting in Poland he destroyed two German aircraft and was wounded. He was evacuated to Rumania but escaped from hospital, took a Greek ship to Malta, made his way by devious means to France, fought with the French until that country fell and then moved on to England.

Henryk Szczesny knew nothing about England or the English people, except that Great Britain was a big and powerful Empire. He had heard of Shakespeare and Sherlock Holmes and the notorious English fog. He had been told that English people were cool and withdrawn. That was about all. Shaken by the collapse of France he was certain that the British Isles would sink by the weight of German bombs. Through the Kentish fog he had misty hopes that somewhere in the far future the scales of war might turn. "That someone, somehow will manage to stop the invincible Nazi battering ram."

Squadron Leader Henryk Szczesny DFC, KW (and four bars), VM (fifth class). He retired from the RAF in the Fighter Command branch on March 27, 1965 living out his retirement in Ealing, amidst many compatriots.

Szczesny was one of 7,000 Polish airmen to escape to England after the capitulation of France and his first base was the training unit at Eastchurch. In May, 1940, the Polish ace was at Manston in charge of a platoon of Polish cadets. In August, he joined 74 Squadron at Hornchurch and moved to Biggin Hill with his CO, the great South African fighter pilot, Sailor Malan. With his colleagues, he struggled to learn English, enjoyed great success with the girls and carried out long, heroic and strenuous duties. Henryk Szczesny was one of the best, destined to become the most decorated Flight Lieutenant in the RAF. As a Squadron Leader in 1943 he was shot down in France and became a POW in Stalag Luft III.

Air raid precautions had been talked about for many years prior to the war and exercises carried out at frequent intervals. One of the earliest was in May 1938 when aircraft from Manston "bombed and machine-gunned" towns in the Thames Estuary. More "bombs" fell on Rochester Bridge and the town halls of Chatham, Faversham and Sittingbourne. More than 2,000 volunteers took part and children were given half day holidays so that their schools could be used as first-aid centres.

ARP exercises continued to be carried out after war was declared and one showed, in theory, how ARP units from other areas would help in the event of a large scale bombing attack. On this occasion Chatham and the Medway towns were "devastated" and hundreds of Civil Defence workers in London and all over Kent were called into action.

Among the 390 vehicles of all types and 1,500 personnel to take part, were these firemen from Dartford wearing breathing apparatus. It was to be many more months before they were in action for real but the practice showed how effectively the units worked together.

Many dark hours as road casualties escalate

THERE had been much anxiety and uncertainty in Kent during those early days of the war and the authorities had made arrangements to deal with thousands of expected casualties — but the blitzkrieg did not happen. Instead the county was bombarded by regulations urging the public to save, dig, work, buy war bonds, not to travel, spread rumours and, most important, to observe the black-out.

By mid-September, the black-out was total. Local shops had long since sold out of black curtain material, street lights were a thing of the past, cars had dimmed headlights and householders were warned that even a chink of light from their windows could lead to a heavy fine.

People became used to the wardens' cry of 'put your lights out' and courts were tough on those who broke the law. Arthur Nash of Ramsgate was among the first to be prosecuted. The local court heard how a hostile crowd had threatened to throw stones through his unscreened upstairs windows. With no sign of enemy action, more people began to appear before magistrates, including a Tunbridge Wells ARP warden. He was fined 4s.

Road casualties in the county began to escalate. The first people to be killed in the black-out were motor-cyclist, Eric Dixon and his pillion passenger, Joan Humphrey who died at Watling Street, Strood. on September 2nd. Such tragedies forced the Government to ease vehicle lighting restrictions by allowing one headlight to be lit and introducing white lines on major roads to help drivers.

An early white-line ARP experiment at Gravesend

Bill Lamie of the Royal Exchange Hotel, Chatham was not going to risk a black-out fine. But he had some messages painted on his shutters for his customers — and Hitler!

Anxious moments as Kent waits for the real war

BY mid-September 1939 black-out material had disappeared from Kent shops. So had brown paper, black paint, drawing pins and number eight size torch batteries. Shoulder bags for gas masks were scarce and sandbags had increased in price from 3d each to 6d or even 9d because many speculators had bought up large stocks. On September 22nd, petrol rationing was introduced, preceded by a rush of panic buying.

As the people of Kent waited for war to begin, there was one moment of great anxiety. A 'German attacking force' of about 200 aircraft was plotted heading towards the Thames Estuary. Fighter Command issued a preliminary warning and radar showed the 'bandits' were flying up the Thames. The sirens sounded, the squadrons were scrambled, the anti-aircraft guns exploded into action, the battle began and the casualties quickly mounted.

Sadly, the aircraft were friendly. There had been a technical fault in the radar and the RAF had intercepted itself. Two Hurricanes were shot down by fighters and a Blenheim by the gunners. One pilot was killed The combat was to be known as 'The Battle of Barking Creek'.

Sandbags, piled round doors and windows of shops and public buildings to deflect blast, were a feature of those early days of war. The Government supplied 400 million to local authorities and thousands more were made up by voluntary labour. Priority was given to hospitals, historical buildings and town halls. Some parents had refused to allow their children to be evacuated. "We'll face the war together", they said. So, many schools were sandbagged and re-opened.

As the phoney war continued, restrictions were slackened. First, football matches were permitted, then cinemas were allowed to re-open.

Meanwhile the sandbag gangs worked on. There was controversy at Canterbury where lorries laden with earth were allowed to drive through the Great West Door of the Cathedral. Here, thousands of tons of earth were deposited in the Nave and a trolley on wheels carried a great quantity in to protect the Quire. It was the same at Rochester Cathedral where a huge mountain of sandbags rose above the West Door.

At Maidstone, County Council staff worked in shifts to fill sandbags and then helped to hump them from lorries, placing them in front of County Hall.

Gravesend Town Hall was well sandbagged and strengthened so that it could be used as an ARP centre. Sevenoaks Police Station (below), then in the High Street, had similar treatment.

No-one knew quite what to expect when (and if) the air raids began, so they continued with the task of gas-proofing refuge rooms at home and utilising whatever convenient natural shelters they could find elsewhere. None could have been safer than the shelter dug under the rocks at Tunbridge Wells (above). Certainly it seemed far more secure than the Anderson shelter which every family was urged to acquire (right). The Marley Tile Company, based in Riverhead, Sevenoaks manufactured its own arch-type shelter which accommodated six to eight people. Meanwhile many people were converting cellars and basement rooms and stocking them with all the essential foodstuffs.

More wedding bells than sirens as men are called up

AS the winter of 1939-40 approached there was a flurry of activity — not in the skies or the streets, but in the churches. The girls were determined that Hitler was not going to stop them marrying, even if they could not have the wedding they had planned in their dreams. The numbers in Britain reached 459,000 couples before November and by then almost a million Britons had been called up to join the services.

One couple who were married during that period was David Ashenden and his bride Mildred, of Rosemary Cottage, Benenden. He was a Terrier based in Ashford so "Mem" as she was known, made all the arrangements and even bought her own wedding ring. They had no bridesmaids, no honeymoon and only their parents and a brother were in church. She kept a diary and of this September day she wrote: "I am happy beyond words! The uncertainty of our future is forgotten at this moment. I believe, somehow, all will be well for us. I think David and I will have our life together".

They did. They had a son in the first year of marriage. David spent most of the war in the Middle East. His civilian career was in banking and he became Barclay's manager in Cranbrook and Ashford.

When the men were first called up the wives and families they left behind often experienced great financial hardship. The pay of a private soldier, naval rating or aircraftsman was 2s. a day of which married men allotted half to their wives. Meanwhile the cost of living was rising by more than ten per cent.

The enterprising old soldier (with the dog) is Mr R.H.Ellis of Shakespeare Road, Gillingham. He had built a dug-out in his garden to the same specifications as the one he made at Gallipoli during the Great War.

Scores of ships were held up as they passed through The Downs at Deal. They were then inspected by officers from "Contraband Control" and anything likely to help the enemy was confiscated. This job was undertaken by The Mission to Seamen.

In his broadcast to the nation on October 1st, Mr Churchill said: "We have captured by our efficient Contraband Control 150,000 tons more German merchandise — food, oil, mineral and other commodities — for our own benefit than we have lost by all the U-Boat sinking put together. The total for the first five weeks was 350,000 tons and much came from the vigilant officers off the coast of Deal."

Meanwhile the war at sea was escalating. Many Kent people died on HMS Royal Oak, torpedoed at anchor in the Scapa Flow with the loss of 800 lives.

79 Squadron is the first to draw blood

ONE American had already made an early impact on this war. Now there was to be another. Flying Officer Jimmy Davies of 79 Squadron, temporarily based at Manston, was patrolling the Kent coast in his Hurricane on November 21st when the Controller's voice came through on his radio telephone. "Hello Pansy Yellow Leader. Sapper Control, Vector 115 Degrees. Angels 15. Buster." He understood the message. He was yellow leader. Pansy was the code name for 79 Squadron. Sapper was Biggin Hill

Control and Angels 15 told him the height of a bandit.

Swinging onto a new course over the sea off the coast of Deal, Davies spotted a grey and blue Dornier 17, twin-engine reconnaissance bomber, known as the "flying pencil" because of its slim fuselage. He chased it, opened fire and watched it hit the sea and explode.

The next day an enemy aircraft was shot down into the sea by anti-aircraft guns and another driven away. The war in Kent had begun.

Eleven Kent men who objected to war

IN November, 1939 eleven Kent men appeared before a tribunal to explain why they wanted to be registered as conscientious objectors. A greengrocer from Crayford asked the tribunal: "Can you imagine Jesus with a bayonet in his hands and a national flag on his shoulder releasing poisonous gas against innocent people?" He, and all those who objected to war on religious grounds, were told that they could register instead for agriculture or forestry.

A clerk from Elham, an agnostic, said he saw no distinction between killing in war and murder. He was told to report for military duty. So was a motor mechanic from Faversham who denied the right of anyone to be the judge of his conscience and a printer from Gillingham who said it was not Britain's quarrel so he saw no reason why he should fight.

One man, a book-keeper, who was born in Margate during an air raid in the last war, said his nerves had suffered ever since. He was registered as a conscientious objector.

In the two months since war was declared thousands of women in Kent had been recruited as volunteers for the women's services — WRNS, ATS, WAAF and the nursing services. Others had joined the Land Army, some were with the Air Transport Auxiliary while the WVS now boasted more than 50,000 members nationwide. Here, ambulance drivers showed the importance of keeping fit.

Improvisation was one of the balloon barrage's greatest assets — they made themselves comfortable wherever they were!

Pilot had 300 collisions with balloon cables

BY Christmas, 1939 the people of North and West Kent were becoming accustomed to a new sight in the sky, which was a passive, seemingly innocuous, but vital part of Britain's air defence — the balloon barrage.

The idea was to force enemy raiders to fly higher and, given the limited technology at the time, bomb far less accurately. The tough steel cable which kept the balloon tethered to the ground was another defence aid, for it could amputate the wings of any bomber which flew too low. The fact that they were also lethal to our own aircraft was an unfortunate by-product.

The balloon barrage was manned by the men of RAF Balloon Command. The balloons were filled with hydrogen and winched to the required height in just a few minutes. Unfortunately production was unable to keep pace with demand and in those early weeks of the war there were 444 balloons flying around London and only 180 elsewhere. There were also many losses due to unexpected changes in the weather and squadrons were forced to conserve their stocks by keeping many deflated.

One fighter pilot who knew what it was like to fly into the balloon's cables was Canadian, Flight Lieutenant Johnny Kent who deliberately flew into them to see what would happen. He carried out more than 300 collisions and for his

Flight Lt Johnny Kent

work on balloon cable research he was awarded the AFE. On one occasion he lost three feet of wing but managed to land safely. Kent, then a Farnborough Test Pilot, went on to command 92 Squadron at Biggin Hill shortly after the Battle of Britain.

1940

Dunkirk, the Blitz and the Battle of Britain

January 1st: A total of two million men between the ages of 20 and 27 were now liable for call-up into the armed services, following a Royal Proclamation.

January 1st: Frittenden, often referred to as Kent's forgotten village because of its remoteness, was bereft of all its young men. No community had responded to the call of arms more quickly or more loyally.

January 8th: Rationing was introduced. Housewives had to register with retailers for butter, sugar and bacon.

January 20th: Kent was in the icy grip of one of the most severe frosts on record. Sheep on the Downs were frozen to gorse bushes. All references to the weather were censored until 15 days after the event.

February 2nd: Rabbit meat had increased in popularity, particularly in Kent's rural households as fish became scarce and meat rationing was introduced.

February 6th: A nationwide campaign was launched to stamp out war gossip under the slogan — "Careless talk costs lives".

March 1st: About six million BBC listeners were reported to be tuning in to Lord Haw Haw's propaganda broadcasts from Hamburg. There was great speculation over the identity of the man.

April 10th: Allied forces evacuated Norway, and Germany's blitzkrieg, in the form of parachutists and heavy panzers, rolled into the Low Countries annihilating the Dutch and Belgians.

May 25th: The British Expeditionary Force and remnants of French and German units were trapped in a pocket of land surrounding the port of Dunkirk. It was decided to evacuate the troops.

May 26th-June 3rd: In nine days no fewer than 338,682 men were evacuated from the beaches of Dunkirk under relentless enemy attack. The killed, wounded or missing numbered 68,000. All told, 222 naval vessels and 800 civilian craft joined in the operation.

June 10th: Benito Mussolini, Italy's Fascist dictator joined Hitler's victorious Panzers and declared war on the Allies.

June 22nd: France surrendered. The armistice was signed in the same railway carriage at Compiègne in which the Germans had been forced to surrender at the end of the 1914-18 war.

July 10th: The German raids on Channel coastal shipping had become so intense that the part of Kent between the North Foreland and Folkestone was christened *Hellfire Corner*.

July 13th: Hitler announced his plans for the invasion of Britain and issued a military directive to the effect that Germany must first gain superiority over the RAF. On the same day Lord Beaverbrook appealed for aluminium which could be turned into fighter aircraft.

August 1st-13th: The Luftwaffe's attempt to destroy the RAF in preparation for the invasion moved into top gear. Relentless and intensive fighting in the air, over the Channel and above the orchards and villages of Kent continued as German bombers with fighter escorts attacked harbours, radar installations, airfields and factories.

August 20th: By now the Kentish airfields of Biggin Hill, Lympne, Hawkinge, Eastchurch, Manston and West Malling had taken a terrible hammering and the last one had temporarily ceased to operate as a front-line fighter base. But Fighter Command was reluctant to give up and the pilots continued with their heroic struggle.

August 22nd: German batteries shelled Dover from cross-Channel guns. Two people were killed. The people of Dover took refuge in caves in the cliffs.

August 31st: Against advice from his generals, Hitler gave orders for the invasion of England to go ahead. He planned a landing on a 200-mile front from Ramsgate to Lyme Regis. The invasion, codenamed *Operation Sealion,* was to be on September 13th.

September 7th: 350 German bombers attacked the London docks and repeated the raid after dusk, forcing people of Kent to believe that the invasion really was imminent. Church bells were rung, bridgeheads blown up and the Home Guard were put on standby to help repel the raiders.

September 9th: The second evacuation of children began in the wake of continued heavy bombing.

September 15th: The pilots of the RAF were now gaining the upper hand. On this day 61 German aircraft were shot down, leaving Kent littered with the smoking wrecks. As the demoralised enemy scampered back to their bases in France, the RAF claimed that victory was almost theirs.

September 17th: Hitler postponed *Operation Sealion.*

November 26th: The Government banned further imports of bananas to save shipping space for essentials.

December 18th: Hitler ordered his generals to prepare for the invasion of Russia under the codename of *Operation Barbarossa.*

December 30th: Many of London's most cherished buildings were set on fire in a series of incendiary raids. 23,000 bombs were dropped by 136 aircraft.

Luftwaffe inspects new runway at Biggin Hill

January 1940 was one of the most bitter months ever known in Kent. Snow, whipped up by piercing winds from the east, heaped into huge drifts. Villages were marooned and supplies of fuel and food were dangerously low. To the Germans it was a mystery how Fighter Command could continue to operate but, of course, they knew nothing about the frenzied efforts of pilots, administrative staff, ground crews and WAAFs to keep the runways clear of snow. The flying conditions were appalling but many pilots managed to keep airborne for an average 100 hours a week.

The snow also hampered the work of construction gangs attempting to lay a new concrete runway at Biggin Hill and excavate deep shelters. "The Luftwaffe inspected Biggin Hill's new runway today", announced Lord Haw Haw, "and will shortly finish it off."

The wreck of the Dunbar Castle half submerged in the Channel off Ramsgate.

Liner's back broken by a German mine

THE 10,000-ton liner *Dunbar Castle* was sunk by a German mine on January 9th, 1940 off Ramsgate. The ship's back was broken in the explosion and 152 people died, including many children.

The magnetic mine, dropped by parachute, was the first of Hitler's "secret weapons" and it proved that Germany had seized the initiative at sea. Hundreds of mines were laid in sea lanes — particularly in the Straits of Dover and the Thames Estuary where 250,000 tons of shipping were lost in the first three months of the war.

One who escaped when the *Dunbar* exploded was John Stewart, 18, of Birchington who broke his wrist in the blast but managed to help some passengers into a lifeboat.

As the ship listed he was thrown into the sea but managed to swim to another boat — the last to leave the liner. He was reported "missing" but, to his parents' relief, he came home to Park Avenue to describe his great escape.

Sea pilot, James Bishop of Parrock Road, Gravesend was on the bridge of the *Dunbar Castle* when she struck the mine. "I was with the fourth officer when I saw a flash from the starboard side and there was a terrific explosion. I was thrown in the air. Pulling myself together I saw the deck disintegrating and the ship breaking in two. She listed so badly that only the lifeboats on one side could be used." Bishop was picked up by a Portugese steamer; he was one of the lucky ones.

Chatham welcomes the "Ajax twins"

IN January, 1940, the people of Chatham gave a tremendous welcome to the British cruiser, *Ajax* as she sailed into the dockyard for essential repairs. Among her crew were many local sailors including 17-year-old twins Charles and John Tubb of Petham, near Canterbury, then known throughout the country as "the Ajax twins".

One month earlier, on December 15th, the cruiser had played a momentous role in the furious Battle of the River Plate which resulted in Germany's finest "pocket" battleship, the *Admiral Graf Spee* seeking refuge in Montevideo harbour, where she was permitted to stay for just 24 hours.

As the *Ajax* waited in the harbour, people all over the world wondered how the captain of the *Graf Spee* would end the drama. He asked for instructions and was given a choice — scuttle or fight it out on the open sea. Just before the three-mile limit the ship stopped and the crew took to the lifeboats. Minutes later came a series of shattering explosions and the burning ship sank to the river bed.

The *Graf Spee* went down with her full load of guns, stores and ammunition and Hitler was bent on revenge. He knew the *Ajax* had entered Chatham and orders were given to destroy her. Days after her arrival in the yard, a Dornier 17 unloaded a series of bombs. The *Ajax* was lying next to the Upnor wall and fitters thought they saw one fall into the ship's funnel. It turned out to be a near miss. The bomb had hit the jetty, killing a crane driver.

To fool the Germans, the *Ajax* was returned to Number 9 dock and her place alongside the Upnor wall was taken by a C class cruiser undergoing conversion. Her upper decks were burnt away and she looked a complete wreck. A German aircraft spotted the damaged cruiser and within a few hours Lord Haw Haw was proclaiming the loss of the *Ajax*.

It was a perfect bluff and the "Ajax twins" — six-foot tall were in great demand, particularly by the Simon Langton School, Canterbury, to tell the story of their contribution towards the ignominious defeat of the once-great battleship.

The British cruiser, Ajax, which sailed triumphantly into Chatham.

Stirling and Sunderland were Rochester prototypes

DURING the early 1940s the activity at Chatham dockyard was hectic. Apart from the construction of new ships, First World War veterans were converted into anti-aircraft gun ships and smaller vessels were fitted with de-gaussing gear to neutralise their magnetic attraction to mines. Unskilled workmen took the place of artisans and up to 2,000 women took over such jobs as driving cranes and operating machines.

Further along the river at Rochester, the Shorts aircraft factory was working on a specification for a long-range high speed bomber which was to carry a crew of seven and be powered by four 1,600 hp Hercules engines. The first production model of the

Stirling, designed by Arthur Gouge of Northfleet, was completed in May 1940. It could carry seven 2000lb bombs over 2,000 miles and had a maximum speed of 300 mph. Eventually 145 Stirlings were built at Rochester but they ceased to be front-line equipment with the advent of the Halifax and Lancaster.

Another Rochester prototype was the S25 Sunderland, really an Empire flying boat with power-operated gun turrets. The Sunderland had four 1,010hp Bristol Pegasus engines, a range of 1,670 miles and top speed of over 210 mph. It was in production until 1945.

The normal employment at Shorts had been around 14,000 people but this rose during the war to 20,000.

When the Kent Messenger appealed for books and magazines for the Expeditionary Forces in France, the response was overwhelming. Thousands were delivered to KM offices throughout the county and willing helpers helped to pack them for transportation.

Everybody was willing to knit for the Forces. Members of the Regional Supplies Office of the British Red Cross and Order of St John of Jerusalem at Matfield are seen here weighing out 900 lbs of wool to be knitted into garments in Kent. Left to right: Mrs B. Pott, Miss Eeles, Miss V. Hubbard, Lady Bennett (Regional Officer), Miss S. Bland and Miss Rankin.

The Regional Commissioner for the South-Eastern Region, Sir Auckland Geddes, who was based at Bredbury, a large house on Mount Ephraim at Tunbridge Wells, addressed members of the Civil Defence Services from all over Kent at the Royal Naval Barracks at Chatham on Sunday January 20th, 1940. This is a fraction of his large audience.

Sandbags and shelters and over-zealous wardens!

BY January 1940, Kent was a county of sandbags and shelters. The bags, piled high around the windows and doorways of public buildings, shopfronts, churches and schools were beginning to turn green and leak at the edges. The shelters, erected in such a frantic rush in September, had hardly been used. But Kent, representing the first English target for the German bombers and invaders, was still waiting for the action to begin.

The Ministry of Home Security, formed at the beginning of the war, was convinced that mass bombing with gas attacks was imminent. The Ministry was responsible for Air Raid Precautions and from this had created twelve Civil Defence administrative regions. Tunbridge Wells (Region No. 12) was responsible for the vital South Eastern area and, in turn, was sub-divided into districts.

The regions, devised in the light of experience from the Spanish Civil War, contained two vital reporting agents — police and wardens. The wardens' job in the event of an attack was to direct people to the nearest shelter, allay panic and give assistance whenever required. They were also given the responsibility of reporting all incidents as accurately as possible.

In the first few months of 1940 the wardens' popularity was on a par with the black-out. Many people regarded them as draft dodgers and letters to Kent papers criticised them as grown men playing war games and using up valuable petrol. In a way, though, the job was hazardous — not from German action but from objects thrown out of windows in retaliation to the zealous cry — "put that bloody light out".

Invasion of Kent was thought to be imminent and the LDF, later to be called the Home Guard, was ready to repel the raiders.

Come on, Hitler — we're ready for you!

THE invasion of Denmark began at 5 am on April 9th. Three German troopships sailed silently into Copenhagen harbour and the only resistance came from a policeman with a pistol. Within 24 hours, Denmark had fallen. This was followed by the German advance into Norway. After two weeks fighting, British and French forces evacuated the country and Hitler's blitzkrieg rolled into the Low Countries. Stuka dive bombers struck at airfields, crippling the tiny Dutch and Belgian air forces and spreading panic. When the ground forces appeared, 200,000 strong, they were backed by heavy Panzers with 37mm guns. Holland, Belgium and Luxembourg were crushed and France braced itself for a Nazi attack. The phoney war was over.

With the Germans advancing into France, War Minister Sir Anthony Eden gave his clarion call for men "not presently engaged in military service between the ages of 17 and 65 to come forward and offer their services".

As he was speaking, volunteers in Gillingham and Cranbrook were signing on and, at Folkestone, men were still enrolling at midnight. Senior pupils at King's School, Canterbury and Maidstone Grammar signed on and one volunteer at Canterbury, who was 85, gave his age as 65.

In his book *Front Line County*, Andrew Rootes described the spirit of improvisation at Maidstone where Brigadier-General H. Franklin, who had been appointed zone commander for Kent, contacted Colonel W. Baker on

May 15th to ask him to form a local force. He was given 200 rifles which he stored at Maidstone police station and Leeds Castle. Eight men volunteered to form the first patrol of Maidstone LDF, collected their rifles and ammunition and went on duty, each with a white handkerchief tied round his arm as the only sign of his official standing.

Within a week, 250,000 men had enrolled nationally; there were more than 1,000 in Kent and Maidstone's army had grown from eight to more than 400. Many of them were veterans of the Great War and they carried a great array of weaponry — aged rifles, shotguns, cutlasses and broomsticks, converted into pikes with carving knives. It was the first citizens' army since Napoleon had threatened invasion in 1803.

The new army was known as the Local Defence Force but in Kent it was better known as the "Parashots", because it was assumed they would soon be attacking invading German parachutists. Uniforms were scarce but good use was made of anything available. Parades were begun immediately and those who had no rifle attended instruction classes just the same.

By July, when the LDF had democratically elected its officers, the Prime Minister referred to them in a speech as the Home Guard. This was to become their new and lasting name.

The men of the Southern Railway LDF whose job was to provide military protection at all points of importance on the rail network. Like all volunteers they were poorly equipped but there was no doubting their enthusiasm, or ability with the rifle. In Maidstone, the town's army which grew from eight to 400 in a week was a thousand strong by the end of June, 1940. The men had no uniforms, they received no pay or expenses and they had to share the rifles; in fact when the force was first formed, patrols of 20 men were sent out with five rifles and 20 rounds of ammunition between them. Kent's great citizens' army went about its business in a serious way and it was no surprise to see officers of the Great War standing shoulder to shoulder with former privates, bank managers, bishops and schoolboys.

Maidstone Grammar School boys marched to the police station to volunteer.

Certain now that Hitler was about to invade, road blocks were hurriedly constructed on all main roads and some side roads in the county. Many bridges were mined. Here at East Peckham, a steam roller, water carts, rails and a village bobby are ready to obstruct the invading army.

Hitler's panzers would have had some difficulty with this lot. The road block outside the trolley-bus depot at Barming consisted of cement, reinforced by iron bars.

The road block at Tonbridge was made of tar barrels. There were concrete posts on the Chatham Road, oak trees at Chilham and barbed wire on many side roads.

Meanwhile all signposts were taken down. The expected wave of German paratroopers must not know where they had landed.

Above: Tommies serving abroad with a battalion of the Buffs (Royal East Kent Regiment) buy dairy produce from a mother and daughter. Left: Two other Buffs give this farmer a helping hand with his barrow load of straw. The smiles of the soldiers and their relaxed manner contrasted with the seriousness of the situation on the Continent. In Belgium, the Germans were closing in on the Belgian army, the French 1st and 7th armies and the bulk of the British Expeditionary Force (BEF). It was feared that up to 300,000 men could be taken as German prisoners. France would fall and the invasion of Britain would follow.

Churchill and Vice-Admiral Ramsay together pore over the plans for the evacuation. Ramsay wrote to his wife on May 25th: "Days and nights are all one. My staff are worn out".

Get those men off the beaches

AS the troops of the British Expeditionary Force and the French First Army pulled back into a diminishing pocket of land centred on Dunkirk, the Government ordered the immediate evacuation of as many men as possible. Vice-Admiral Bertram Ramsay was put in charge of the operation and given less than a week to prepare. In his underground bunker, deep within the cliffs of Dover — a room which held electrical plant in the last war and was known as the Dynamo Room — Ramsay codenamed the evacuation plan *Operation Dynamo.*

Originally it was planned that 30,000 men a day should be evacuated from the ports of Calais, Boulogne and Dunkirk but on May 25th Boulogne was captured and the following day Calais fell. 400,000 British and French troops were pushed back into a 30-mile stretch of coastline running from Gravelines through Dunkirk to Nieuport. Inland, near Lille, six French divisions were surrounded by seven German ones. The men were under constant attack. The situation was desperate.

By May 26th, Ramsay had assembled 15 passenger ferries at Dover and a further 20 at Southampton. These were ordered to embark troops direct from the quays at Dunkirk. To help with the evacuation and to provide escorts for the merchant ships, Ramsay had a force of destroyers, corvettes, minesweepers and naval trawlers, augmented by cargo vessels, coasters, pleasure steamers, London Fire Brigade boats and some 40 Dutch self-propelled barges. All ships of the British merchant marine had their normal civilian crews but near continuous bombing and shelling began to take their toll and naval personnel were drafted in to help.

Ramsay believed he had two days before the Germans overran the beach-head. In that time he had to keep the Channel clear of mines, provide the bombardment of German batteries at Calais, drive off U-boats and depend on the RAF to hold back the Luftwaffe. His aim was to rescue 45,000 troops from the clutches of the enemy. What he achieved was much, much more — an operation later described by Churchill as "a miracle of deliverance".

In that network of tunnels in the Dover cliffs there was a frantic round-the-clock effort by men and women who had little sleep and suffered sheer exhaustion. There were calls to Nore Command for further destroyers and to the Ministry of Shipping for more merchant ships; calls to the Admiralty for tugs, weapons, ammunition, medical supplies, fuel, rations and trained personnel and calls to Southern Railway for special troop trains.

All the time the military situation was changing and worsening. The Germans reported that the British were retreating nearer and nearer to the beach-head, some running along breakwaters in a desperate effort to escape. They also reported that the Isle of Man steamer *Mona's Isle* had been mined and sunk and 90 men of the Royal Norfolk Regiment captured and slaughtered.

Heroes of Kent rescue the heroes of Dunkirk

By May 28th when Belgium capitulated, the British and French troops seemed doomed, but evacuation from Dunkirk beaches had already begun.

Operation Dynamo
May 26th — June 3rd, 1940

AGAINST a lurid backcloth of a burning city and under relentless enemy attack, a staggering 338,226 British and Allied troops were plucked from the beaches of Dunkirk and taken to England. In Kent, which was the disembarkation area for most of them, Southern Railway provided nearly 2,000 locomotives and carriages in a bid to transport the men as soon as they had landed.

This was an extraordinary military manoeuvre, unprecedented in history, and it took seven days to complete. All told, 222 naval vessels and 800 civilian craft joined the operation. Six destroyers and 243 ships were sunk and the killed, missing or wounded numbered 68,000. "It was", said Churchill, "a miracle of deliverance" even though there had been a "colossal military disaster".

On May 26th, the first day of *Dynamo*, only 4,247 troops were rescued. Minefields and shelling from the German batteries had forced the convoys to take longer routes to Dunkirk and only the passenger ferries *Royal Daffodil* and later the *Canterbury* succeeded in berthing. For two days rescue was painfully slow and because of the shallow waters, destroyers could not approach within a mile of the shore. There was, however, an alternative. Stretching into the seas from the eastern side of Dunkirk harbour was a spindly concrete-legged structure with a narrow timber walkway, known as a mole. It was not designed to withstand ships berthing beside it but Captain Tennant, in charge of the Dunkirk shore party, ordered the *Queen of the Channel* alongside and 950 men quickly boarded.

From that moment small ships went to the beaches and large vessels queued for the mole. As the rescue operation gathered momentum, Ramsay appealed for more ships. Destroyers were sent from Portsmouth and from Kent all available seaworthy pleasure craft went in flotillas to Sheerness Dockyard where they were told to await final sailing orders.

Among them were lifeboats, fishing smacks, dredgers, drifters and trawlers. A mudhopper joined the party and so did the paddle steamer, the *Medway Queen*. Tugs came from the London Docks and cockleboats from Leigh-on-Sea.

The 'Little Ships' sailed at 22.00 hours on May 29th. They streamed across the Channel in seemingly unending lines. On board were volunteer crews, many of whom had never been out of sight of land before. Among them were

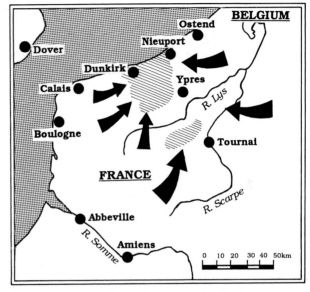

factory employees from Gravesend, ARP volunteers and dockyard workers. The 'Little Ships' headed for the beaches with fuel, rations and charts. They also carried rafts and ladders made by the men at Sheerness Dockyard.

As they approached Dunkirk on calm waters, they had to risk the constant shelling and bombing which was battering the sea approach. And they saw a huge pall of smoke rising from the harbour, which gave some protection from the Luftwaffe. The men were plucked off the beaches and the Little Ships joined the destroyers and the minesweepers on the journey back to Kent. At Dover, the busiest port, they berthed, unloaded their troops, refuelled and returned to Dunkirk.

The troops, hungry, exhausted and many dressed only in tattered rags, were given food and clothing. The first job of the port authorities was to sort out the living from the dead and the new Customs Shed at the Marine Station was used as a mortuary. Lorries took stray dogs away which had boarded the vessels at Dunkirk.

Trains were waiting at the station to take the men away and then return for more. Dover had 327 trains and moved 180,982 men, Ramsgate carried 783 men on 82 trains. 64 trains were supplied at Folkestone, 75 at Margate and 17 at Sheerness. Headcorn and Paddock Wood were used as eight-minute food stops, where catering headquarters were established, the food was prepared and carried to each train in turn.

At Headcorn, 207 trains pulled up for their eight-minute

Thousands of British troops stranded on the beach at Dunkirk — and the waiting seemed interminable. One by one they were picked up by the small boats which took them out to larger vessels and then home through the dangerous Channel waters to those waiting trains. The volunteers who crewed the Little Ships played a great part in saving the men — and Britain.

stop. The little Weald village had never seen such activity before, or since. Forty soldiers dished out the food helped by 40 to 50 local women who worked in eight hour shifts for nine days and nights, cutting up 2,500 loaves each day. Nineteen stoves were on the go day and night to produce tea and coffee. Beef was roasted on spits in open trenches, a million sardines were supplied along with bully beef and 5,000 eggs. On one evening 5,000 meat pies, 5,000 sausages and 5,000 rolls were delivered and they were all eaten by early the following afternoon.

All the time, the 'Little Ships' and their bigger sisters were picking up the troops and risking acute danger. The destroyer, *Jaguar* was damaged. *HMS Grenade* was hit and later blew up, the paddle-steamer *Waverley* was bombed with the loss of 400. Passenger ships *Lorina* and *Normannia* were bombed and sunk. The French destroyer *Bourrasque*

with 800 on board, hit a mine. *HMS Wakeful* was torpedoed with 600 passengers. *HMS Grafton* went to pick up survivors and, she too, was torpedoed.

The sunken ships made navigation quite hazardous. *Brighton Belle* hit a wreck and sank but the *Medway Queen* steamed to the rescue and picked up 800 troops floundering in the water.

Goering had boasted that his Luftwaffe would annihilate the BEF, but his aircraft were often grounded by bad weather and could not operate at night. Despite their best efforts the RAF could only give limited protection and inevitably there were times when there was no air cover at all. "Where is the RAF?" was the bitter cry of the anxious troops on beaches, who knew nothing of air battles being fought out of their sight.

Even so the Kent squadrons were in

DUNKIRK Daily evacuation figures	
May 26th	4,247
May 27th	5,718
May 28th	18,527
May 29th	50,331
May 30th	53,227
May 31st	64,141
June 1st	61,557
June 2nd	23,604
June 3rd	29,641
June 4th	27,689
TOTAL	**338,682**

The Destroyer, HMS Whitehall (D94) had to wait her turn at the berth at Admiralty Pier in Dover to unload her human cargo. Ships were crowded to bursting with every last space on deck and below taken. At the height of the evacuation, 64,000 men were brought back in a single day. Many soldiers, shaken by the army's defeat, feared a hostile reception when they arrived in Dover, but instead received an overwhelming welcome. Many local children ran to the shops to buy "Doverbags" — a pennyworth assortment of sweets — not for themselves but to give to the soldiers.

the thick of the action, many men were lost and every pilot had a harrowing story to tell. Sergeant Wilson of 610 Squadron baled out from his blazing Spitfire and landed in the Channel. Flight Lieutenant Ellis tried to draw the attention of a destroyer only to be shot down for his pains. In seven days, Goering lost 107 aircraft and Fighter Command, 106. "There was a victory inside this deliverance", said Churchill. "It was gained by the Royal Air Force."

As they plied the men with tea, food and cigarettes, the people of Kent did not see the evacuation as defeat. They welcomed the Dunkirk survivors as heroes.

Fags, food, tea and a waiting train to take them home. The welcome was warm and wonderful and the boys responded with the biggest grins they could manage — but many had endured hours of grief on those beaches. One soldier, Sgt Leonard Howard said: "I lay in the sand dunes and slept because I was exhausted. The next morning I went into the water in the hope of being picked up and there was no hope. But there was panic. Eventually a small boat came in and we all piled on to such a degree that it was in danger of capsizing. The chap in charge had to take action — so he shot a hanger-on. As we sailed away I saw chaps running into the water screaming. Mentally it had been too much for them".

The crowded deck of a troopship as officers and other ranks of the RAF were rescued.

Sandwiches had never tasted like this before. Exhausted troops had been starved of both food and sleep.

The ladies at Headcorn worked in eight hour shifts for nine days and nights, cutting up 2,500 loaves each day. Some said they never wanted to see another sandwich again!

One of the feeding stations was at Paddock Wood. At nearby Tonbridge, the wife of the stationmaster organised a collection for wounded soldiers in Pembury Hospital.

Southern Railways played their part in the great evacuation. The train in Dover Priory, steam billowing, waited for British and French troops to board. At Paddock Wood (below) the Canneries provided helpers and tins to serve as mugs for tea.

At Sandgate there was an opening in the defences for those who wished to bathe but only "organised parties under an officer".

Hitler misses his chance to invade

THE British Army had abandoned much of its modern equipment in France. The 1st London Division, responsible for the defence of the coast from Sheppey to Rye had no anti-tank guns, no Bren guns, only eleven 25-pounder field guns, four 18 pounders and eight 4.5 inch howitzers from the Great War. Morale was low and Hitler, so everyone thought, was now certain to invade.

Kent began to strengthen its fortress. No visitors were allowed on seafronts. Gun emplacements and pill-boxes, disguised as chalets and tea-stalls began to spring up. Scaffolding and concrete blocks covered beaches and piers were cut off from the shore. Barbed wire was everywhere; in fact the longest train to go through Ashford was a train carrying barbed wire.

Convinced that the German paratroopers and troop gliders would be the first wave of invaders, efforts were being made to make landing difficult. Open spaces, the Downs, golf courses, straight roads were strewn with obstacles, including old cars, buses, carts and even iron bedsteads.

Hitler would have had a good chance of success in those days immediately after Dunkirk but, still hoping that there could be peace with Britain, so that he could be free to launch an assault on Russia, he was not ready to strike — but he did want control of the English Channel.

On June 17th, the White Star liner, *Lancastria,* converted into a troopship, was attacked by five German aircraft in her berth in St Nazaire. More than half of the 5,000 on board died. It was the forerunner to a month of attacks on British convoys in the Channel.

On the same day, Churchill gave another inspirational performance in the House of Commons: "Let us brace ourselves to our duty and so bear ourselves that if the British Commonwealth and Empire lasts for a thousand years, men will still say: This was their finest hour".

A month later, on July 16th, Hitler retaliated by issuing a new War Directive: "As England, in spite of her hopeless military position, has so far shown herself unwilling to come to any compromise, I have decided to begin preparations for and, if necessary, to carry out the invasion of England.......if necessary, the island will be occupied. The landing must be a surprise crossing on a broad front from Ramsgate to the Isle of Wight....The invasion is to be codenamed Sealion".

THE criticism and derision levelled at the ARP services during the phoney war disappeared in those days after Dunkirk and, in the face of a threatened invasion, wardens were taken seriously. One of their jobs was to recruit fire watchers and they toured their districts enrolling men between the ages of 16 and 60.

In the event of incendiary, or even heavier, bombs falling, the fire watchers were to detect and combat fires, particularly in business and industrial districts. Women and children were encouraged to play their part and steel helmets and armbands with the initials SFP (Street Fire Party) were issued.

The photograph shows a firewatcher being recruited in a house in Old Farm Avenue, Sidcup. In many areas stirrup pumps and sandbags were given out on a "free on loan" basis and in places where no water receptacles existed, the street parties had to provide their own. This arrangement was eventually superceded by the Fire Guard Service introduced in August 1941. In Kent they were to prove their worth.

Merchant ships under attack in the Channel

IT was not only Royal Navy ships which were under attack in the Channel. Passenger steamers, fishing and merchant vessels were now prime targets for the Luftwaffe as they steamed up and through the Straits of Dover.

The first air attack on a British merchant ship had actually taken place on March 20th, 1940 when the SS *Barn Hill* with a gross tonage of 5,439 tons, en route from London to Halifax in Canada was singled out by the Luftwaffe. On board was a crew of 34.

Several bombs struck the ship, one penetrated her deck and killed four members of the crew. The ship's engines halted and she took on a list to starboard as fire swept through below deck. A Dutch vessel responded to distress calls and took off 18 men, but the ship went down.

The loss of the SS *Barn Hill* was the first of many in Channel waters at the hands of the Luftwaffe.

An old soldier with his hands full. London children enjoyed the summer of 1940 near Canterbury.

It was not so pleasant in the towns. This is Tonbridge, where barbed wire separated the pavements from the road with very few exits for crossing.

An anti-landing device. This was a lethal steel cable, strung across the main road at Eltham.

Luftwaffe ordered: knock out the RAF

HITLER'S plan was to invade England with 20 divisions to be put ashore between Ramsgate and Lyme Regis. The preparations had to be ready by mid-August, the sea routes cleared of mines and guns brought up to protect the coastal front area. The most favourable time for moon and tide was established. Operation Sealion was set for September 21st.

The German Army saw the invasion as similar to a river crossing on a broad front; in place of bridging operations the navy would keep the sea lanes secure against British attacks. The navy, however, were less certain of success. In the absence of purpose-built landing craft they could not guarantee to protect the river barges being towed across the Channel. How, they also asked the Generals, do you propose to get horses across the Channel under fire?

The attack on Kent was to be carried out by men from the 17th and 35th Divisions of the XIII Corps of the 16th Army who were to land between Folkestone and Dungeness. Paratroopers would be the first to drop on high land around Lympne and Lyminge, capture the ground, secure crossings over the Royal Military Canal, establish a road block on the Canterbury to Folkestone Road, link up with other airborne troops and expand a bridgehead so that they would hold a line running from Canterbury to Ashford. Meanwhile more bridgeheads were to be established in Sussex. Within 20 days, the Germans planned to capture the country from Gravesend to Portsmouth.

It was simple. All the Luftwaffe had to do was knock out the RAF.

A new name for Kent — "Hellfire Corner"

AS the German raids on coastal shipping became even more intense, a new name was given to the part of the Kentish shore closest to the enemy in France — "Hellfire Corner".

On July 18th, Dover harbour was bombed and the 11,500 ton Admiralty tanker *War Sepoy* had her back broken. On July 27th a surprise attack was carried out on the harbour by 120 aircraft. The destroyer *Codrington* was sunk. On July 29th Junkers (Ju87) "Stuka" dive-bombers protected by Messerschmitt fighters screamed out of the sky at Dover. Buildings shook and windows were smashed by the concussion of bursting bombs.

This time the RAF was ready. Hurricanes and Spitfires tore into the enemy formations, already heavily engaged by anti-aircraft defences. Twelve German planes were shot down for the loss of three British and, for the first time, it became clear that the "Stukas" — so effective in France — were sitting ducks for the British fighters.

All coastal convoys in the Channel were stopped. Dover was abandoned as a base for anti-invasion warships. Destroyers were withdrawn to Sheerness. The Germans had daytime control of the Channel. News came through of a battery of heavy coastal guns being set up near Calais.

The people of "Hellfire Corner" braced themselves for a new bombardment.

Monday August 12th was the day nominated by the Germans to be Eagle Day, Adlertag. For the people of Dover and Folkestone it began with a new form of enemy action that was to plague the two front-line coastal towns for more than four years — the firing of shells from cross-Channel guns. On this day two people in Dover were killed and three seriously injured. In Ramsgate a new type of oil bomb was reported which sprayed to a distance of 75 feet. The photograph is unique. It was taken by the Germans and shows the first round of hundreds of shells which were fired from Pas de Calais.

This extraordinary picture was taken just seconds after a Messerschmitt crashed onto a house in Hardy Street, Maidstone on September 5th, 1940. See page 58.

Hit and run raids precede Eagle Day

THE fighting in the air over the Channel and the Kent coast became even more relentless during those early weeks of the Battle of Britain. August 10, 1940 was the day nominated by Hitler and Goering as *Adlertag*, the "Eagle Day" which was to commence the annihilation of the Royal Air Force. In the meantime, the Luftwaffe continued to attack harbours, naval bases and airfields in an attempt to strangle Britain's supply lines. The Hurricanes and Spitfires of Biggin Hill, Manston, Hawkinge and Gravesend flew hundreds of sorties and in four weeks, 227 enemy aircraft were destroyed for the loss of only 96.

Because of bad weather, Eagle Day was postponed and it was not until August 12 that the rain and mist relented. On that morning 12 Spitfires of Biggin Hill's 610 Squadron were engaged in a hectic dogfight with nine Messerschmitts. Two 109s were destroyed but only 11 Spitfires flew home to Biggin Hill.

The pilot of the twelfth was Flight Lieutenant Edward Smith whose Spitfire was hit by cannon shells. The engine stopped dead, the cockpit filled with smoke, flames licked around the instrument panel, the aircraft went into a dive and the hood wouldn't open. Smith thought he was dying but refused to panic. He reduced speed, managed to slide open the hood, released his seat harness, rolled over and was very quickly outside. Pulling the ripcord he found himself swinging gently to earth. There were no fighters in sight and no sound except a slight silken rustle from above. Ten minutes later, buoyed up by his Mae West, he was floating in the Channel.

Within the hour he was being picked up by a motor torpedo boat, taken to Dover Hospital to have his burns treated and then back to Biggin Hill.

Smith had become the first pilot to be shot down as the curtain rose on *Adlertag*. The Battle of Britain was now in full fury.

The Luftwaffe had a plan for Eagle Day — to attack and put out of action all known radar stations between the Thames Estuary and Portland. Two were in Kent —— one on top of the cliffs at Dover and the other at Dunkirk, near Canterbury. Bombs were dropped all around but no vital damage was caused. However, two other stations, at Rye and Pevensey, were silenced and a 100-mile gap torn in the radar chain.

This gave the German fighters the opportunity to attack the airfields at Lympne, Hawkinge and Manston. At Lympne, 141 bombs were dropped causing considerable damage. At Hawkinge, two hangars, the station workshops and four fighters on the ground were destroyed. At Manston, 18 Dorniers dropped 150 bombs and machine-gunned the airfield in a raid that lasted only 20 minutes. Workshops, hangars and a Blenheim night fighter were hit and the airfield was cratered. Spitfires took off but the raiders had disappeared.

Within 24 hours, Hawkinge and Manston and the two radar stations were back in operation. With massive help from the Army, the airfield staffs had worked through the night — but once again Hellfire Corner had lived up to its name.

Lord Beaverbrook, the buccaneer publisher and Minister for Aircraft Production made a dramatic appeal to the women of Britain: "Give us your spare pots and pans and we will turn them into Spitfires, Hurricanes and Wellingtons". The response in Kent was fantastic. One woman, aged 80, walked a mile or so to the depot to donate a saucepan. Hundreds of tons were collected in just a few days and this included an artificial leg, an abandoned racing car and aluminium tennis racket presses. This photograph shows the collecting point at Canterbury where the man on duty received another precious kettle.

THE BATTLE OF BRITAIN

HUNDREDS of books, pamphlets and accounts have been written about the Battle of Britain in the summer of 1940 when the defeat of the RAF seemed certain, the invasion of Britain likely, and the existence of the free world hung in the balance. It was, without doubt, the greatest air battle in modern history and the battleground was the skies above Kent and the orchards, fields and villages below where hundreds of aircraft crashed.

Historians have decreed that the battle officially began in July 1940 and ended on October 31st. Only the aircrew involved in operations between those dates qualified for a Battle of Britain clasp.

Because of the enormous scale of the battle, the squadrons, the scrambles, the sightings, the interceptions, the combats and the casualties suffered by each side, it is impossible to give a full picture in a book which covers the entire war.

However, the next few pages contain an example of the men and machines who were involved in this legendary 'field of human conflict' as it affected the county of Kent. There are profiles of some of the famous aces, the action from the front-line fighter stations, the bombing of the Kent towns and a diary of the action during the critical period between August 12th and September 15th, the crucial day when Hitler postponed his invasion of Kent and Britain.

Accompanying the text are some of the amazing photographs from the archives of the *Kent Messenger*.

Churchill's immortal words were spoken at the conclusion of the battle: "The gratitude of every home in our island, in our Empire, and indeed throughout the world, except in the abodes of the guilty, goes out to the British airmen who, undaunted by odds, unwearied in their constant challenge and mortal danger, turned the tide of the world war by their prowess and by their devotion. Never in the field of human conflict was so much owed by so many to so few."

A pilot snatches sleep when he can between periods of mortal conflict in the sky.

Sapper Control here — good hunting, old chaps!

Battle of Britain from August 13th to September 15th

THE RAF was always rich in an idiom that was technical and necessary but the Controller at Biggin Hill, in giving precise instructions to pilots of the three coastal stations, Manston, Lympne and Hawkinge, must have sounded like a cricket captain just before sending his team into battle: "Hello Dog Rose Leader. Sapper* here. Receiving you loud and clear. Vector 120 degrees. Nine bandits approaching. Angels 10. Good hunting."

The men were playing a game and a highly deadly one. In the blue skies of this late Kentish summer, the greatest air battle in history was fought. For those whom Churchill called "The Few" were attempting to thwart Hitler's preparation for an invasion of Britain.

The average fighter pilot flying his Spitfire, Hurricane, Blenheim or Defiant in that summer of 1940 was 21 years old, unmarried, interested in fast cars and girls and loved the RAF slang. "Angels" signified height, to "scramble" was to take off and to "pancake" was to land. The fight was played out in a dramatic 15 weeks of aerial combats, many of which happened above the towns and villages of Kent. At one time it was called The Battle of Tonbridge; eventually it was known by the world as The Battle of Britain.

Every one of those courageous young men who fought in the battle and all those who worked behind the scenes — the fitters, mechanics, controllers, drivers, administrators, caterers and, of course, the WAAFs — had a story to tell. Some have been told elsewhere; many will never be told.

Here is a brief diary of the battle for one month from August 13th to September 15th as it affected Kent.

Tuesday August 13th: *(07.00)* : 74 Dorniers on bombing raid of naval base at Sheerness and Coastal Command's airfield at Eastchurch. Harassed by Spitfires from Manston. Five Eastchurch Blenheims and one Spitfire destroyed. 14 soldiers and airmen killed. *(17.16):*

40 Ju 87s (Stuka divebombers) attacked Detling airfield housing the Ansons of 500 Squadron. Hangars and messes wrecked, station commander killed, 22 aircraft destroyed.

Wednesday August 14th: *(12.30):* 42 Hurricanes and Spitfires from Biggin Hill, Hawkinge and Manston in combat with 120 Messerschmitts, escorting 80 Stuka divebombers. Furious dogfight over Dover involving more than 200 aircraft. Eight barrage balloons destroyed. Goodwin Lightship bombed and sunk. Three Hurricanes damaged. Six Messerschmitts destroyed. Manston airfield also attacked. Three Blenheims destroyed. Four hangars set on fire. Two raiders brought down by AA gunfire.

Thursday August 15th: The Luftwaffe's biggest assault of the whole battle. More than 500 enemy bombers, escorted by 1,256 fighters, attack British airfields in five massive assaults. Hawkinge, Eastchurch, Manston, Rochester and the partly completed West Malling airfield damaged. The cables which carried power to the radar stations at Dover, Rye and Foreness severed at Hawkinge, Lympne put out of action for several hours. Manston lost two Spitfires on the ground and 16 people were injured. Two airmen killed at West Malling. One of the biggest raids was on the Shorts aircraft factory at Rochester where Britain's first four-engined bombers, the massive Stirling, were being

produced. One man killed and several injured. Six Stirlings destroyed, together with all the finished parts, putting production of the bomber back by more than a year. RAF scrambled some 150 Hurricanes and Spitfires to meet the foe. 161 enemy aircraft destroyed.

Friday August 16th: *(10.45):* West Malling attacked again with 24 Dorniers dropping more than 80 bombs. *(12.00):* Enemy aircraft attacked Northfleet town centre. 106 high explosive bombs dropped, killing 29 people. Raiders met by Spitfires from Manston, Kenley and Hornchurch and Hurricanes from Biggin Hill and Hawkinge. One Hurricane and five Spitfires shot down. Acting Pilot Officer William Fiske, from Manston, died of injuries. Acting Flight Lieutenant William Warner, from Biggin Hill, reported missing.

Sunday August 18th: *(12.38):* 300 enemy aircraft reported over Kent. West Malling bombed again but this time Biggin Hill was the target. Low level attack on airfield by nine Dorniers. Intercepted by Hurricanes of 32 Squadron and Spitfires of 610 Squadron. Two Dorniers shot down, two crashed in Channel, three force-landed in France. Biggin Hill badly cratered. In an extraordinary act of bravery, WAAF Sgt Elizabeth Mortimer planted red flags to mark unexploded bombs, an action for which she became the first WAAF to win the Military Medal. Another attack by Junkers followed. 32 Squadron again in action. Flight Lieutenant Humphrey Russell baled out seriously wounded above Edenbridge and applied tourniquet during parachute descent. Flight Lieutenant Mike Crossley baled out at Gillingham to be met by hostile locals who thought he was a Luftwaffe pilot. Junkers shot down by Flight Lieutenant Stanford Tuck of 92

King George VI inspected many gun emplacements, searchlight units and listening posts in Kent on August 15th, 1940. The picture shows an earlier visit on May 13th.

* Sapper is code name for Biggin Hill

Squadron who had to jump out over Horsmonden. *(17.00)* : Medway Towns bombed. 59 casualties. Three killed at Sevenoaks and one at Kemsley, near Sittingbourne. Two Hurricane pilots of 501 Squadron, Gravesend, Flight Lieutenant George Stoney and Pilot Officer John Bland, killed. Six Hurricanes lost.

Monday August 19th: *(15.00)* : Single plane dropped bombs near Dover Castle, killing 14 soldiers and sailors. 20 people injured.

Tuesday August 20th: *(14.20):* 46 fighters from six squadrons scrambled to meet raiding force of 27 Dorniers and 30 Messerschmitts above the Thames Estuary. In furious fighting, two Dorniers and one Messerschmitt shot down.

Wednesday August 21st: *(14.23):* Bombs dropped on row of cottages at Cossington Road, Canterbury by two lone Dorniers. Five people killed. Raid also on Dover but no casualties.

Thursday August 22nd: *(13.00):* The convoy, *Totem,* heavily shelled in the Channel off Deal. No casualties. Messerschmitts harried by Spitfires of Biggin Hill and Hornchurch. *(18.50):* Two people killed at Dover. Further raid on Manston. Hangars, stores and squadron offices damaged. No casualties. Two Spitfire pilots of 54 and 65 Squadrons from Manston and Hornchurch killed during day.

Friday August 23rd: *(7.15):* For the second successive day, Pilot Officer Jan Pfeiffer of 32 Squadron crash-landed at Hawkinge due to combat damage. On the second occasion he landed on one wheel of his Hurricane.

Saturday August 24th: *(12.40):* Enemy raids even more intense after period of bad weather. 20 Junkers accompanied by fighters severely mauled Defiants of 264 Squadron, Hornchurch off Manston. Seven aircraft damaged or lost. Seven airmen killed. *(15.20):* Another attack on Manston forcing its evacuation as front-line airfield. Airfield cratered, living quarters destroyed, buildings lost and telephone circuits severed, 17 casualties. The first-wave raiders created so much smoke and dust that the second wave attackers turned their attention to Ramsgate flying club which had no military value. Many bombs dropped on the town, killing 31 people. Pilot Officer Pawel Zenker of 501 Squadron, Gravesend killed off Dover.

Sunday August 25th: *(19.00):* Biggin Hill's 32 Squadron in combat action over Channel. Two Hurricanes lost. Pilot Officer Jack Rose baled out and was rescued from the sea. Pilot Officer Keith Gillman failed to return.

These two Ramsgate ladies escaped the attack on August 24th because they, and many of the town's 60,000 population, were 70 feet below ground in the shelters which ran for three miles under the town. Those who lost their houses in this devastating raid made the catacombs their home for the rest of the war.

Ramsgate's blackest day

August 24th, 1940 was the most tragic day in Ramsgate's history. Instead of attacking Manston airfield, one wave of enemy raiders turned their attention on the town and dropped 250 high explosive and incendiary bombs. 31 people were killed, 45 injured and 1,200 houses destroyed. Streets in the town were blocked, water mains fractured and unexploded bombs littered the borough. Two auxiliary firemen who were cycling to work when the raid began were machine gunned and badly injured. One of them, although wounded five times and weak from loss of blood, dragged his friend to a sheltered spot and then climbed over masonry and debris to a first aid post. His friend died but he was awarded the George Medal for his act of gallantry. Most of those who died were in the town centre. Five pubs, the town's gas works, lifeboat station and several shops were hit by bombs.

The worst area was Camden Square where the Assembly Hall was demolished. It could have been worse. Most people were sheltering in the tunnels during the attack and it was estimated that these saved up to 11,000 people.

The Maidstone and District bus depot after the Gillingham raid.

Buses blaze in raid on Gillingham

ON August 27th it was Gillingham's turn to suffer its worst day of the war. German bombers attacked at midnight, killed 20 people and seriously injured 22. One bomb scored a direct hit on the Maidstone and District bus depot which blazed through the night; in fact the heat from the fire was so intense that houses on the other side of the road suffered. In a desperate attempt to save some of the buses, depot staff braved exploding petrol tanks but managed to save 70, while 50 were destroyed.

One sailor, who could not drive, found that he could not stop his bus — so he deliberately ran into a telephone kiosk and went back for another! Bombs caused extensive damage in the town. The Co-op store, a newsagent, sub post office and a butcher's shop were hit. An incendiary bomb fell on the theatre where an audience, unaware of the raid, were politely asked to leave. The fire station was also hit in the raid but the men managed to save 21 hoses which were all used to tackle the bus depot fire.

Challock Forest, Hinxhill. Five killed. This was the last daytime sortie by the vulnerable Defiant. *(13.00):* 100 aircraft over Thames Estuary on way to Rochford met by Spitfires of 54 and 56 Squadrons. Flying Officer Al Deere's Spitfire shot down by another Spitfire. Deere baled out over Detling. Aircraft crashed at Stockbury. *(15.15-16.45):* Enemy launched seven attacks totalling 100 aircraft over Kent and Thames Estuary. Met by Spitfires of 603 Squadron, Hornchurch who lost two pilots, and 610 Squadron, Biggin Hill. Pilot Officer Kenneth Cox of 610 Squadron shot down and killed. He crashed into a house at Stelling Minnis. *(19.00):* 60 aircraft approached Kent and 603 Squadron scrambled again. Spitfire crashed at Tenterden. Pilot killed.

Monday August 26th: *(11.30):* A raiding force of 40 Heinkels, 12 Dorniers and 80 Messerschmitts crossed Dover and flew west. Party harried by 40 Hurricanes and 30 Spitfires resulting in furious dogfights over Weald of Kent. Small towns and villages in East Kent strafed and barrage balloons destroyed. Two people killed in Folkestone. Local policeman W. Spain rescued woman from bombed house — an action for which he won George Medal. Pilot Officer Frank Webster of 610 Squadron, Biggin Hill crashed in flames and died attempting to land at Hawkinge. On this day the Kent countryside was littered with the burning remains of crashed Messerschmitts.

Tuesday August 27th: *(23.30):* German bombers attack Gillingham, 20 killed. Many buildings in town centre set on fire. 50 buses destroyed in direct hit on Maidstone and District bus depot. High explosive bomb fell on Co-op store causing severe damage.

Wednesday August 28th: Four major attacks on Kent. *(09.00):* 60 aircraft flew inland between North Foreland and Dover to attack Eastchurch where more than 100 bombs were dropped and several light bombers destroyed. Harried by Hurricanes from 79 Squadron, Biggin Hill and Defiants from 264 Squadron, Hornchurch. Defiants crashed at Faversham,

Thursday August 29th: *(15.00-16.00):* An equal battle in the afternoon above Rye between 12 Messerschmitts and 12 Hurricanes. Flight Lieutenant Harry Hamilton, a Canadian, of 85 Squadron, Croydon was killed when his aircraft crashed near the ruins of Camber Castle. Two other Hurricanes written off. The Spitfires of 610 Squadron, Biggin Hill were also in action. Sergeant Edward Manton crashed at Hurst Green and died. *(19.00):* 501 Squadron, Gravesend, scrambled to intercept enemy fighters over Deal. Two Hurricanes lost.

Pilots from Biggin Hill drinking outside one of their favourite watering holes, The White Hart at Brasted. Landlady Kath Preston said that if the Luftwaffe had chosen to drop a bomb on The White Hart on a Saturday night in the summer of 1940, the outcome of The Battle of Britain might have been very different. Can anyone identify these pilots please?

The bombing of Biggin Hill

Friday August 30th: Another day of hectic activity in which 48 Observer posts in Kent and Surrey reported combats above their stations. Three Hurricanes damaged in morning as 79 Squadron chased off raiding party. *((12.00):* Squadron Leader Eric King of 151 Squadron, Stapleford crashed and died in Temple Street, Strood nine days after taking command. Kenley lost three pilots Pilot Officer David Jenkins and Pilot Officer Colin Francis of 253 Squadron and Flying Officer John Bell of 616 Squadron. *(13.30):* Waves of bombers and Messerschmitts crossed the coast at 20-minute intervals and five fighter stations were scrambled. Bombs dropped on Lympne airfield and five civilians killed. Kent again littered with burning remains of fighter aircraft from both sides. Another Kenley pilot, Sergeant John Dickinson killed. *(16.00):* One of the most devastating raids of the Battle as 740 enemy aircraft crossed the coast. Ten Junkers left the raiding party to attack one of the Luftwaffe's most prized targets — Biggin Hill. They left behind a scene of death and devastation.

THE Luftwaffe's intention on August 30th was to wipe RAF Biggin Hill off the map. It was just after six o-clock when airmen, pouring out of the Mess, saw a small formation of Junkers, machine guns crackling, bearing down on them from the east. They dived for the shelter but there was not room for all. Those outside were the lucky ones for a bomb hit the shelter, the concrete walls caved in and all that was left was a gaping crater with fragments of stones, chalk, uniform and mangled flesh.

The death toll was 39. The havoc wrought over the rest of the airfield was appalling. The workshops, cookhouses, the NAAFI, the Sergeants' Mess, the WAAF's quarters and the airmen's barracks were wrecked. So was 90 per cent of the station transport and two Spitfires on the ground. One hangar had received a direct hit and all electricity, water and gas mains were cut. In another shelter, where WAAFs had been packed like sardines, the girls had listened to the head-splitting inferno outside, the machine guns, the lightweight bombs and the roar of a thousand pounds of high explosive. One bomb blew up the entrance, a hot blast bowled them over and they found they were completely entombed.

Ambulances and stretcher parties, together with the local doctor, were standing by as pilots and erks worked side by side to dig out the girls. Some were hardly recognisable through the dirt and blood but all were alive, save one. Hornchurch took temporary control of Biggin Hill as men worked all night to restore communications. A link was made and the operations room was back on air with No 11 Group headquarters the following morning.

Cup of tea in a country cottage for the Nazi airman

ONE of the greatest talking points in Kent during those hectic weeks of the air battle concerned the number of Nazi airmen who were parachuting out of the sky — "the RAF having made the Heinkels, Junkers, Dorniers and Messerschmitts too uncomfortable to sit in any longer".

The reception afforded to the visitors varied with their behaviour on landing. One landed in a Weald village and was seen by an old lady in a country cottage. She invited him to have a cup of tea and while he was drinking it, she calmly phoned for the police.

Some of the German airmen could speak good English. One said to his captors. "I am a German aviator. Will you take me to the RAF, please?" This must have seemed a little odd at the time considering the tremendous trouble he had just been taking in trying to get away from the RAF.

Not all the Nazi pilots were so tactful. A Kent newspaperman described how many prisoners spat at their captors and frequently insisted on Heil Hitlering!

One German pilot was under armed escort on a train when it stopped at Chatham. A waitress ran out of the station buffet and rattled the Mayor

This Messerschmitt Bf 109E-4 was shot down on Thursday September 5th during a diversionary fighter sweep over Kent and force-landed at Winchet Hill, Love's Farm, Marden. The pilot was Oberleutnant Baron Franz von Werra, one of the most famous German aces, who became known as "the one that got away" — the only German prisoner of war captured in Britain who escaped back to the Fatherland.

of Chatham's Spitfire Fund collecting box at the prisoner. He smiled, pulled a five-mark note out of his wallet and put it into the box.

When a Dornier bomber crashed at Shoreham, near Sevenoaks, the Home Guard were entrusted with one of the uninjured airmen. He was so pale and shaken that they stopped at the Crown

Franz von Werra's aircraft which force-landed at Marden is emblazoned with previous victories.

in the village and bought him a brandy before turning him in. By the end of August the Guards Room at Biggin Hill was full of prisoners. Each one, however, had been entertained in the Mess before being locked up — a custom that continued throughout the war. Few, it seemed, appreciated the splendid Westerham Ale!

Unfortunately for the enemy, the driver of the 403 bus from Sevenoaks to Westerham was not quite so hospitable. He saw a lone parachutist fall on top of a haystack, stopped the bus, alerted the conductor and, armed with spanners, approached the airman who was covered in hay.

The German thought that London Transport uniform represented some kind of military uniform, gave a smart Nazi salute and announced that "Biggin Hill is kapput". The infuriated bus driver hit him over the head with his spanner.

Elspeth Henderson, Helen Turner and Elizabeth Mortimer, Biggin Hill WAAFs, who were awarded the Military Medal for bravery.

Military Medals for three WAAFs

MANY of the Biggin Hill WAAFs, engulfed by chalk and concrete when their shelter collapsed, were on duty the next day. Among them were Corporal Elspeth Henderson who looked after the switchboard and Sergeant Helen Turner who manned the telephone near the Operations Room.

At six o'clock on Saturday August 31st the raiders returned and everyone was ordered to shelter. Sergeant Turner refused and remained at the switchboard until she was dragged under a table, protesting. At that moment a 500 lb bomb crashed through the roof and bounced off the safe. The blast knocked over Miss Henderson who was still in touch with Group HQ.

The plotting screen was smashed, the runways cratered again and all communications severed. Water and gas were escaping, many people were injured and there were fires everywhere. Once again the station was devastated.

Within minutes post office engineers were again at work reconnecting cables and setting up a makeshift operations room in a village shop. They worked through the night, repaired the main cable and established links with Observer Posts throughout Kent. Biggin Hill refused to be beaten.

The two girls were awarded the Military Medal for their bravery, making it three for Biggin Hill — out of six won by WAAFs during the war.

Saturday August 31st: *(07.00-09.30):* All barrage balloons protecting Dover were shot down by Messerschmitts in a dawn assault that was followed by a raid on Eastchurch and Detling airfields. *(12.55):* Dorniers and Heinkels returned to Biggin Hill and bombed the airfield once more. A Hurricane piloted by Squadron Leader Peter Townsend of 85 Squadron, Croydon was hit by a burst from an Me10. He baled out at Hawkhurst and was taken to Croydon Hospital where his left big toe was amputated. 253 Squadron, Kenley was also in action with tragic results; Squadron Leader

Harold Starr was shot down and killed at Hammill Brickworks, Eastry and Squadron Leader Tom Gleave baled out, grievously burned, at Mace Farm, Cudham. *(16.00):* Enemy aircraft carried out a series of raids in the afternoon on the radar stations at Foreness, Dunkirk, Rye, Beachy Head and Pevensey. All were damaged. Sergeant Henry Bolton force-landed at Haliloo Farm, Warlingham and was killed. *(17.30):* Biggin Hill attacked yet again by Junkers and Messerschmitts who dropped 30 bombs on the beleaguered airfield. The operations room received a direct hit and all

communication lines were severed. Minutes later the station lost Flying Officer Edgar Wilcox of 72 Squadron who was shot down in combat over Dungeness. He crashed in Checkenden Farm, Staplehurst.

Sunday September 1st: *(10.55):* A wave of bombers and fighter escorts flew in over Dover along a front that was five miles long. The targets were Biggin Hill, Detling, Eastchurch and the London Docks. The Hurricanes of No.1 Squadron, Northolt and the Spitfires of 72 Squadron, Croydon were among those scrambled. Flight Sergeant Frederick Berry crashed and died at Ruckinge. Flying Officer Oswald Pigg was killed when his Spitfire crashed on Elvey Farm, Pluckley. *(13.40):* 170 Dorniers and Messerschmitts crossed the Kent coast and were attacked by Hurricanes of 85 Squadron, Croydon. Flying Officer P. Woods-Scawen was killed when his parachute failed to open. Scores of aircraft from both sides were shot down, including Dorniers at Lydd and Dungeness, Messerschmitts at Orlestone, Chilham, Winchelsea and Bilsington. *(17.30):* Final wave of seven enemy formations swept in — one to attack Biggin Hill yet again.

Squadron Leader Mike Crossley, the "Red Knight", charismatic CO of 32 Squadron was shot down on Sunday August 18th after a dog fight over the Thames Estuary. He landed in some allotments near Gillingham where a reception committee was waiting with pitchforks and shotguns. They seemed rather disappointed that he was not a Nazi. Less than a week later, on August 24th, he was shot down again, this time crashing at Lyminge. Again he was unhurt. Crossley, who kept the 32 Squadron diary, received the DFC from the King in June, 1940 at a special investiture at Biggin Hill and, two months later, received the DSO. He remained with 32 Squadron until April 1941 when he was sent to America as a test pilot. Back in the UK, Crossley led the Detling wing in 1943 and later contracted tuberculosis.

Monday September 2nd: *(07.00):* The relentless pounding of Biggin Hill continued when nine Dorniers split away from an attacking force of 40 and swept in low over the airfield. This was the sixth raid in 48 hours and there was little left to destroy save the unquenchable spirit of the personnel. After each attack the CO, Group Captain Dick Grice, took pride in reporting to Fighter Command: "Airfield still operational." A big dog fight developed over Maidstone between Spitfires and Messerschmitts and a bomb on the town killed two people. *(12.00):* More than 70 Hurricanes and Spitfires intercepted 250 German fighters and bombers over Ashford. Pilot Officer Charles Woods-Scawen of 43 Squadron, Tangmere was killed when his Hurricane crashed at Fryland, Ivychurch — his brother had died the previous day. *(17.00):* Another 250 raiders crossed the coast and were met by fighters from ten RAF squadrons. Pilot Officer John Bailey, a former Tonbridge School boy, was killed when his Hurricane was shot down over the Thames Estuary. Detling and Eastchurch airfields attacked by 40 Dorniers. Nine aircraft on the ground destroyed. One bomb at Eastchurch hit bomb dump and exploded the 350 bombs, virtually demolishing every building within 400 yards.

Tuesday September 3rd: Most of the day's action moved to Essex and the eastern counties but the Spitfires of 603 Squadron, Hornchurch were involved in combat off Margate. Pilot Officer Richard Hillary was shot down in flames. He baled out grievously burnt and was rescued by Margate lifeboat. Hillary became another of Archie McIndoe's Guinea Pigs after undergoing surgery at the Queen Victoria Hospital, East Grinstead. He is remembered for his book *"The Last Enemy"* published in 1942. On this day a Hurricane crashed at Parkhouse Farm, Chart Sutton, near Maidstone but the identity of the pilot was never established. Today an 'unknown pilot's memorial garden' exists on the site of the crash.

Wednesday September 4th: *(09.15):* Two Hurricane pilots of 111 Squadron, Croydon went missing during combat off Folkestone. *(12.00):* Seventy Heinkels and Dorniers with an escort of more than 200 Messerschmitts split up between Dover and Hastings to attack Canterbury, Faversham, Eastchurch, Reigate and Redhill. Two people died in the village of Bapchild, near Sittingbourne. Nine squadrons of Hurricanes and Spitfires successfully repelled the raiders but Flying Officer John Cutts was killed when his Spitfire crashed at Amberfield Farm, Chart Sutton and Sergeant John Ramshaw died after crashing at Collier Street, near Yalding. He had survived just five days in the front line. Both were members of 222 Squadron, Hornchurch.

501 Squadron, based at Gravesend and seen here in the second week of August, lost many pilots in the Battle of Britain. Left to right: Pilot Officers Stefan Witorzenc and Bob Dafforn, Sgt Paul Farnes, Flight Lieutenant George Stoney (killed August 15th), Pilot Officer "Hawkeye" Lee, Sgt Antoni Glowacki, Flying Officer John Gibson and Sgt Hugh Adams (killed September 6th).

Thursday September 5th: *(10.00):* A Spitfire of 603 Squadron, Hornchurch shot down following combat with Dorniers and Messerschmitts over Biggin Hill. Flight Lieutenant Frederick Rushmer crashed at Smarden and died. *(11.15):* Messerschmitt 109 shot down by Flying Officer Haines of 19 Squadron crashed in Hardy Street, Maidstone.

Friday September 6th: *(09.00):* Tragic morning for 501 Squadron, Gravesend and 601 Squadron, Tangmere following combat in Hurricanes with raiders over East Kent. Pilot Officer Hugh Adams, from Oxted crashed and died at Clavertye, near Elham, Sergeant Oliver Houghton crashed and died at Long Beech,

Charing and Sergeant Geoffrey Pearson was killed at Kempton Manor, Hothfield. In the same dog fight 601 Squadron lost Flying Officer Carl Davis who crashed into the back garden of a cottage at Matfield and Flight Lieutenant William Rhodes-Moorhouse who came down near the High Brooms Viaduct at Southborough. Altogether 12 Hurricanes were shot down as the war entered its most critical period. Earlier in the morning 24 people were killed when bombs fell on a women's block at the County Hospital, Dartford, wrecking many houses in nearby Anne of Cleves Road.

Saturday September 7th: *(16.15):* The men on the Observer Posts in East Kent could not believe their eyes as the greatest attacking force yet, crossed the coast between Deal and Ramsgate. A staggering total of 348 bombers and 617 fighters advanced towards the Thames Estuary along a 20-mile front. All 21 squadrons based within 70 miles of London were in the air or under take-off orders by 1600. Facing them was a massive aerial armada covering more than 800 square miles. One wave of enemy aircraft flew to the London docks and the second to central London and then the East End. Follow-up raids continued until 0430 the next morning and by that time 306 had been killed with more than 1,337 seriously injured in London. Dog fights continued unabated throughout the afternoon and evening and the eventual tally of losses were 41 German aircraft **(continued on page 67)**

(continued on page 67)

Flying Officer Pat Hughes.

On September 7th, Flying Officer Paterson Hughes of 234 Squadron was killed when his Spitfire crashed at Darks Farm, Bessels Green, Sevenoaks. In 24 days of intensive combat, Hughes had accounted for 15 enemy aircraft and his death came when the Dornier he had been attacking blew up with such force that it completely wrecked his Spitfire. Hughes, an Australian, had been married for just one month.

Now just a matter of days

THE constant strain and relentless attrition suffered by the British fighter pilots over the previous weeks continued as the Germans mounted attack after attack. By Friday September 6th, the resources of Fighter Command were stretched to the limit and in a measure aimed at avoiding its inevitable collapse, exhausted squadrons who had suffered crippling losses were henceforth to be classified as training units and withdrawn. Such a move heralded the beginning of the end of Britain's capacity to resist for very much longer. It was now just a matter of days.

On this day, the Luftwaffe, unaware of how near victory they were, lost 30 aircraft on operations — most of them crashing in Kent. Hitler, incensed by the bombing raids on Berlin, switched his point of attack and demanded immediate reprisals. On September 7th the daylight bombing offensive switched to London and the pressure was taken off the heavily attacked airfields in Kent.

Second Lieutenant William Rhodes-Moorhouse of the Royal Flying Corps.

Flight Lieutenant William Rhodes-Moorhouse of the Royal Air Force.

Hero's son killed at Tunbridge Wells

William Rhodes-Moorhouse who was shot down and killed in combat over Tunbridge Wells on September 6th was a member of 601 Squadron who took part in one of the first raids of the war when six Blenheims from Biggin Hill attacked the German seaplane base at Borkum in November 1939. 601 was known as "the millionaire's mob" — former auxiliary pilots keen to prove that they could be equal in combat to the regular pilots — and among them were Brian Thynne, Whitley Straight, Loel Guinness, Roger Bushell, Sir Archibald Hope and Max Aitken.

Rhodes-Moorhouse's father, also William, was the first airman to be awarded the Victoria Cross. As a member of the Royal Flying Corps in 1915, he bombed a railway line at Courtrai, Belgium on a solo mission in a successful attempt to stop German reinforcements reaching the second Battle of Ypres. He was seriously wounded by machine gun fire and died in hospital clutching a photograph of his only son.

The tragedy at Tunbridge Wells had a sequel 25 years later. In 1976 the site of Rhodes-Moorhouse's crash was excavated by the Kent Battle of Britain Museum who unearthed a beautiful intact Rolls-Royce Merlin engine with various cockpit components and the pilot's wristwatch.

The first raid of the war to cause loss of life in Maidstone occurred on September 2nd when a bomb fell on Marsham Street and two people were killed. This photograph, taken within minutes of the incident, shows two lucky survivors.

On five occasions during September 1940, bombs dropped on Maidstone caused fatalities and after each raid the casualty list was posted on the notice board outside the town hall. It made grim reading.

Immediately after the Gravesend raid, Mrs Webster (left) and Mrs Mansell of Raphael Road organised a collection. For a week they collected over £12 a day.

ARP wardens throughout Kent had novel names for their posts. This is the Grand Hotel at Rochester, where the men were on duty, day and night.

Observer Corps 'unsung heroes' of the battle...

THE Observer Corps played a vital part in Britain's air defences during the Battle of Britain — and throughout the war. It was formed in 1925 following an experiment in aircraft reporting at Cranbrook. At first the men were enrolled as Special Constables but they were so effective in their reporting and plotting role that, by 1938, observation posts had been established all over the country.

These posts were set about 10 miles apart and, in Kent, were linked by a telephone line to the operations centre at Maidstone. Here the reports of various aircraft were numbered and assigned to an RAF sector. The aircraft were plotted across a gridded map table with coloured counters, bearing track, designation, height, number and aircraft type.

Photograph (above) shows the No 1 Group centre at Maidstone in September 1940, buzzing with activity. The operations room moved from the Corn Exchange Buildings to Fairlawns in the London Road in 1942. Here, the uniformed plotters were using arrow-shaped counters for visual plots and shields for sound plots. Other counters indicated crashed aircraft or lost plots.

There is no doubt that the Observer Corps "won its laurels" during the Battle of Britain by maintaining a service in the most difficult conditions. They really were the "unsung heroes".

The operations room of the Observer Corps at Maidstone. It was in April, 1941 that the King designated the description and style, Royal Observer Corps.

Coastal Artillery also did great work in the Straits of Dover. Every movement of enemy ships was checked and many were sunk. Here Brigadier C.W. Raw watched members of the ATS plot the movement of enemy ships. When the ships were in range, the Channel Guns were invited to speak!

The spy who called at the Rising Sun

THE Rising Sun at Lydd occasionally served beer after hours to thirsty airmen but few people tried to snatch a pint BEFORE the pub had opened! Imagine the surprise of the landlady, Mabel Cole, when a well-dressed young man knocked at the door at 9.30 am on September 3rd and, in a foreign accent, said he wanted a glass of cider and some cigarettes. Having every reason to be suspicious Mabel sent him across the road to Tilbeys Stores for his cigarettes, told him to come back for his drink, and summoned help.

The young man — Carl Meier, a Dutchman — was one of four spies who had landed in Kent with instructions to look for information of military importance and to send back coded messages to Germany, prior to the invasion of Britain.

Meier returned to the Rising Sun where he was immediately arrested by an RAF officer, taken to the police station and interrogated. The next day police spotted a man walking across farmland near the Lydd to Dungeness road. Rudolph Waldberg, a German, was also arrested and admitted being in possession of a wireless set, five batteries and a morse key.

The other spies were Dutchmen, Charles van der Kieboom and Sjord Pons. The four men had crossed the Channel in two dinghies; Meier and Waldberg had landed at Dungeness, while Kieboom and Pons came ashore near the Grand Redoubt at West Hythe. Like their colleagues they didn't get far. Both were seen by privates of Somerset Light Infantry — and quickly captured.

The four spies were tried at the Old Bailey on November 22nd under the Treason Act. Waldberg, Meier and Kieboom were hanged at Pentonville while Pons, who claimed he had intended to give himself up and had a fairly plausible story, was found not guilty.

On September 11th, 1940 the hop-pickers huts at Beltring, Paddock Wood were bombed as the hoppers slept. Fortunately the casualties were light.

They fled to the hopfields

WHEN the heavy bombing of London began on September 7th, thousands of people fled from the East End. Some trekked to Epping Forest and camped there and many more took lorries to the Kent hopfields where they slept on straw in the hop-pickers' huts. They didn't stay away for long — the majority returning to face the foe in a neighbourhood renowned for its spirit of defiance.

While the adults were coming and going, the Government quickly organised a more official second evacuation scheme in which half a million children were to leave the capital at the rate of 2,000 a day. As the London children poured into Kent once again, the county was making its own evacuation arrangements. The air raids were far too serious and thousands of children and their mothers moved to Wales, the Midlands and the West Country. Others were evacuated to the Dominions and the United States.

From the East End blitz to the air-raid trenches in the Kent countryside, London children had their eyes trained to the sky.

Gravesend's gunners — who claimed three Dornier 17s.

The gunners who made it too hot for Jerry

IT was "drinks on the Major" for this battery of anti-aircraft gunners at Gravesend who claimed three Dornier 17s inside one minute on Sunday September 8th, 1940 in an extraordinarily accurate burst of shooting.

Records show, in fact, that they certainly shot down two bombers, both of which crashed near the Farningham Road railway station at 12.45. The crew of the first Dornier were all captured, wounded, while the second Dornier lost three of its crew and the fourth was wounded. Nobody seems to know what happened to the third Dornier but on that day a Junkers failed to return to its base in France and was believed to be a victim of ground defences. Aircraft and crew were lost, presumably in the sea.

The destruction of the aircraft was a triumph for the gunners who consisted mainly of lads of 19 and 20. They described how the Dorniers formed the spearhead of a squadron bound for London and the docks. "The call for 'action stations' came", said one of the gunners. "The Jerries came through the clouds at 15,000 feet and we let rip. We were right on target. The first round blew the leader to pieces and it exploded in mid-air. The second and third fell in flames."

The major who stood the round of drinks said the boys, who were Territorials before the war, had been in operation all night. "We've a grand lot of chaps here. They are giving the Jerries a hot time, I can assure you."

Walthamstow Hall School, Sevenoaks was badly damaged when a bomb landed nearby on September 8th, 1940.

Direct hit on Knoll Road, Bexley on September 14th, 1940.

and 18 British. There were several fatalities including Sergeant A.F.C.Saunders and Sergeant J.W.Davis of 600 Squadron, Hornchurch, whose Blenheim crashed on its back from 200 feet at East Close, Rainham. The bombing of London strengthened the feeling that an invasion was imminent and there was great confusion in Kent when a codeword warning to this effect was issued. Church bells were rung, country road-blocks were closed and in many places road bridges were demolished. The Germans did not come. The great invasion was reserved for another day.

Sunday September 8th: Several Dorniers were shot down over Kent by anti-aircraft fire and Hurricane pilots before their fighter escorts could interfere. Some had penetrated as far north as Sheppey and the Thames Estuary. Sub-Lieutenant Jack Carpenter, a Fleet Air Arm pilot on loan to 46 Squadron crashed on Bearsted Golf Course. He baled out but was killed. In a separate incident Flying Officer William Scott crashed in flames and died during squadron patrol off Dover — the victim of a surprise attack by Messerschmitt 109s. Bombs killed four people in the Dartford Rural area, one at Dover and one at West Malling.

Monday September 9th: *(16.00):* Another great day for the RAF as a big bomber raid on London was thwarted and broken up by determined fighter opposition. Turning for home and harried both by Spitfires, Hurricanes and anti-aircraft fire, the German bombers scatttered their bombs on random targets in Kent. In a raid that lasted just five minutes Canterbury suffered badly. Fifty five bombs of various sizes fell on the city at 5 pm damaging property in several roads and killing nine people. One bomb scored a direct hit on the East Kent bus garage in St Stephen's Road where three buses were destroyed. In Dover, four people were killed by shelling. It was a sad day also for 607 Squadron, Tangmere. Three Hurricane pilots were killed in combat — Pilot Officer Stuart Parnall, who crashed at Lime Trees Farm, Goudhurst, Pilot Officer John Lenahan, who crashed at Mount Ephraim, Cranbrook and Pilot Officer George Drake whose aircraft crashed at Bockingfold Farm, Goudhurst. As evening fell, the sirens began wailing in London again which then received its third successive night attack. On this day the Germans lost 27 aircraft and many pilots were captured or killed.

Tuesday September 10th: Owing to a low blanket of cloud which covered Europe, this was a day without any major attack but single Junkers came over Kent and turned their attention to Whitstable, where three people were killed and Sevenoaks, where four died. `

When the sirens wailed the people of Kent were quick to take cover but motorists needed extra help. Here an ARP warden puts out the notice warning that a raid was imminent.

As the raids grew in intensity and the German bombs claimed more and more victims, schoolteachers and their classes became even more vigilant. Children out walking always took their gas masks.

Wednesday September 11th: *(15.45-16.45):* Enemy activity by day consisted of one major attack by 250 aircraft on the Kent coast and, of those, about 30 penetrated to London. Bombing and shelling of Dover and Deal were carried

Flight Lieutenant David Hughes, aged 22, of 238 Squadron failed to return from intercepting a Junkers 88 south of Tunbridge Wells on September 11th. A few months later he was awarded the DFC, posthumously presented to his wife Joan by the King.

out simultaneously and more than 26 bombs were dropped causing vast damage in Dover where the Grand Hotel, the Sailors' Home and the Sussex Arms pub were all hit. Property in Townall Street was devastated. Some people on

the top floor of the hotel fell to the ground floor when it received a direct hit. Altogether 16 people died and 13 were seriously injured. Two people were also killed in Tunbridge Wells. During the day's activity 21 British fighters and at least 60 enemy aircraft were shot down. 92 Squadron, Biggin Hill — destined to be the top-scoring squadron in the Battle of Britain — lost two pilots, Pilot Officer Harry Edwards who crashed into a wood at Smeeth and Pilot Officer Frederick Hargreaves who crashed into the sea.

Thursday September 12th: *(17.00):* Tunbridge Wells was to suffer again when a single aircraft, presumed to be on a reconnaissance flight, suddenly circled the town, picked its point and dropped its cargo of bombs. 11 people were killed in the town's highest death-toll of the war.

Friday September 13th: *(09.45-13.55):* Because of bad visibility, interception by British fighters was virtually impossible so the 90

German bombers which attacked London had things their own way. The raid caused the longest daylight warning in London yet experienced. Bombs also killed four people in Maidstone. During the night, British aircraft of Bomber and Coastal Command attacked the docks at Calais, Dunkirk, Le Havre and Boulogne for the second successive night, destroying hundreds of landing barges intended to be used for the invasion. Hitler, angered by the news, postponed Operation Sealion until September 27th.

Saturday September 14th: More bad weather made fighter interception so difficult that Spitfires were responsible for three Hurricane casualties. Two pilots of 73 Squadron, Debden survived but a third was killed near Tonbridge. A Hurricane pilot, Sergeant W. Higgins of 253 Squadron, Kenley, crashed in flames and died at Swanton Farm, Bredgar. High explosive bombs fell in Swanscombe during the afternoon and killed five people.

Hundreds of German bombers and fighters crashed on Kentish soil during the Battle of Britain, including this Dornier 17Z of the 'Blitz' Geschwader, KG3 which fell victim to fighters and ground fire on August 31st, 1940 before belly-landing on the Sandwich Flats with four wounded crew members aboard. Photograph shows the burning aircraft with Pegwell Bay in the background. The pilot, Oberfeldwebel Lange and another crewman, were marched off to captivity. Local people said that after 40 years the remains of the Dornier were still visible at low tide.

The odds were great, our margins small, the stakes infinite — Churchill

September 15th, 1940

IT looked like a dense black swarm of insects; in fact it was a solid phalanx of bombers and fighters in the sky above the Kent countryside, bound for London. This was the morning of September 15th, 1940 — now celebrated as Battle of Britain Day — the turning point in Nazi Germany's bid for the subjection of Britain and her Empire.

Twenty one squadrons were scrambled to meet the wheeling, snarling fray and were soon caught up in the fiercest, most confused and most widespread fighting of the whole battle. By nightfall the RAF had shot down 61 German aircraft, 34 of which were bombers, for the loss of 26 fighters. It was a day later recognised to be the last classic intercept of the Luftwaffe by the RAF. In the morning the Battle of Britain had reached its climax. By the evening the invasion was no longer feasible.

Squadron Leader Douglas Bader of 242 Squadron described the day as "the finest shambles I have ever seen". Squadron Leader Brian Lane of 19 Squadron thought "I was facing the whole might of the Luftwaffe on my own". Flight Lieutenant Brian Kingcome of 92 Squadron said it "was an electrifying, adrenalin-filled day. One long, sustained high".

The Biggin Hill squadron (92) was one of nine squadrons in action in the morning; scrambled to intercept a formation of 100 Dornier bombers and a massive fighter escort as they crossed the coast. Brian Kingcome was "driving the train". The pilots' reports were eloquent: "Sighted large enemy formation, dodged fighters and climbed into the sun, attacked Dorniers head on...." "Dived and attacked a Do 17 in the middle of the formation. Did not have time to observe results as there were 109s above..." "Gave it a burst from above and behind and it spun into the Thames Estuary..." "He burst into flames. I then spun down to get away from 109s...." "Received cannon shell which forced me to return to base..."

This was a tremendous assault as 160 Spitfires and Hurricanes suddenly appeared and smashed into the formation. The German raiders dropped their bombs at random and fled but not before eight British fighters had been shot down.

Pilot Officer G.L.J. Doutrepont of 229 Squadron was killed when his Hurricane crashed on Staplehurst railway station. Sergeant L.Pidd of 238 Squadron smashed into an oak tree at Kent College, Pembury. He baled out too late and was found dead. Flying Officer A. Pease of 603 Squadron died in his Spitfire at Chartway Street, Kingswood. Hurricane pilot Sergeant M. Brzezowski of 303 Squadron crashed into the Thames, east of Gravesend. 501 Squadron, Kenley, lost their charismatic Belgian pilot Albert Emmanuel Alix Dreudonne Jean Ghislain van der Hove d'Erstenrijct who bravely wrestled with the controls of his damaged machine which had been hit by an Me 109 over Ashford. At 200 feet it exploded above East Stour Farm, Chilham and fell into the River Stour. Pilot Officer J. Gurteen of 504 Squadron dived full throttle into a house at Hartley, Longfield and his colleague Flying Officer M.Jebb died of his injuries in Dartford Hospital.

The second raid on this eventful day consisted of three waves of more than 150 Heinkel and Dorniers with escorts. This time 13 British squadrons tore into them from above and, in the whirling dog fight that ensued, the skies were filled with curling tracers, smoking aircraft and the crackle of ammunition. For the people of Kent who watched from below it was impossible to distinguish friend from foe. Again the raiders fled and suddenly, as if by magic, the skies were empty except for the fading plumes of vapour trails.

There was just one civilian death in Kent on that memorable day, when a German fighter crashed in flames on a building at Bilsington, near Ashford. The house was completely gutted, a small shop nearby was wrecked and the force of the explosion scattered wreckage over a wide area. A widow living close to the scene found a wheel in her living room and a machine gun on her bed upstairs.

The fields, orchards, gardens and villages of Kent were littered with the smoking burnt out remains of German aircraft. Messerschmitt 109s crashed at St Michaels near Tenterden, Pluckley Brickworks, St Margaret's-at-Cliffe, Brenchley, Smarden, Bekesbourne, Bearsted, Biggin Hill, Dymchurch Redoubt, Lympne, Hothfield, Hartlip Churchyard and the Isle of Sheppey.

Dorniers came down at Chatham, off Herne Bay, Cranbrook, Barnehurst Golf Course, Isle of Grain, Marden, Sturry, Herne Bay, Shoreham and Underriver

There were Heinkels at Foulness, Tripcock Pier, Woolwich, Sandhurst, Frittenden, Benenden and West Malling. Many others crashed into the sea and some limped back to base badly damaged.

92 Squadron, based at Biggin Hill, achieved fame as the most successful in Fighter Command during the Battle of Britain. Certainly they had a good "score" on September 15th, 1940. One of those who came through was Flight Lieutenant Brian Kingcome (left) who "drove the train". On October 15th Kingcome was shot down in combat with Bf 109s and baled out wounded. He was admitted to the Royal Naval Hospital, Chatham. He is seen here after returning to action the following year with Wing Commander Jamie Rankin who became CO of 92 in March 1941. Due to the accuracy of his shooting Rankin became known as "one-a-day Rankin".

Hitler postpones invasion of Britain

MONDAY September 16th, when the weather was too poor for large scale fighting, was to be an historic one for Kent and Britain. German aircraft losses were so huge that Luftwaffe commanders warned that their force could "bleed to death". Bitter inquests were held in Pas de Calais and Hitler announced his decision to postpone the invasion "until further notice". The War Diary of the German Naval Staff recorded: "The enemy air force is still by no means defeated — on the contrary it shows increasing activity".

Churchill, with his genius for timing, had chosen September 15th to visit the Underground Ops Room at Group HQ and watch the battle on the plotting board. For him it was a tense day, its crisis points marked by the red bulbs glowing on every squadron panel beside the words — enemy intercepted.

He said: "Yesterday eclipses all previous records of the Fighter Command. Aided by squadrons of their Czech and Polish comrades, using only a small proportion of their total strength and under cloud conditions of some difficulty, they cut to rags and tatters three separate waves of murderous assault upon the civil population of their native land. These results exceed all expectations and give just and sober confidence in the approaching struggle."

The open parachute was a frequent sight for those in Kent during the Battle of Britain. Brian Kingcome said: "There were intensely sad moments as well as exciting ones. I lost many old friends as well as making new ones and the worst part was watching them die, spiralling down with a smudge of smoke, watching for the parachute to blossom, the relief when it did, the sick feeling when it didn't."

This Junkers (Ju88A-1) was on a night bombing mission of London when it was intercepted by a Defiant crew who opened fire. The Junkers crashed in Maidstone and the pilot, Leutnant Ganslmayr and his crew were all killed. This is from an original oil painting by Ralph Bristow.

Part of the fuselage of the Junkers 88 which paid a call on this house in St Andrews Close, Maidstone at 11.45 pm on the evening of September 17th, 1940. The Junkers was shot down by the pilots of a Defiant night fighter, Sgts George Laurence and Wilfred Chard, following a chase that was plotted on the school blackboard at Biggin Hill where the Operation Room was temporarily housed. "Stuffy" Dowding Commander-in-Chief of Fighter Command was a guest observer. The Defiant pilots were with 141 Squadron which had just returned to its birthplace at Biggin Hill.

Dive bombers in revenge attack on Maidstone

THE drama in Maidstone on the night of September 17th aroused enormous excitment in the town. Leutnant Ganslmayr and his crew were buried at the Sutton Road cemetery three days later with full military honours and the gutted house at St Andrews Close was demolished.

There was, however, even worse to come. As if to avenge the loss of the Junkers crew, 16 dive bombers appeared above Maidstone at noon on Friday September 27th and created havoc from Allington Castle on the Medway to Barton Road, south of the town.

A bomb dropped next to St Faith's Church, made a huge crater and the church tower was split almost from top to bottom. Another crashed into the museum gardens, wrecking the gardener's cottage and damaging the almshouses. One fell in the station goods yard, damaging the railway line. Clothes and toys were set alight when a bomb fell through the roof of Hills and Steele store in Week Street and two auxiliary firemen were injured when another dropped on the Walls ice cream depot next to their station in Hope Street.

Several soldiers had a lucky escape when a bomb fell near their bus and hop-pickers on another bus threw themselves on the floor as flying fragments smashed through the windows.

This was to be Maidstone's worst raid of the war. About 50 high explosive and incendiary bombs were dropped, 22 people were killed and 44 seriously injured. More than 100 properties were damaged.

Milkman Bill Phipps carried on with his round despite the danger, accompanied by Princess. Wally Scarboro removes the barrier to let them through. Sidcup, September 1940.

Parachute mines fall on 12 Kent towns

A new terrorist tactic was introduced during the night of September 16th/17th, proving beyond doubt that the enemy had abandoned all pretence of aiming at military objectives. Six aircraft flew over Kent and dropped parachute mines on Woolwich, Orpington, Rochester, Swanley, Bellingham, Swanscombe, St Mary Cray, Bromley, Chislehurst, Chelsfield, Chipstead, Beckenham and several south London sites.

Another 36 were reported on September 19th causing Churchill to send a note to his Chiefs of Staff: "This is an act of terror against the civil population. My inclination is to say that we will drop a heavy parachute mine on German cities for every one he drops on ours..."

The mines had a high charge ratio of 60 to 70 per cent explosive and created considerable blast damage wherever they fell. Officially the existence of parachute mines was not disclosed to the public until 1944.

Few people were killed in those first mine explosions, called "Luftmines" by Home Security and merely "Tpe C" by the Admiralty who had the job of defusing them.

The crippled Junkers on the Graveney Marshes.

The battle of Graveney Marshes

WHEN a huge force of Junkers 88s missed the rendezvous with their fighter escorts on September 27th, 1940, the German pilots foolishly decided to press towards London unprotected. Hurricanes and Spitfires were scrambled to meet them and, like a pack of hounds, cornered a dozen bombers and picked them off one by one.

The first broke up over Cudham and another came down at South Holmwood, near Dorking. Five plunged in the Channel and others crashed in flames at East Grinstead, Horsmonden, Penshurst and Sevenoaks, where one of the crew survived and was taken prisoner.

The twelfth unfortunate Junkers 88 was damaged by anti-aircraft fire and then chased by pilots of 66 and 92 Squadron. What happened next turned out to be one of the most fascinating stories of the war.

Piloted by Underoffizier Fritz Ruhlandt, the lame Junkers was easy prey for the British pilots who raked it with gunfire and then closed in for the kill over North Kent, east of Faversham. Ruhlandt skilfully brought the bomber down on the Graveney marshes just a few hundred yards from the Sportsman Inn on the South Oaze sea wall.

The wounded captain and his crew crawled out of the maimed aircraft and were immediately confronted by troops of the 1st London Irish Rifles who happened to be billeted in the Sportsman Inn. Imagine the surprise of the soldiers when the German airmen opened fire with two machine guns and a sub-machine gun just as they were preparing to arrest the crew and take charge of the aircraft

before it was destroyed.

The captain in charge deployed his men in a line and they crawled along the dykes of the marshes prepared for a vicious land battle. When they were within 100 yards, one of the Junkers crew waved a white flag. The soldiers pounced, there was a fight and two of the crew were hurt. When the riflemen reached the aircraft a time-bomb was discovered and successfully removed — but as the prisoners were being taken away one of them was heard to remark that the aircraft would "go up any time now".

Captain Cantopher who had arrived on the scene went back and found another time-bomb, which he removed. The aircraft was thus saved from destruction and proved to be a new type, only two weeks old. It provided the experts at the Air Ministry with highly valuable information. For his timely action, Captain Cantopher was awarded the Military Medal.

It is claimed that the skirmish between the German bomber crew and the London Irish Riflemen was the only occasion of armed conflict between British and German forces on English land during the war, replacing the ill-fated mission in February 1797 when 1,200 French troops were routed by Pembrokeshire Yeomanry near Fishguard as the last battle on British soil. However, on that occasion the invaders did not fire a shot. The precedent, therefore, may be far more distant.

The Battle of Graveney Marshes has a significant place in history.

Secret army to harrass the invaders

THE invasion had been postponed and Hitler, for the time being at least, was not going to despoil the Garden of England. However, the furious battle in the skies continued and the Kentish people were as vigilant as ever — none more so than Peter Fleming, a captain in the Grenadier Guards and brother of the creator of James Bond. For he was in charge of the county's anti-invasion preparations.

While the Fuhrer was planning his landing tactics, Fleming was forming a secret army from his hideaway at The Garth, Bilting, near Ashford. Few knew of his work or of the existence of the armed guerrillas who would have hassled the invaders in the same way that the resistance movement was causing havoc in occupied France.

Captain Fleming began to form his patrols in the summer of 1940 with the help of four soldiers, several drivers and two batmen. He also had two RAF radio operators and a platoon of Lovat Scouts. Each patrol operated independently and had between four and eight men and its own hide-out as a base. They were part of a national resistance movement which had its headquarters at Coleshill, near Swindon.

The civilian members of Fleming's patrols were armed with pistols, a rubber truncheon and commando knife. They also had use of a tommy gun, two rifles, hand grenades and plastic explosives. Training was carried out in the grounds of The Garth where the men were taught how to kill silently and use their weapons effectively.

Nobody knew of the men's dual role — not even their wives — and nobody knew of the 25 hide-outs which existed all over Kent. One of the most impressive was an enormous underground chamber in Godmersham Park. It was called The Airship because it housed one during the 1914-18 war and was so massive that it could accommodate up to 120 people.

Having established his resistance patrols, Fleming was replaced at Bilting by Lieutenant-Colonel Norman Field. He took over in November 1940, dug an underground observation post on the crest of Charing Hill and made certain that all hide-outs were ingeniously concealed.

Eventually there were more than 1,000 hide-outs in use in the country before it was decided Hitler would never invade and the patrols were disbanded. In Kent they existed at Baddlesmere, near Faversham, Wickhambreaux, near the mouth of the River Stour, Challock, Hastingleigh, near Wye, Manston, Wootton, near Folkestone, Lydden, near Dover, Minster, Staplehurst, Sutton Valence, Frith Wood, near Hawkhurst, Rolvenden, Tenterden, Bethersden, Brookland, Ash and Pluckley.

In his book, *Operation Sealion*, Peter Fleming wrote: "It seems unlikely that the Auxiliary Units would have been able to achieve very much.....but before melting away in the white heat of German ruthlessness, it might have struck some useful blows....."

* In the event of a German invasion in 1940 the newspaper owners of Kent had plans to produce a clandestine journal, probably called Invicta. Journalists and printers in the local underground would bring out a single sheet, 16 in by 11 in printed for as long as possible on the Kent Messenger presses in Maidstone.

If large parts of the county were over-run a mobile printing press would operate from the Kent Territorial Association offices at Yalding, with the Godmersham farm of the KM's proprietor, Henry Pratt Boorman and farm buildings at Withyham, East Sussex, as fall-back locations.

Stay put in your fortress, or you will be shot

HAD the Germans landed in 1940, all Kent towns of any size would have become citadels — to be defended in a series of "Stalingrads". The most important fortress of all would have been the county town of Maidstone where defenders would have fought over every inch of rubble and used every method possible to keep the enemy at bay.

A 52-page manual released in the early 1970's under the "30 year rule" showed that Mr Henry Vann, wartime chief constable of Maidstone, was in charge of turning the town into a fortress. His instructions were to ring it with barbed wire and anti-tank traps, protected by Army units. As far as the civilian population was concerned a 'stay-put' policy would have been implemented.

Had the Maidstone defences been breached, the Army would have fallen back into the town. Helped by the civilians and Peter Fleming's secret sabateurs, every building would have been defended and everything useful to Fifth Columnists destroyed. Orders would have been relayed to the defenders, or "Triumvirate" as they would have been called, by piped radio. There were code words for all instructions.

It was anticipated at the time that thousands of Maidstone people would have deserted their homes and fled into the countryside, despite the order to stay put. If this had happened the police were instructed to use force to prevent any panic evacuation.

Each town in Kent had its own plan to make life as difficult as possible for the invaders.

Meanwhile the people of Kent were showing the spirit of defiance that was now their hallmark. So that pickers could be near to their bomb shelters and homes, hops were brought by farmers into the village of Marden to be picked. And, in Greenhithe, Sunday services were held in one of the chalk tunnels which was used as an air raid shelter. Photograph shows the Rev. Stanley Morgan and his underground congregation.

Many killed as bombs blast Kent pubs

AS autumn arrived and the nights drew in there was no respite in the bombing of Kent towns. Eight were killed in Middle Street and Union Street, Deal on October 4th when single aircraft arrived in quick succession and created havoc. The old Victory pub and four houses were demolished and rescue parties searched for bodies for hours. High explosive bombs were dropped in Ordnance Street and Rochester Street, Chatham the following day. The raid killed eight people.

On October 6th, Folkestone was bombed twice. A total of 13 people died. An officer of Folkestone fire brigade received the OBE for saving the life of a trapped child. Bomb-carrying Messerschmitts, being chased by Spitfires, scattered their deadly cargo over Ashford, Canterbury and Folkestone on October 11th. Nine died in Canterbury and one bomb fell within 100 yards of the Cathedral.

Nights out in Kentish pubs were hazardous affairs in those tragic days. The Royal Oak at Wrotham Heath was crowded with customers on Tuesday October 15th when a bomb scored a direct hit on the inn, killing at least three people inside and six in the village. The Star pub in Swanscombe also received a direct hit on November 10th and the death toll rose to 27.

It was Ramsgate's turn again on Saturday November 2nd. An air raid warning had sent people rushing for the shelters but the All Clear quickly sounded and shoppers returned to the town centre. Without warning 25 aircraft swooped out of the clouds and released more than 60 bombs sending hundreds of people scurrying for cover. One woman who survived returned home to find her own mother and her two children dead in the ruins of her house.

By the end of October there had been bombing incidents involving multiple deaths in Margate, Dover, Rochester, Penshurst, Headcorn and Beltring.

On Thursday October 10th, 1940, Sergeant Harold Allgood of 253 Squadron, Kenley was on patrol over Maidstone with eight other Hurricanes when his aircraft, at 20,000 feet, went out of control and into a steep dive. Sergeant Allgood, apparently suffering from oxygen failure and hardly conscious, wrestled weakly with the controls as the plane skimmed across the roofs of several houses. There were reports that he was trying to steer it towards open ground but the Hurricane bounced off the roof of Albion Stores and smashed into the two houses next door in Albion Place at the top of Union Street. Petrol from the wrecked aircraft spewed all over the buildings which burst into flames, killing eight people and injuring two. Firemen found the body of the pilot in the cellar together with his parachute and parts of the engine.

Wardens, civilians and servicemen stared at the mangled remains of a Messerschmitt 109 which exploded under attack by Pilot Officer Bryan Draper of 74 Squadron on October 20th, 1940, then fell apart and crashed at Wickham Street, Welling. The pilot was killed. Draper survived many more sorties but died in Rangoon in the last year of the war.

The bus driver was due to report for work but during the night a bomb fell near his home in Bexleyheath, partially wrecking it. The smiling faces, so common during this period, showed the determination of the people of north Kent to face the onslaught. The message to Hitler was simple. Bomb us if you will, but you're not going to win!

Poor Maidstone, it seemed, had been singled out by the Luftwaffe for special attention. On October 31st, bombs were again dropped on the town, killing and seriously injuring 14. This was Mill Street at 9 am. A naval officer was actually driving this car when it plunged into one of the bomb craters. He and his wife were both rescued unhurt.

Why "Millie" was the toast of Tenterden

THE last airman to die following action with enemy fighters over Kent during the Battle of Britain was a young South Australian, Pilot Officer William Henry Millington. Engaged in sporadic fighting at 1.00 pm on Wednesday October 30th, Millington and his Hurricane failed to return and he was reported missing, almost certainly drowned in the Channel.

The 23-year-old was then with 249 Squadron, based at North Weald and had been flying with the RAF for little more than a year. Two months earlier this unlucky airman had been the toast of Tenterden following one of the bravest decisions of the whole campaign and one in which he won the DFC.

On August 30th, Pilot Officer Millington, then with 79 Squadron, was chasing a Dornier, streaking for home after unloading its bombs on Biggin Hill. The Australian suddenly found himself alone with two Messerschmitt 109s. He sent one spinning to earth near Romney Marsh and made the fatal error of watching the pilot crawl out of the wreckage. In those split seconds the second 109 pumped cannon fire into

"Millie's" Hurricane which started a flicker of flame that suddenly burst into his cockpit.

Blinded by scalding oil, Millington forced the hood back and prepared to jump. Below was a small town which he assumed to be Tenterden and there were villages all around. The young pilot instinctively knew that a crashing Hurricane would bring tragedy, perhaps to scores of people. Somehow, he fought back the urge to save his own life, righted the aircraft and crash-landed in an open field at Conghurst Farm, Hawkhurst. Badly burned, he dragged himself clear and the Hurricane exploded.

The last German aircraft to crash in Kent during the official period of the Battle of Britain were all 109s and each incident occurred on the afternoon of Wednesday October 30th. The first exploded over Brook Farm, Meopham and the pilot was killed, the second crash-landed in a hop field on Court Lodge Farm, East Farleigh and the pilot was captured and the third crashed in flames at Leylands, near Meopham. The pilot baled out, slightly wounded.

The thirteenth century chancel of the Cathedral of the Marsh was destroyed by German bombs, which fell in the town of Lydd, on October 15th, 1940.

The terrible scene at Swanscombe where the Star pub was totally wrecked.

Carnage at the darts match

THERE was an important darts match at The Star pub, Swanscombe on the evening of Sunday November 10th, 1940. The teams and regulars turned up and, by 8 pm, the pub was crowded with customers. Above the banter, the excited chatter, the piano playing and the cheers as the darts match got underway, no-one heard the air-raid alarm and no-one heard the German bombers as they droned overhead on their way to East London.

One bomb was dropped as the raiders flew over and, by chance, it scored a direct hit on The Star. The party was abruptly broken up by an enormous explosion and the building just fell apart. Outside a column of smoke rose into the wintry sky. Victims, covered in blood and horribly injured, tried to claw their way to safety. Some were yelling hysterically. Others were silent and motionless.

All that was left of the small bars where the pub had stood was a heap of smouldering debris and twisted rafters. The staircase leading to the clubroom upstairs was still in place but there was a gaping hole in the cellar and, inside, there was carnage.

The people of Swanscombe heard the explosion and those with relatives known to be in the pub rushed out of their homes and shelters. Some also came out of the local cinema. They had not heard the alert. They were confronted by a distressing scene, as they waited for news of the casualties. Firemen, civil defence personnel and rescue squads recovered the bodies one by one. Women, many weeping hysterically, stood by the street corner watching the activity, waiting for the moment when the official casualty list could be posted. The death toll rose from 10 to 19 and then to 27, with six seriously injured.

The landlord died in the bombing but his wife and daughter survived. The barmaid on duty that night was also killed and so was a seaman and his father who were having a drink. It was Swanscombe's worst incident of the war.

It is possible that people were sheltering in the old lime pits at Swanscombe when the bomb fell on November 10th. In 1940 the old railway tunnel which led to the pits was fitted out by the local authority as an air raid shelter and was soon in regular use. Children here were looking across one of the lakes towards the scene of the pub carnage.

Bombs fell nearby, but the threshers toiled on

WITH machine gun bullets raking the ground around them and bombs crashing nearby, two farm workers from Deal continued to operate their threshing machine high on the cliffs and well within the range of the guns of France. For six weeks they were under fire but they continued to work from dawn to dusk and their reward was the George Medal.

The two men, Reginald Blunt and William Harris knew their work was important. Mr Blunt said: "Certainly it was hot. Twice, enemy planes deliberately gunned us. Bullets spattered all around and we could see sparks fly up as they struck hard ground. On other occasions shells from the French coast and bombs fell near us but we managed to keep going, starting work again at dawn the next day".

Kent pilot won the Victoria Cross

FLIGHT Lieutenant Roderick Alistair Brook Learoyd who was born at Folkestone in 1913 won the Victoria Cross (VC) for an act of bravery that was oustanding, even in 1940, when deeds of valour took place almost every day.

On August 12th, 1940, Learoyd was detailed to attack a target in the Dortmund-Ems Canal which was heavily defended. He approached through a lane of anti-aircraft guns and made his attack at 150 feet. His aircraft was repeatedly hit by flak and large pieces were torn away. He was almost blinded by the glare of searchlights but Learoyd pressed home his attack with the greatest resolution and skill.

Incredibly, the intrepid pilot brought home his wrecked aircraft through more flak and, on August 23, was awarded the Victoria Cross, the nation's highest award for valour. Learoyd was one of only two pilots to win the VC during the summer of 1940 and immediately became one of the country's best-known war heroes, particularly in Littlestone where he lived with his family.

An equivalent award for bravery for civilians is the George Cross, which came into being on September 24th, 1940. All holders of the Gallantry Empire Medal were requested to exchange it for a GC and this included Flying Officer Anthony Tollemache, Auxiliary Air Force who crashed-landed at Manston on March 11th. He tried in vain to save his passenger, sustaining serious injuries.

A posthumous award of the GC went to Squadron Leader Eric Moxey of the RAF Volunteer Reserve who attempted to defuse two unexploded bombs at Biggin Hill on August 27th. He was killed when one went off.

Sub-Lt John Babington of the Royal Navy Volunteer Reserve was another recipient of the George Cross. On December 27th at Chatham he tackled a bomb with a new type of fuse knowing that a similar device had recently killed an expert. He could not remove it but much was learned from his brave attempt.

There were many commendations for bravery during 1940, including Albert Rigden of Folkestone who rescued colleagues after a bomb had hit a laundry on August 20th and Dr Henry Warren and his wife, Winifred who entered a basement at Maidstone on September 27th which was in danger of collapsing. In the most harrowing conditions they rendered first aid to people who were trapped.

For details of all Kent's Victoria and George Cross award winners, see pages 220 and 221.

Anson heroine rescued pilot as bomb exploded

A BURNING Anson returning home from action over the Channel spluttered and coughed as it approached Detling, then landed heavily on the airfield with its bombs still on board. Among those watching the drama from the ground was Corporal Daphne Joan Pearson, a WAAF medical orderly who immediately took an ambulance to the blazing Anson and saw two men dragging out a third. Running up to them she told them to leave the injured man with her and get into the ambulance waiting on the grass.

Corporal Pearson noticed the injured man, Pilot Officer Bond, slightly regain consciousness and heard him whisper that there were bombs on the Anson. Realising that the aircraft could explode at any moment she gave her tin hat to the airman and dragged him towards a ridge in the grass. As she did so a 120 lb bomb went off and splinters of metal and burning fuel rained down all around them.

In June 1940, Corporal Pearson received her commission and the following month she was awarded the EGM for bravery. Later this was exchanged for the George Cross and the King told her that she was the first woman to win the coveted award.

Courage of the Margate firemen

CHIEF Officer Albert Twyman and Fireman Frederick Watson of Margate Fire Brigade both won the George Medal for bravery. With their crew the men were called to Manston airfield on August 22nd which had been devastated by low-level bombing.

Twyman led his men into a blazing building without breathing apparatus and, by forming a chain, saved the whole stock of valuable equipment. Watson, meanwile, worked the pumps from an underground tank and refused to stop despite the presence of an unexploded bomb nearby.

The other crew members, Herbert Evens, Arthur Harrison, Michael Wicks, Gabriel Nye, Donald Setterfield and Albert Watson, all of Margate, received commendations for their gallantry.

Two days after this incident the crew were called to Manston again to deal with more fires following another raid. Fireman Herbert Evens said at the time: "As we tried to get a clear view of the blazing buildings, we saw a number of enemy aircraft return. We dived into a slit trench and crouched in terror as they headed straight for us, released their bombs and fired machine guns and canon bombs. We were lucky, we escaped without casualties.

"A GPO man who had been working at the top of a telegraph pole before the second attack was still there and still working. He had ignored the raiders. The damage to the airfield was vast. The hangars had gone, there were craters everywhere and most of the auxiliary buildings were either completely devastated or severely damaged. The airfield was now out of action."

Among those who defied bombs and shells were Mr and Mrs G.W. Mitchell and tractor driver Grace Harrison whose farm was on the Dover cliffs.

Military Medals for Detling WAAFS

There were two more awards for the brave WAAFs of Detling. During a heavy raid on August 13th, Corporal Josephine Robins, a non-commissioned officer was in a dug-out by the Operations Room when it received a fatal hit. Several men were killed and two seriously injured as the blast ripped through the shelter. Dust and fumes filled the air but Corporal Robins went to the assistance of the wounded and stayed with them until they could be evacuated.

During the same attack, WAAF Sergeant Youle was on duty in the station telephone exchange when it received a direct hit. As bombs exploded nearby and debris and splinters rained down, Sgt Youle carried on "with coolness and complete efficiency at a most dangerous time for all". The citation finished: "It is praise indeed for all the women's section to say that the Ops Room and all essential services were back in operation the next day."

Both Corporal Robins and Sergeant Youle won the Military Medal.

Goodwill abounds — after 4,000 air raids!

PEACE on earth. Goodwill to all men. The carols and Yuletide messages seemed entirely out of place as Kent faced its most desperate Christmas ever. The county newspapers were of one accord in asking if we could, in all sincerity, sing such words. The editor of the *Sevenoaks News* wrote: "Can we, amid all the horrors of war and when hate so becomes the predominating passion, hope they will ever ring true?"

Sir Auckland Geddes, south-east regional commissioner for the Civil Defence gave his message to the county: "Since we welcomed back the men from Dunkirk and the women of Kent were proud to feed the 350,000 that came home, more than 4,000 air raids and local attacks have been delivered by Germans and Italians on this area alone. Thousands of homes have been destroyed..."To all of you, to the police, fire services, wardens, rescue squads, de-contamination squads, WVS and to all the men and women who by their gallant fortitude have kept life and work going on, in the farms, in the villages, in the seaside resorts and in the inland towns, I say, well done. Sterner trials lie ahead. Be vigilant and wary and don't talk to strangers".

Kent, however, did its best to observe the traditions of the season. The Assembly Hall at Tunbridge Wells was fully booked for its dance on Christmas Eve and pantomime, *Red Riding Hood* on Boxing Day. The Majestic Cinema, Sevenoaks announced that it would open on Christmas Day for the Laurence Olivier film *Conquest of Air* and The Regent at Cranbrook had a special showing of *Tom Brown's Schooldays*. Elsewhere in the county, people were flocking to the new Hollywood blockbusters, *The Wizard of Oz*, Disney's *Pinocchio* and Hitchcock's *Rebecca*. Hughie Green and his Gang were appearing live on stage at The Hippodrome, Dover alongside a daring and "exotic" young lady called Lolita. Circle seats were priced at 1s.9d.

The favourite song seemed to be the rather sophisticated *A Nightingale Sang in Berkeley Square* but everyone was delighted by a plumber's daughter from the East End who sang with the Ambrose Dance Band such songs as *Faithful For Ever* and *We'll Meet Again*. The BEF had voted Vera Lynn their favourite singer.

Many towns were concerned with their targets for War Weapons Week. Sevenoaks announced that it was aiming for £250,000, while Tunbridge Wells proudly declared that it had set out to raise £250,000 but the final effort was an amazing £510,225 — and the population was only 35,000. Maidstone went a lot better. The people of the heavily bombed county town had raised more than a

My Goodness — My GUINNESS

million pounds.

Newspapers were full of pleas for help. More munition workers were wanted in the Medway towns. Sevenoaks asked for more volunteers for the Auxiliary Fire Service — they were desperately short in the rural area. Ambulance drivers were wanted in Tunbridge Wells and Tonbridge called for recruits to the Home Guard.

The Tonbridge department store, Frank East, announced they would open for business on December 21st, 23rd and 24th unless an air raid was in progress. George King, photographers, of Sevenoaks said they were selling the new Home Cine, which could be used in the shelters.

Throughout the county there had been many heroes but none greater than a 10-year-old boy scout from Tonbridge. Royston Newman was awarded the silver medal of gallantry for saving the life of his younger brother, Michael, aged one. A raider raked his Tonbridge street with gunfire when the two boys were in the front garden of their home but Roy threw himself across Michael's pram and received a bullet wound in the back. He was not seriously injured.

1941

Night bombing, desert offensive, Pearl Harbour

January 20th: Men and women aged between 16 and 60 had to register for part-time Civil Defence Service work and fire-watching became compulsory.

January 28th: *The Daily Worker,* the communist party newspaper, was shut down by order of Herbert Morrison, Home Secretary because of its anti-war propaganda.

February 4th: Britain's war costs had risen to more than £11 million per day. In April standard rate income tax was increased to 50 per cent.

March 8th: The Luftwaffe began its new night bombing assault on London as part of its spring offensive with heavy attacks on other British cities.

March 9th: Ernest Bevin, Minister of Labour, appealed for 100,000 women to come forward and sign up for munitions work.

April 16th: It was decided that the last remaining tower of Crystal Palace should be demolished as it was such a distinctive landmark.

April 17th: Yugoslavia surrendered.

April 20th: There were heavy raids on London and Birmingham with parachute mines.

April 27th: Allied troops evacuated Greece as the German army advanced into Athens.

May 5th: Emperor Haile Selassie returned to Ethiopia after years in exile.

May 7th: Seven nights continuous bombing devastated Liverpool.

May 11th: The height of the Blitz when over 500 German bombers reduced London to a city of rubble.

BUILDERS
IT'S A RACE AGAINST TIME

No man can do more for his country to-day than the building operative who works his best to complete the job in advance of time. *The team spirit wins.*

Ministry of Works

May 17th: Rudolf Hess was imprisoned in the Tower of London after being brought down by train from Scotland where he had parachuted from his crashing Messerschmitt. He said it had been his flight to bring about peace.

May 24th: *HMS Hood* was sunk off the coast of Greenland. Only three of the 1,416 crew survived. In revenge the German battleship *Bismarck* was torpedoed and sunk in the Atlantic on May 27th.

June 1st: Clothes were now rationed and margarine tokens had to be used until new ration cards were printed.

June 22nd: A German attack on the Soviet Union took the Russians by surprise along an 1,800 mile front from the Baltic to the Black Sea.

July 4th: A new restriction on coal rationing — only one ton per month from now on for domestic use and even that could not be guaranteed.

July 20th: Churchill launched the "V for Victory" campaign.

August 14th: The Atlantic Charter was announced after five days of secret meetings between President Roosevelt and Winston Churchill.

September 8th: German and Finnish soldiers surrounded the city of Leningrad, then went on to sieze Kiev.

September 17th: Mashed potato sandwiches and potato pastry were recommended in a campaign to get the British public to eat more root vegetables, of which there was no shortage.

September 23rd: Charles de Gaulle formed his national committee in London as France's government in exile.

October 1st: Children were obliged to share pencils and margins were abolished because of the paper shortage.

October 12th - 13th: RAF bombers made their first large-scale night raid on Nuremberg.

October 31st: The Army Catering Corps was formed, enlisting professional caterers to advise on feeding the troops.

November 7th - 8th: RAF Bombers attacked Cologne, Berlin and Mannheim in heavy night-time raids.

November 14th: The *Ark Royal* was sunk by a U-boat off the coast of Gibraltar.

December 4th: Unmarried women between the ages of 20 and 30 were called up to serve in the police, fire service and armed forces.

December 7th: Japanese air force attacked Pearl Harbour and the following day President Roosevelt signed America's declaration of war on Japan.

December 25th: Hong Kong surrendered to the Japanese.

Hitler had announced the postponement of his invasion plans but no-one trusted him. It was essential to be vigilant and here a private of the Buffs keeps his eyes intently focussed on the grey waters of the Channel from his sandbagged command post high on the chalk cliffs of Dover. The lookout continued without respite throughout the war and the soldiers on duty had an unenviable view of the battle in the air, the shelling of the coastal towns and the constant skirmishing between German E-boats and the Royal Navy's Motor Torpedo Boats and Motor Gun Boats. In the tunnels below, all the activity was monitored and appropriate action taken. Information flowed in to the Combined Headquarters from coastal observers, pilots, warship commanders and from the radar chain whose lattice masts were a prominent feature on the cliff top east and west of Dover castle.

Amy Johnson drowns in the Thames Estuary

AMY Johnson, the airwoman who made history with her 10,000-mile solo flight to Australia in 1931, was killed on January 5th, 1941 when the aircraft she was flying ditched in the Thames Estuary. Miss Johnson, aged 38, had been flying aircraft for the Air Transport Auxiliary from factories to RAF bases for the previous six months. There was no enemy activity at the time and it was believed she lost her way in bad weather and ran out of fuel.

Eyewitnesses from the mainland said the aircraft's engine appeared to cut out before it crashed into the sea. The captain of a naval trawler, Lieutenant Commander W.E. Fletcher saw her bale out. He dived into the sea, reached her but despite valiant efforts could not support her. He died later in hospital from hypothermia.

Amy Johnson was among the scores of women who worked for the ATA, ferrying new aircraft to the front-line squadrons in Kent.

The Buffs did not spend the entire war on front-line duty. Here, a smiling group is photographed at the foot of the monument to William, Prince of Orange, at Brixham. They were training in the West Country.

The Commanding Officer and officers of a Battalion of the Queen's Own Royal West Kent Regiment who were on duty in Hellfire Corner in 1941. During the war the ten battalions of the West Kents saw service in France, Belgium, Malta, Palestine, Western Africa, Iraq, Syria, Italy, Leros, Samos, Greece, Burma, Germany and Austria.

Actors and artists join Cazalet's Little Army

ONE of those who had spoken out strongly against the growth of the Nazi regime was Victor Cazalet, proprietor of the racing stables at Fairlawne, Shipbourne, near Tonbridge, who was also an officer during the 1914-18 war, a Member of Parliament and long-time friend of the Royal family.

Cazalet joined the Auxiliary Air Force on the outbreak of war but resigned when the War Office suggested something more suited to his talents. He was offered command of the 16th Light Anti-Aircraft battery, then forming in the Sevenoaks area and personally recruited the first members.

His battery captains were his brother Peter and Lord (Tony) Mildmay, his partner in the racing stables. In the ranks were people from a cross-section of the best families in the Sevenoaks area — actors, writers, stockbrokers drilling side by side with bus drivers, journalists and most of the jockeys and grooms from the stables.

Cazalet's Little Army, or Cazalet's Cuties as they were known because of the high proportion of actors in the ranks, had the best camp concerts in the British Army and an excellent canteen, presided over by the glamorous actress Heather Thatcher. There was hardly any ammunition for the guns and no uniforms at first but Cazalet pulled rank outrageously in bullying the War Office to supply the best for his battery.

The rush to join the Cuties soon doubled. His original four batteries became eight, and half were taken away to form the nucleus of new ones. He was lucky in retaining the services of the Dorchester Hotel chefs recruited to give his cookhouses a little style. The star-studded battery attracted much publicity and Beverly Nichols wrote about their "deadly secret weapons", which could only have been worn-out Lewis guns.

By the beginning of 1941, some 80 per cent of the Cuties' gunners had been commissioned and the War Office, well satisfied with the success of its scheme to get into uniform the sort of people who would attract others, re-formed the original units in various guises to fight at El Alamein and later in the glider force at Arnhem.

Cazalet's career as a gunner major ended with his appointment as military adviser to the Polish Prime Minister in exile, General Sikorski, who lived at Great Swifts, Cazalet's other house at Cranbrook. On July 4th, 1943 Cazalet and Sikorski were killed when the Liberator bomber in which they were flying crashed and sank off Gibraltar.

Tributes came from all over the world. The *New York Herald Tribune* said of Victor Cazalet: "There can be few other Englishmen of our time who have so touched so many nations and so many individual citizens upon terms of understanding and friendship."

Happy, healthy, fit and away from the bombs that were falling with such regularity in north Kent. These were some of the girls of Sittingbourne County School who went to Hengoed, South Wales. This was April 1941.

Chatham, home of the Royal Navy, was a prime target for the Luftwaffe. By January, 1941 there had already been five attacks on the town involving loss of life and now there were to be two more. On the 10th, three people were killed when a bomb fell in Mount Road and, on the 18th, houses in Palmerston Road (above) were badly damaged. During the war, civilian casualties at the dockyard totalled ten.

Churchill's plea to America: "Give us the tools..."

IN a speech of praise and encouragement for both the forces and civilians, Winston Churchill broke five months of radio silence by saying: "We have stood our ground and faced the two dictators in the hour of what seemed their overwhelming triumph and we have shown ourselves capable, so far, of standing up against them alone".

The Prime Minister also spoke of the vital importance of American aid. "We shall not fail, or falter", he said, "we shall not weaken or tire. Neither the sudden shock of battle, nor the long drawn trials of vigilance and exertion will wear us down. Give us the tools and we will finish the job."

The Queen inspected the WRNS at Chatham in May 1941.

A happy note during a grim period was struck when the Hayes May Queen and her retinue toured the bombed areas after being crowned on May 10th, 1941.

15,000 people lived in the "town below ground"

AS the bombing raids intensified, thousands of south Londoners moved underground into a vast network of pre-historic tunnels that were extensive enough to accommodate a large surburban town. And that is just what they became. The Chislehurst caves, deep and safe, was the "town below ground" for hundreds of families.

During the spring raids of 1941 there were more than 8,000 people living in the caves; by the end of the year the number was closer to 15,000. At first they were there unofficially because Chislehurst and Sidcup Urban Council disapproved of their use and was concerned about health and safety but eventually a "cave committee" was elected and ran their town with clockwork efficiency.

The committee charged 6d a week for a family pitch. They did not have to sleep in the caves every night but they lost their pitch if it were not used for three successive weeks. There was water and electricity, the WVS ran canteens and supplied clothing to those who had been bombed out. There was a cinema, a church, telephone kiosk, national savings bank, shops, post office and first aid centre.

There were many distinguished visitors including the Duke of Kent and General Charles de Gaulle, the French leader, who lived for a while at 41 Birchwood Road, Petts Wood. Each section had a 'cave captain' who made sure that there was no music after 9 pm and lights were out by 10.30.

St Peter and St Paul Church, Bromley was destroyed on April 16th, 1941 during a raid in which 198 bombs were dropped on the borough, killing 74 people in Bromley alone and causing 365 fires. More than 1,500 people were made homeless. It was during this raid that three Chislehurst men, Leslie Hammond, Edward Smith and Sidney Windall were awarded the British Empire Medal for rescuing people from a demolished house while bombs were still falling and gas was escaping.

One-bob meal in the British Restaurant

THE scarcity of food and the restrictions caused by rationing were biting deep into the average family's way of life. Many people were receiving food parcels from the Dominions, others were self-sufficient thanks to their skills in the garden and allotment, recipes for carrot jam and nettle tea became more popular and so did the dried egg which encouraged people to keep chickens. Women's Institutes throughout Kent set up a network of Preservation Centres to prevent fruit being wasted and the Government-introduced British Restaurants opened in many Kent towns. Here, the price of a meal was 1s, or even less, with soup for 1d and tea at the same price.

One of the staple foods of which there was no shortage in Kent was the potato which retailed at 1d a pound. There were also plenty of carrots and swedes and the Ministry of Food, in recommending that all Britons should eat more vegetables, introduced a cartoon character called "Potato Pete".

On June 1st, 1941, clothes were also rationed, joining food and petrol. It was agreed that every man, woman and child should be given 66 coupons to last for a year. The coupons varied according to the size of the garment; women needed 14 coupons for an overcoat while men required 13 for a jacket and eight for trousers. The new regulations paved the way for second hand clothing shops to be established.

One month later on July 4th coal was rationed, principally because of the call-up of young miners. It was announced that only one ton per month of coke, coal or any other type of solid fuel could be supplied for domestic use. Ernest Bevin, the Minister of Labour appealed for miners to return to the pits.

There were more than 300 fires in Bromley following the raid of April 16th — and one of the biggest was at Dunn's furniture store in the Market Square. Several incendiaries had fallen and within minutes it was blazing. So, too, was a printing works in Green Lane, Penge and a block of flats in Southover on the Downham Estate.

19 Beckenham firemen killed on duty

Nineteen members of the Beckenham Auxiliary Fire Service, who had responded to a call for help from London, were killed on Saturday April 18th, 1941 when a bomb hit the building above and completely buried them under tons of debris.

In one of the saddest occasions in Beckenham's history, the men were buried in Elmer's End Cemetery. Two colleagues who died with them were buried at West Wickham. The funeral was the largest ever seen in the Borough and fire brigades all over Greater London were represented.

The 19 dead heroes were laid to rest in one large grave by the main walk where an inscription recorded: "We remember proudly the heroic men martyred in the cause of liberty".

Kent watched as London burned

THE people of Kent slept uneasily on the night of May 11th, 1941. The weather conditions were perfect, with a full moon, a very low Thames ebb tide and every indication that the German bombers would take full advantage. They were not mistaken. The air raid warning sounded soon after 11pm and 15 minutes later the greatest concentration of enemy aircraft ever seen crossed the coast and droned on towards the capital.

By dawn, London was burning. More than 550 German planes had dropped hundreds of high explosive bombs and 100,000 incendiaries and, even Londoners, hardened by the horrors of nine months of the blitz, were shaken by this greatest raid of all.

Many living on the higher ground in North Kent came out of their shelters to watch the carnage from afar. In Sevenoaks, people looked out of their windows and stood on flat roof tops to see great fires lighting the sky and to hear the thunderous explosions. When dawn broke the sky above London was a dark pall of brown smoke which continued to blot out the sun, turning a spring day into a wintry one. The air smelt acrid. Charred clothes were floating in the breeze and shreds of burnt paper rained down into the country villages of the North Downs.

Those who were due to take the morning train to London knew it was impossible, for every main line terminus was out of action. More than 5,000 houses were destroyed and the provisional figures for casualties indicated that 1,400 were dead and 1,800 badly injured. 2,200 serious fires were burning, streets were impassable and burnt-out incendiaries littered the pavements.

Much of historic London suffered. The chamber of the House of Commons was reduced to a heap of rubble. Big Ben was scarred. The roof of Westminster Hall was ablaze and the tower of Westminster Abbey had fallen in. The British Museum and St Paul's Cathedral were badly hit — and, for the first time people were seen weeping in the streets in despair.

The guns of Anti-Aircraft Command in Kent were in action and two bombers were shot down. RAF squadrons were also scrambled and a Defiant crew singled out a Heinkel over Gillingham and raked it with gunfire. The bomber crashed at Gore Farm, Upchurch at 2 am where three people on the ground and three crew died. Two others baled out and were taken prisoner.

This was the start of a spring offensive described by Nazi High Command as "a reprisal for the methodical bombing of the residential quarters of the German towns, including Berlin".

There was one other intriguing incident on that day — many miles from Kent. Rudolph Hess, Hitler's deputy, parachuted from a crashing Messerschmitt near Glasgow and claimed he was on a peace mission. He was taken prisoner and lived until 1987 when he died in Spandau Prison.

Some of the 1,000 girls who attended the rally in Maidstone.

Land Girls wore their badge of courage with pride

IN their green jerseys, brown corduroy breeches and slough hats, the Land Girls of Kent attended a rally at Maidstone Zoo Park in July 1941. Nine girls were presented with badges at the rally for "sustained courage under dangerous conditions" and Lord Cornwallis, who presented the badges said: "I don't think we could have carried on without you. You belong to the first county to have more than 1,000 members."

Before the war the girls, who were now dodging bombs and working hard on farms throughout Kent, had such occupations as dress designers, artists, hairdressers, waitresses, factory girls and domestic servants. By the summer of 1941 their hair was untidy, their hands and face dirty and their pretty frocks packed away and long forgotten — but life in the countryside was making them gloriously fit and the keen air was doing wonders for their complexion, even if the air raids were a bit of a problem.

The Invicta was awarded to nine girls. They could not qualify for the badge unless they had worked for at least six months while dog fights were raging and bombs and shells were falling. Most of the recipients came from East Kent. They were:

Miss A. Eke, previously a library assistant, Miss L.M. Gardner, children's nurse, Miss B. Gimbert, shop assistant who all worked on farms around Dover for more than a year. Their employers spoke highly of their courage under machine gun fire and shelling.

Miss T. Ledger, aged 17, a schoolgirl who had remained at her job through numerous bombing attacks including one occasion when her cow sheds were hit. Miss R. Lloyd Evans, dramatic student who set an example for courage to the rest of the farm workers throughout the Battle of Britain. Miss V. Markham, shop assistant who continued working despite machine gun fire, bombing and shelling. Miss C. Payne, who had been a member of the Land Army in the last war. Huge bomb craters completely encircled the farm where she was working but she carried on.

Miss D. Walker, a cook, worked just across the road from an aerodrome which was repeatedly bombed and Miss M. Walker worked continuously in a glasshouse while bombs were falling. Also commended for their bravery were Miss Keyse, Miss Coventry and Miss Heaton.

The Land Girls worked on farms all over the county. The most popular jobs were milking and driving but there was great demand for pruners, diggers, fruit packers and even tree fellers. In fact the farm girls of Kent so outnumbered the jobs available that many of them had to be sent to other counties.

Dorothy Ebers at the wheel of her tractor.

Two cheerful Land Girls, Freda Penn and Rachel Nottidge, off to feed the pigs.

In April 1941 many women were officially registered in order to fill positions normally undertaken by men. They took jobs in munitions and shell-filling factories. They delivered goods and milk, became butchers, printers, postmen and even blacksmiths.

This unlikely lady blacksmith worked at the Southern Railway works at Ashford.

They worked for the National Fire Service as Despatch riders, became railway porters and telephone linesmen.

To overcome the problem of insufficient baths, troops were allowed to bathe in a beer vat at one of Maidstone's Breweries. The vat contained hot soapy water and not the excellent Style and Winch best!

The girls of St Mark's School, Tunbridge Wells look quite contented knitting in their shelter.

The 'secret' tunnels in Hellfire Corner

WHEN France fell in June, 1940 and Hitler promised the invasion of Britain would follow, Dover became the country's front-line town. German troops, it was feared, and their armoured divisions with Panzer tanks, would soon be storming across the chalk cliffs into the Garden of England. Frantic preparations were made to counter the invasion and Dover Castle was supplied with enough provisions to withstand a six-week siege. The invaders did not arrive but the town and harbour were pounded with bombs and shells and thousands of people sought refuge in the secure tunnels beneath the Castle.

The tunnels had already assumed great importance as naval headquarters with liaison officers from the army and air force. Gun batteries from the North Foreland to Hastings were controlled from the tunnel HQ and, by the spring of 1941, the strength of coastal artillery in this sector was almost 4,500 troops. The navy employed fluent German speakers who worked next to the Cipher room in the Admiralty Casemate. Here they listened to wireless transmissions from Germany and attempted to confuse the enemy by broadcasting misleading orders.

In the summer of 1941, three army tunnelling companies began work on extending the system in three different places. One, to be used as a hospital and dressing station, eventually became dormitories. The second was for the use of the GPO who had charge of all the land communications and needed space for the telephone and teleprinter systems.

The major excavation work in 1941 was intended to provide a vast new Combined Headquarters complex for all three services, which would be available if the main operations centre at Portsmouth was put out of action. However, there were serious rock falls and subsidence and the project, half completed, was finally abandoned.

This was a major setback but, in 1942, a further grid of tunnels was excavated 50 feet below the Napoleonic tunnels and the Combined Headquarters was finally brought into operation.

The conditions in the tunnels and the lack of facilities for those escaping from the bombs were far worse before

A whist drive in progress in Dover's tunnels.

the extra accommodation was completed. The atmosphere was chill and damp and the lack of daylight, the background roar of the battle, the absence of any ventilation and the constant anxiety made it very difficult to sleep at night.

The caves and the tunnels, however, provided a safe haven for the people of Kent's most-bombed town — the hottest part of Hellfire Corner. Many of the cave-dwellers came from Athol Terrace which faced across the Channel to Occupied France. Each evening when bedtime arrived mothers picked up their children and carried them into the caves. One boy, Michael Culley was born in the caves on April 23rd, 1941 and for years he never knew what it was like to sleep in a bed in his own home.

Michael and his family were among those who survived the dive-bombing attack on Dover on Thursday October 2nd when the town was hit by three waves of raiders between 7.30pm and midnight. Many bombs fell in the St Margaret's area but the worst casualties were near Folkestone Road where a concert in the Wesley Hall had just ended and the audience was walking home. As the bombers approached one woman was thrown to the ground by a soldier who then shielded her with his body. He was seriously injured and had to have a leg amputated.

More bombs fell in Dour Street and more than 100 incendiaries on the slopes at Western Heights. The raids left eight people dead and 13 seriously injured. Six houses were completely wrecked and 1,800 homes needed repairs.

Tea and buns were served when the shelling began.

After an air battle the air-sea rescue launch was quick to search for and pick-up survivors.

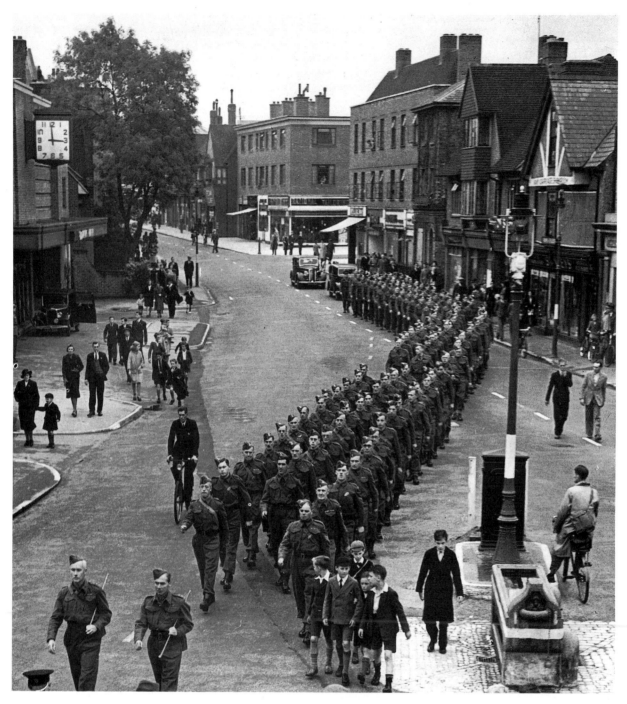

There was a good muster at the Sevenoaks Home Guard Parade for the Drumhead Service on Sunday August 24th — an event held in most towns throughout the county. Captain C.M.Oliver, in charge of the parade congratulated his men for "their military picture of smartness".

A few weeks earlier, a Home Guardsman had appeared in Sevenoaks Court, not as the defendant, but as a key witness in the case against Mrs Anna Webb of Hillingdon Rise, Sevenoaks who had left a light shining in her bedroom window while a heavy raid was in progress.

The Home Guardsman, Mr E.J. Wallis, was so appalled by the sight of the unscreened window that he threw a stone through the pane and reported the owner who was fined.

Prisoners and casualties as Sevenoaks is invaded

DURING the weekend of July 5th/6th many Kent towns were "invaded" by the "enemy" — but this was a military training exercise carried out by the Home Guard. Sevenoaks was one of the towns chosen for a large-scale mock battle in which the "enemy" was the Woolwich contingent of the Home Guard. Armed men were spotted on the roofs of buildings, coming from the direction of Knole Park and helmeted heads popped around almost every corner. The defenders set up road blocks while the ARP dealt with imaginary fires and took "casualties" to hospital. Many "prisoners" were also captured.

There was a similar "war" at Hawkhurst during the same weekend involving the men of Cranbrook, Ticehurst, Sandhurst and Hawkhurst while the Bromley battalion had to deal with three mock attacks with the action spreading to Orpington, Chislehurst, Hayes, West Wickham and Beckenham. It was all considered to be of great value should the invasion ever happen.

The "street battle" in Canterbury as parachute troops advanced under cover of a smoke screen.

Parachute troops 'capture' Canterbury

IT was Canterbury's turn to be "attacked" at the end of October 1941. Parachute troops who were dropped on the outskirts of the city, advanced towards the centre and, in a great mock battle, captured the East and West railway stations and the Westgate Towers.

The exercise, carried out by the Army, Civil Defence and Home Guard, was most realistic. Gun fire and smoke filled the air and bitter fighting broke out around the mediaeval buildings of Canterbury, while aircraft dive-bombed from above. Parachute troops crossed the river in boats supplied by the "Fifth Column" and approached the town centre under the cover of a thick smoke screen.

Officers from a number of Allied countries watched with interest as the Canterbury defenders coped with a gas attack, the first-aid team dealt with casualties and the fire brigade was on hand to quell the many blazes. Several people were "blown up" in the manoeuvres including the town clerk, Mr George Marks.

There was a tragic touch of irony about the whole affair. Less than a year later, the town clerk was killed by a bomb, Canterbury was burning, casualties were horrific, and it was all a reality.

'Radar' secret is revealed

UNTIL the summer of 1941 the people of Kent had never heard of the term, "radar". The stations that existed at Dover and Dunkirk were called Air Ministry Experimental Stations, for security purposes, and they were part of a Chain Home network that existed all round the coast of Britain. In June, 1941, however, the public was let into the secret for the first time when Sir Philip Joubert of RAF Coastal Command paid tribute to Robert Watson-Watt, the scientist who pioneered the system which did much to help win the Battle of Britain.

Sir Philip gave no technical details but he did say it was a system of rays "which are unaffected by fog or darkness and any aircraft or ship in the path of this ray immediately sends back a signal to the detecting station".

The system was called Radio Direction Finding or RDF — the term "radar" being introduced in September 1943 to conform to the United States terminology to avoid confusion between the Allies.

In Kent there were also two smaller stations at Whitstable and Foreness which were used for detecting aircraft attempting to approach below the coverage of the stronger powered stations at Dover and Dunkirk.

The Kent stations with their huge 360-foot tall transmitting towers and 240-foot receiving towers could not be camouflaged and quite naturally received considerable attention from the Luftwaffe. Dover was one of the targets on August 12th, 1940 and the WAAF plotters in the nerve centre of the station had the uncomfortable task of reporting enemy formations on their screens heading straight for them. They remained at their post until taking cover at the last possible moment.

Dover was badly damaged and so were other RDF stations but Air Chief Marshal Sir Hugh Dowding said the Chain Home stations would continue to transmit regardless of the damage suffered, either with their own heavy equipment or lighter equipment provided in such emergencies.

The Luftwaffe quickly realised that the radar stations could not be permanently destroyed and no more attacks after August 18th.

One of the towers that supported the transmission aerials on the cliffs to the east of Dover. In between the towers were the blocks housing the generators and the operations room which was protected by blast walls and camouflaged.

Villagers look rather bemused by the aerial mine which fell in Halstead.

There was nothing unusual about bomb craters in Kent during the war; most communities had at least one and some had a few hundred. Bearsted children found an original use for one. They decorated the crater and then asked passers-by to contribute to the Kent Spitfire Fund. This was one of the many enterprising acts during the war..

There'll be blue-birds over, the White Cliffs of Dover...

IN July 1941 a company from New York, called Shapiro and Bernstein, produced a song that was destined to become a war-time favourite and the one that symbolised the hope that peace would soon return to England.

"The White Cliffs of Dover" was written by an American, Nat Burton at a time when this front-line town was at the height of its suffering and "tomorrow" really did appear to be a long way off.

All Kent knows Burton's stirring words, but here (for the younger generation) is the first verse and chorus.

Verse One:

I'll never forget the people I met
Braving those angry skies;
I remember well as the shadows fell,
The light of hope in their eyes.
And tho' I'm far away, I still can hear them say,
"Thumbs up!"...........For when the dawn comes up:

Chorus:

There'll be blue-birds over The White Cliffs of Dover, tomorrow,
Just you wait and see.
There'll be love and laughter and peace ever after, tomorrow,
When the world is free.
The shepherd will tend his sheep,
The valley will bloom again,
And Jimmy will go to sleep,
In his own little room again.
There'll be blue-birds over, The White Cliffs of Dover, tomorrow,
Just you wait and see.

The Spirit of Kent — one of the Spitfires of 131 Squadron which carried the Invicta motto. Right: Proof of purchase. The actual cheque.

Kent buys a squadron of Spitfires

WHEN the Battle of Britain was at its most furious, counties and some big towns in England made it known that they would each attempt to raise enough money to buy a Spitfire. Kent went several times better. The county promised to buy a whole squadron!

And they did. By November 1941, every town and village had contributed towards the Spitfire Fund. Kent was the first county to achieve such a target.

It was on September 7th, 1940 that the *Kent Messenger*, in an inspired challenge, said: "It would be a wonderful tribute to the gallant airmen who are defending Kent if there was an "Invicta" Squadron with each plane bearing the name of the borough or district which raised the necessary money. The county should be proud to be able to say to Lord Beaverbrook that, by local effort, the county was giving the nation a complete squadron".

Donations began to pour in immediately. The fighters were priced at £5,000 each and most towns aimed at that figure and exceeded it. The smaller towns and villages began to join in. Westerham's first instalment was £36 18s 6d which included a cheque from Mrs Churchill. An agricultural worker from Brenchley collected £80 from his friends and neighbours and then added £55 the next week.

The Association of Men of Kent and Kentish Men were put in charge of the fund with Lord Cornwallis as chairman. The target was £100,000 but, in November, 1941, £108,000 was handed over to Colonel Moore-Brabazon, the new Minister of Aircraft production. The 22 aircraft provided were given the following names: Beckenham, Bexley, Bromley, Chatham, Canterbury, Chislehurst and Sidcup, Fair Maid of Kent, Gravesend Shrimp, Garden of England, Kentish Man, Man of Kent, Medway, Meteor, Faversham, Folkestone and Hythe, Robinson (Mr Stanley Robinson who donated £5,000), Rochester, Royal Tunbridge Wells, Pride of Sheppey, Weald of Kent, Spirit of Kent and Yeoman of Kent.

The squadron adopted the motto "Invicta" and eventually became known as the 131 (County of Kent) Fighter Squadron. It was disbanded on December 31st, 1945 after distinguished service in which five commanding officers were awarded the DFC.

A Bofors Gun was mounted on Maidstone Bridge during Army manoeuvres in November 1941.

Boy Scouts of St George's Home, Tunbridge Wells, bringing in a load of waste-paper salvage for the war effort. They collected more than 30 tons.

Sturry High Street. Soldiers, Civil Defence workers and Chislet miners dug in the debris to rescue those buried.

Mines tear the heart out of Sturry

THE air-raid alarm sounded in the village of Sturry, near Canterbury, just before 7 pm on the evening of Tuesday November 18th, 1941 and a few minutes later a lone aircraft could be heard circling above. In the pitch-black of this winter's evening, villagers braced themselves for a possible attack. It was more than that. Two parachute mines were dropped and the heart of the Kent village was completely torn out.

Only 15 people died and that, in itself, was something of a miracle. For in those few terrifying seconds Sturry had become the most wrecked village for its size in the country. The mines fell within yards of each other, one directly in the main street outside the Red Lion pub and the other in open ground near allotments.

Several shops were demolished and every building in the street was damaged in some way. Some people were lying dead in the street including a small girl who was clutching a bag of buns. The bodies of a married couple, their two children and a visitor were found in a wrecked house, another woman was found lying across her two

children as if she was trying to protect them. They were all dead. It was rumoured at the time that two soldiers, sitting in their car outside the Red Lion, were never found.

Rescue parties, made up of of soldiers, the Home Guard and villagers, were formed immediately. Miners came from Chislet with lamps and floodlights and a local doctor gave priority to some children who were trapped in the debris. They were not alive. A large house near the town, Milner Court was turned into a first-aid post and the injured were taken there.

The work went on throughout the night. One man was trapped in his wrecked house for more than eight hours but he was able to give directions to those trying to reach him and other trapped victims.

The morning brought a scene of utter despair and destruction. In addition to the 15 killed, 11 were seriously injured, 12 houses and shops were wrecked and 20 were unfit to live in. Gas and water was cut off and the main road was closed for several days.

The massive crater made by one of the parachute mines which devastated the village of Sturry and completely changed the picturesque High Street. Half timbered houses, small shops and the Red Lion pub were all blown to smithereens.

In November 1941 the German guns at Calais began shelling once more and one person in Dover was killed. Most of the civilian population would have been in their shelters or caves waiting for the All Clear which always sounded an hour after the last shell had fallen. During the shelling the Dover bus routes were wisely diverted as this notice clearly indicates.

DIY was born in 1941. People whose homes had been blitzed came to the local council repair centre to collect tarpaulins, tiles, wood and accessories so they could do their own repairs. This one was at Rochester.

Women called up for Britain's war drive

ON December 4th, 1941 in what Mr Churchill described as "another instalment of toil and sweat", unmarried women, between the ages of 20 and 30, were called up to serve in the police and fire services and armed forces. Married and single women up to the age of 40 were registered as 'available labour' and directed to industry. The age of call-up for men was reduced to 18 years and six months, those between 41 and 50 were now liable for armed service and boys aged 16 were encouraged to join the Home Guard. Among men, lay preachers and farm workers were some of those whose "reserve occupations" kept them out of uniform.

Sailor Malan, one of the most fearless and skilful pilots in Fighter Command, was among the first airmen to put his signature on the famous blackout screen at the White Hart, Brasted. At the end of 1941 he led the Biggin Hill Wing, having relinquished command of 74 "Tiger" Squadron and, in January 1943, he took command of Britain's "number one" fighter station. This photograph was taken after the war.

When Sailor Malan beat Joe Davis at snooker!

MUSIC and entertainment was an enormous morale booster and, as the third Christmas of the war arrived, stage and screen stars continued to entertain the troops in Kent. RAF Biggin Hill, which had looked like a battlefield a year earlier, was now being rebuilt and reward for the hundreds of people who worked so hard came with the theatrical shows. During 1941, Laurence Olivier and Vivien Leigh visited the station. So did Bea Lillie, Carroll Gibbons, the Gang Show, Jack Warner and Noel Coward.

Just before Christmas, the great snooker player, Joe Davis, gave a dazzling exhibition on the NAAFI table and then challenged "Sailor" Malan to a game of snooker giving him 12 blacks as a start. "Sailor" won and received the champion's cue as a memento!

In Dover there were continuous performances at The Hippodrome in Snargate Street, which was to be so badly damaged by the shelling. Almost every week there was a stripper and on one photograph of a near-naked girl the censor wrote: "Dover is more interested in strip than Blitz. Where the LCC has no authority, Dover can put on shows that the Forces like and this strip-tease act is very popular".

The boys of Biggin Hill never tired of their own music hall. It was sentimental and low, leggy and hilarious. The laughter was infectious and the girls, of course, were always a great success. There is no caption available for this particular troupe but the photograph was discovered among the archives at The Bump.

Cabaret time for the boys

FIGHTER pilots from all over Kent besieged Biggin Hill for the popular cabaret acts during Christmas 1941. It was pleasant compensation for the endless patrols which they had endured for so long. One VIP visitor was the film star Leslie Howard who was gathering material for his portrayal of R.J.Mitchell, designer of the Spitfire which was entitled "The First of the Few". Another regular visitor was the Prime Minister who loved to have a drink in the Mess on his way to and from Chartwell.

The word austerity did not have quite the same meaning for the people in uniform but it was a word that was not likely to be forgotten in a hurry. Men wore austerity suits with drainpipe trousers, no turn-ups and few pockets. The trousers were kept up by braces which had no elastic in them and they wore absurd austerity socks which only came three inches up the leg. These were supported by suspenders with no give in them, so they cut into the leg.

Women endured austerity frocks and underclothes, wore shoes with wooden soles and felt miserable in stockings with no shape to them. Children played with austerity toys.

The clothes rationing was hard to bear. Board of Trade films were made to show how father's old overcoat could be made into a coat for a child. The sacks that contained flour could be saved to make dresses for little girls.

By Christmas 1941, most families in Kent had their own allotment or piece of land where they could grow vegetables. They used railway embankments, parks, edges of football pitches, window boxes and even the roofs of air-raid shelters.

RATIONING
of Clothing, Cloth, Footwear
from June 1, 1941

Rationing has been introduced, not to deprive you of your real needs, but to make more certain that you get your share of the country's goods—to get fair shares with everybody else.

When the shops re-open you will be able to buy cloth, clothes, footwear and knitting wool *only if you bring your Food Ration Book with you.* The shopkeeper will detach the required number of coupons from the unused margarine page. Each margarine coupon counts as one coupon towards the purchase of clothing or footwear. You will have a total of 66 coupons to last you for a year; so go sparingly. You can buy *where you like* and *when you like* without registering.

NUMBER OF COUPONS NEEDED

Men and Boys	Adult	Child	Women and Girls	Adult	Child
Unlined mackintosh or cape	9	7	Lined mackintoshes, or coats (over 28 in. in length)	14	11
Other mackintoshes, or raincoat, or overcoat	16	11	Jacket, or short coat (under 28 in. in length)	11	8
Coat, or jacket, or blazer or like garment	13	8	Dress, or gown, or frock—woollen	11	8
Waistcoat, or pull-over, or cardigan, or jersey	5	3	Dress, or gown, or frock—other material	7	5
Trousers (other than fustian or corduroy)	8	6	Gym tunic, or girl's skirt with bodice	8	6
Fustian or corduroy trousers	5	5	Blouse, or sports shirt, or cardigan, or jumper	5	3
Shorts	5	3	Skirt, or divided skirt	7	5
Overalls, or dungarees or like garment	6	4	Overalls, or dungarees or like garment	6	4
Dressing-gown or bathing-gown	8	6	Apron, or pinafore	3	2
Night-shirt or pair of pyjamas	8	6	Pyjamas	8	6
Shirt, or combinations—woollen	8	6	Nightdress	6	5
Shirt, or combinations—other material	5	4	Petticoat, or slip, or combination, or cami-knickers	4	3
Pants, or vest, or bathing costume, or child's blouse	4	2	Other undergarments, including corsets	3	2
Pair of socks or stockings	3	1	Pair of stockings	2	1
Collar, or tie, or pair of cuffs	1	1	Pair of socks (ankle length)	1	1
Two handkerchiefs	1	1	Collar, or tie, or pair of cuffs	1	1
Scarf, or pair of gloves or mittens	2	2	Two handkerchiefs	1	1
Pair of slippers or goloshes	4	2	Scarf, or pair of gloves or mittens	2	2
Pair of boots or shoes	7	3	Pair of slippers, boots or shoes	5	3
Pair of leggings, gaiters or spats	3	2			

CLOTH. Coupons needed per yard depend on the width. For example, a yard of woollen cloth 36 inches wide requires 3 coupons. The same amount of cotton or other cloth needs 2 coupons.
KNITTING WOOL. 1 coupon for two ounces.

THESE GOODS MAY BE BOUGHT *WITHOUT* COUPONS

¶ Children's clothing of sizes generally suitable for infants less than 4 years old. ¶ Boiler suits and workmen's bib and brace overalls ¶ Hats and caps. ¶ Sewing thread. ¶ Mending wool and mending silk. ¶ Boot and shoe laces. ¶ Tapes, braids, ribbons and other fabrics of 3 inches or less in width. ¶ Elastic. ¶ Lace and lace net. ¶ Sanitary towels. ¶ Braces, suspenders and garters. ¶ Hard haberdashery. ¶ Clogs. ¶ Black-out cloth dyed black. ¶ All second-hand articles.

1942

Singapore, Dieppe and El Alamein

January 1st: The United Nations, representing four fifths of the world's population, signed an agreement to fight against the Axis and not negotiate a separate peace.

January 6th: President Roosevelt announced that American land, sea and air forces would be sent to Britain.

January 20th: The first Japanese air raid on Singapore killed 50 people.

January 29th: A huge vote of confidence was given to the government in the House of Commons in support of its war strategy by 464 votes to one.

February 9th: Soap rationing came into force with an allowance of 4oz of household soap or 2oz of toilet soap per person per month.

February 19th: Singapore surrendered to the Japanese, claimed to be the greatest military defeat in the history of the British Empire.

April 14th: In a "sacrifices for victory" budget, purchase tax was doubled to 66 per cent.

April 15th: The island of Malta was awarded the George Cross in recognition of its people's bravery in the face of repeated bombing by the Axis.
On the same day embroidery, appliqué and lace on women's and girl's underwear was banned.

April 18th: The Americans carried out air raids on several large Japanese cities, including Tokyo.

April 25th: Princess Elizabeth, aged 16, registered for war service.

April 26th: Hitler assumed the position of "Supreme Judge" of the Reich and gave himself powers to act independently of the law.

April 28th: Pay and prices were frozen in America and rationing of petrol and sugar were introduced.

May 14th: Women were asked not to wear stockings in the summer so as to conserve supplies for winter. This started a fashion for dying legs with onion skins and drawing-in seams with eyebrow pencil.

May 20th: The Japanese completed their capture of Burma.

May 31st: RAF bombers devastated Cologne in the largest raid in the history of aerial warfare. Rommel launched his attack in the Western Desert.

June 1st: The first Baedeker raid on Canterbury. 43 people killed.

June 21st: Rommel captured Tobruk.

June 24th: Allied PoWs were put to work by the Japanese to extend the 294-mile Singapore to Bangkok railway line north through the jungle to Rangoon.

June 25th: Dwight David Eisenhower was appointed commander of US forces in Europe.

July 26th: Sweets and chocolate were rationed from today, half a pound per person every four weeks.

August 9th: Mahatma Gandhi was arrested after riots across India for independence.

August 12th: Montgomery took over command of the British Eighth Army in North Africa.

August 15th: The first summit meeting between Stalin and Churchill took place in the Kremlin.

August 20th: Allied forces suffered defeat in Dieppe with over 4,000 killed, mostly Canadians.

August 31st: "Utility" furniture went on sale in three different designs.

October 24th: Montgomery launched attack at El Alamein. RAF Lancaster bombers made their first attacks on Italian towns, including Genoa.

October 26th: Cakes in shops were limited to only one layer of jam or chocolate with a maximum price of 1s 6d per pound.

October 31st: In a copycat raid, adopting RAF tactics, the Luftwaffe bombed Canterbury. In a single incident ten people died in an attack on a bus. In total, 52 tons of bombs were dropped.

November 3rd: Rommel, the Desert Fox, ordered a retreat at El Alamein. "Good old Monty" hailed as a hero.

November 15th: Church bells, silent since June 1940, rang out to celebrate the victory at El Alamein.

November 22nd: Herbert Morrison, Home Secretary, replaced Sir Stafford Cripps in the war cabinet.

December 31st: The Red Army celebrated the defeat of the Germans at Stalingrad but Leningrad was still under siege.

More people were killed on the roads in 1942 than on the battlefields of the first two years of the war. This was despite of a drop in the number of private cars from two million in 1939 to 718,000 in 1942.

Hard labour for miners' leaders who went on strike

THE Government had made it illegal to go on strike during the war, but that made little difference to the miners of Betteshanger Colliery who found themselves in dispute over a pay claim and, on January 9th, 1942, voted to stop working until the matter was settled.

The strike lasted 19 days before the claim was settled in the miners' favour. However, the Minister of Labour had stepped in and, on January 29th, more than 1,000 underground workers were prosecuted at Wingham Petty Sessions held in Canterbury. Only 50 of them, including the secretary and chairman, appeared in court — on a charge of breaking the law by coming out on strike.

The miners pleaded guilty. The secretary of the Betteshanger branch of the Kent Mine Worker's Association, William Powell, was sentenced to two month's hard labour, the secretary, Tudor Davies, and a committee member, Isaac Methuen received one month, a number of workers at number two face were fined £3 each and the rest £1 each.

The leaders served 11 days of their sentence at Maidstone Prison before they were released. Very few of the pit workers paid their fines; coal was vital to the war effort and the Government had no intention of provoking the men into more action.

Tragedy of the Swordfish assault

THREE of Germany's most powerful ships, the battle cruisers *Scharnhorst* and *Gneisenau* and the heavy cruiser *Prinz Eugen* made a daring dash up the English Channel in broad daylight on February 12th, 1942. They passed the Straits of Dover at noon and, by the evening, were within reach of the safety of the German ports.

The cruisers had been sheltering at Brest where they were constantly under attack but Hitler wanted them in Norwegian waters and personally ordered the breakout. The Resistance had heard of the plan and told the British who sent 18 Wellington bombers to Brest to thwart the operation. They succeeded only in delaying it.

RAF Spitfires spotted the German ships in the Dover Straits at 11.09 am. The Castle guns fired but fell short and the Dover torpedo boats sped out but could not get within range because of the powerful German escorts.

Torpedo-carrying Swordfish.

The rendezvous with the German Fleet was left to six torpedo-carrying Swordfish of the Fleet Air Arm based at Manston, with 72 Squadron from Gravesend and 124 and 401 Squadrons from Biggin Hill, providing cover. The Swordfish were led by Lieutenant Commander Eugene Esmonde. Some of the fighters headed straight for the open sea hoping to overtake the Swordfish but missed them and returned to Manston. Here they found they had already left and headed for the open sea again, losing vital minutes in the confusion.

It was 12.30 when the Swordfish and just 10 Spitfires sighted the battle cruisers and their escorts. Esmonde ignored the enemy fighters and led his section straight for the big ships. He was shot down almost at once and killed.

Through a deadly curtain of flak the remaining Swordfish flew towards their targets and released their torpedos before they too were shot down. Not a single Swordfish escaped and only five of their crews were rescued from the sea.

By now, Spitfires of 124 and 401 Squadrons had arrived to join in the fierce battle. A Messerschmitt was shot down onto the deck of a destroyer and four others badly damaged. As the day wore on, several other attacks were made on the fleet until the RAF mustered 242 bombers to attack the ships off the Dutch coast. Eventually one of the battle cruisers was seriously damaged.

Hitler had needed the cruisers in Norwegian waters because he feared an invasion of Norway by the British. It was one of the most audacious acts of the war and one in which the RAF lost 42 aircraft. For his bravery, Esmonde was awarded a posthumous VC.

All over Kent, women were now working in the factories and they made everything from ammunition and uniforms to aircraft. Often factory work meant moving away from home with higher pay and more independence but they still received less money than the men. At Shorts in Rochester the women received £2 3s a week and the men £3 4s. for doing the same job. The girl in the photograph, working on a lathe, was training for a highly skilled job.

The "Immortal Tuck" — a prisoner of war!

ONE of Kent's best-loved fighter pilots and one who thrived on action was in the news on January 28th, 1942. Robert Stanford Tuck who was born in Catford, lived in Kent and had become Station Wing Leader at Biggin Hill, set off with a colleague to put a juicy target out of action — the alcohol distillery at Hesdin, inland from Le Touquet.

Tuck found his target, roared down, pumped cannon shells into the building and saw smoke and flames soar into the sky. Craving more excitement he spotted a stationary locomotive and dived towards the engine. As it exploded into a geyser of scalding steam, Tuck found himself trapped in the crossfire of the Boulogne defences. With black oil and glycol streaming out of his Spitfire he made a forced-landing in a field.

The pilot who was known as the "Immortal Tuck" was now in enemy hands and no-one could believe it. In less than 18 months he had baled out over Horsmonden, glided 15 miles before landing on a dead engine and had been shot down over the Channel. Now he was to have more adventures as a prisoner of war, finally escaping to fight alongside the Russians.

A week without a single air-raid warning. That was the unbelievable situation in Dover towards the end of March 1942 — and it made people quite uneasy. As expected, the raiders returned. On the 23rd, five aircraft dropped 20 heavy bombs on the town. One fell on the air-raid shelter belonging to the East Kent Road Car Company in St James Street and killed most of the staff inside and another hit the Carlton Club where more died. Altogether there were 16 fatalities and numerous injuries. Photograph shows a typical "front-line street in Folkestone"

Many prisoners from Kent as Singapore falls

IN March 1942, scores of Kentish families were receiving the grim news that their soldier husbands and sons were in the hands of the Japanese following the fall of Singapore.

The invasion by Japanese assault troops had taken place on February 9th and so invincible were the enemy divisions that the British commander, Lt-Gen Arthur Percival chose not to counter attack, despite orders to do so. A telegram from Churchill had read: "Battle must be fought to bitter end. Commander and senior officers should die with their troops."

The official surrender which came on February 15th was believed to be the greatest military defeat in British history. Tokyo was ecstatic with victory fever, the lives of one million civilians were in jeopardy and 130,000 British and Imperial troops were preparing for a long ordeal as prisoners.

In March, Britain heard that most British PoWs were at Changi where 50,000 men were squeezed into four barracks and the human density was worse than the Black Hole of Calcutta.

BY March 1942 the country was desperately short of metal for making tanks, bombs and guns and the Parliamentary Secretary to the Ministry of Works, Mr George Hicks visited each county to talk to local authorities and voluntary organisations. He came to Maidstone in March 1942 and the Kent Messenger, on his behalf, was able to emphasise the urgency of the problem. As usual the county rose to the challenge.

One half of a threshing machine came from a farmer at Five Oak Green, pre-war automobiles were taken to the collection yard at Sevenoaks, a man from Pembury gave two floating mines from the last war, the owner of a windmill at Benenden offered two large wheels which he estimated would yield a ton of metal and youngsters from Pembury searched the area for broken iron bedsteads!

Every type of metal object was handed in. Our photograph shows a steam roller at Tunbridge Wells flattening a load of tins that had been collected in the borough. They were then sent away to a munitions factory.

There were queues everywhere during the war, but none were longer than those outside shops and by bus stops. This photograph was taken in Tunbridge Wells on March 24th, 1942 and the people were waiting for the Maidstone and District double-decker bus. There may not have been room for all!

More big raids on Hellfire Corner

THERE were several more serious raids on "Hellfire Corner" during the spring of 1942. The first was on Good Friday, April 3rd, when raiders, intent on bombing the Priory railway station at Dover, instead hit the concrete shelter in Union Road where 30 people were sleeping. Nine were killed. Nearby, two houses in Priory Gate Road collapsed and eight people were trapped in the wreckage. A postman and his wife were among those who died.

The miners at Betteshanger Colliery. having recovered from any bad feelings that may have lingered over the pay dispute, had further problems to occupy their minds on April 26th when a bomb fell on the power house, damaged the machinery and trapped some of them at the pit face for many hours. Eleven men were injured, two seriously.

Just over a week later, on May 6th, seven people were killed in nearby Deal when bombs were dropped in the Park Lane and Alfred Square areas. Ten homes were completely wrecked. Forty-eight hours later, while the people of Deal were busy clearing the debris and finding lodgings for the homeless, the raiders returned and on this occasion three people died.

Folkestone had braced itself for a big attack for many weeks — and when it came a great tragedy was averted by just a few minutes. On Sunday May 17th a bomb fell on Christ Church, Folkestone just before Matins. The congregation of a hundred or so moved to the church hall where they held a thanksgiving service instead.

During May there were more raids on East Kent. Two died at Hythe and one at St Mary's Bay on the 10th and two were killed in Deal on the 18th.

New chief for Bomber Command appointed

BY March, 1942, Bomber Command had a new commander-in-chief, Air Marshal Arthur Harris, who made it quite clear that he believed in strategic bombing and could be relied on to carry out orders to attack civilian morale in Germany.

Harris, aged 49, had once flown worn-out Bristol Fighters against the tribesmen in the North West Frontier and Vickers Vernon transports against Iraqi rebels. His last appointment was Commander, No. 5 Bomber Group.

The new chief, known as Bert and greatly respected by Churchill, had a reputation at the time for being a rather stubborn individual.

Pigeons belonging to Kent carrier pigeon fanciers were used by the Royal Corps of Signals and especially by guerilla forces in Nazi-occupied Europe to bring home important messages. It was all part of the Army Pigeon Service.

May, 1942. Land girls helped with the haymaking at Harrietsham. It was to be a wonderfully hot summer.

Haw Haw warns — Canterbury for Cologne

OPERATION Millennium was the codename given by Air Marshal Arthur Harris to the largest raid in the history of aerial warfare. The plan was to obliterate the giant German industrial city of Cologne and demonstrate the power of Bomber Command.

On Saturday May 30th, more than 1,000 aircraft, crewed by 6,500 young men, dropped 1,455 tons of bombs and achieved the most devastating results. In just 90 minutes Cologne was transformed from a healthy, thriving and beautiful historic city to a pathetic, shattered skeleton. More than 3,000 buildings were destroyed and almost 10,000 damaged. The great cathedral was among the victims. 480 people were killed and it was estimated that 85 per cent of the city was reduced to rubble.

The Luftwaffe was certain to retaliate; many smaller English cities had already been bombed by what came to be known as the "Baedeker Raids". The targets had been picked from the famous guide book of that name.

The people of Canterbury heard the news of the devastating raid on Cologne on their wireless sets on Sunday morning. On this warm summer's day, many of them remembered something else — Lord Haw Haw's warning that, should Cologne ever be bombed, then Canterbury would be the responding target. The thought chilled them to the bone.

At the same time, somewhere in Occupied Europe an enormous squadron of Luftwaffe bombers was being loaded with high explosive and incendiary bombs. The target was Canterbury.

Luftwaffe retaliates — and Canterbury is destroyed

THE sirens of Canterbury sounded in nerve-tingling harmony soon after midnight on the clear, cloudless, perfectly still, moonlit morning of June 1st. The city was tense. The Baedeker raids on British cities had all occurred at 12.45 am and the sirens seemed to signal that Canterbury was next on the menu. Tugboat Annie gave her throaty distinctive warning and, in the distance, the noise of a single aircraft grew slowly, tantalisingly into a roar. The bombers were on their way. The waiting was almost over.

The first raiders circled the city and dropped 16 parachute flares. They fell slowly, producing a bright blue and yellow light and, for those who dared to watch, the historic city with its fine detail of architecture was brilliantly illuminated. As the flares hung in the sky, a great wave of bombers, coming from the direction of Herne Bay, were heard in the darkness. Then came another wave and then another.

For more than an hour the people of Canterbury experienced unmitigated terror as a mixture of high explosive and incendiary bombs exploded on the city. One raider swooped low over the Cathedral precincts and, as he headed for Bell Harry tower, incendiary bombs clattered on to the roof of the Cathedral. The fire guards were waiting. With bombers zooming overhead they pushed the sizzling incendiaries over the roof to burn out on the grass below. Others that had flared up were quelled

before any damage could be caused. They were unable to save the Victorian Library by the Chapter House. As they worked, they could see the awesome sight of Canterbury burning.

RAF fighters and anti-aircraft guns were quickly in action, but to little avail. The bombers had got through and were dropping thousands of high explosives onto large areas of the city. Building after building became engulfed in flame and the sound of crashing masonry was almost as deafening as the noise of the gunfire and the exploding bombs. From their brick shelters and Morrison shelters people could feel the heat. It was intense.

Gradually the bombers left — their terrible mission completed — and the gunfire eased. All that could be heard was the crackle of fire, the brave voices of the firewatchers, the frantic activity of the firemen and the sudden shattering sound of another historic building crashing to the ground. The All Clear sounded at 2.10 am. People ventured outside and found the air filled with the acrid smell of burning. The raid had lasted for 75 minutes, Canterbury was reduced to rubble and the smokescreen that hung over the city was so thick that no-one knew whether the Cathedral had survived.

It had survived but not unscathed. A four-ton bomb, the heaviest ever to be dropped on Kent, had fallen near the entrance to Warrior's Chapel and the stained glass windows in the nave were blown out. The homes of Canon Shirley,

*The smoking ruins of the once-elegant Royal Fountain Hotel in St Margaret Street,
once used by Queen Victoria on her visits to Canterbury. This whole complex was
destroyed. Today it houses the Marlowe Arcade shopping centre.*

Canon Macnutt and Lady Davidson were destroyed. So
was the Norman staircase and part of King's School
buildings. The Old Palace survived and so did its famous
resident, Archbishop William Temple and his wife, who
sat huddled together under the old stone stairs.

More than 200 firemen from all over Kent were called
in to tackle the fires and, together with the rescue workers,
they worked for 24 hours without a break. They managed
to contain many fires by sacrificing some streets, such as
Butchery Lane, as firebreaks. By dawn, they had managed
to extinguish most of the big blazes. Members of the Civil
Defence, aided by troops, helped to dig people out of the
collapsed buildings. Rest centres and first-aid posts were
set up and the British Restaurant handed out emergency
food supplies. Few people slept and those who lived on
the outskirts, fled into the countryside, away from the
bombs. Here they could see Canterbury Cathedral,
illuminated by the light of 100 fires, glowing defiantly
high above the inferno.

Monday dawned to a scene of utter desolation. Hundreds
of buildings had been lost in the town centre bordered by
The Burgate, Lower Bridge Street, Lady Wootton's Green,
Monastery Street, Longport, Lower Chantry Lane, St
George's Place, Upper Bridge Street, Watling Street,
Stour Street, the High Street, The Parade and Butchery
Lane. Some timber frame buildings were completely
burnt out and others were levelled flat. The churches of
St George and St Mary Bredin and the Congregational
Church were just smouldering shells. Baker's Hotel, Rose
Hotel, Royal Fountain Hotel — the birthplace of the poet
Christopher Marlowe — had gone. The Payne Smith
School was totally destroyed.

Canterbury's famous pubs did not escape. The Crown
in Burgate, the Royal Oak in Longport, the Fountain Tap
in Rose Lane, the Comet in Broad Street, the Coach and
Horses in St George's Lane, the White Lion in St George's
Street and the Riding Gate Inn in Upper Bridge Street
were among the victims. The Longmarket, the Corn
Exchange and the terrace of large town houses along the
city walls — all Georgian — were gutted.

About 100 high explosive and 6,000 incendiary bombs
had been dropped, affecting almost six acres of the city.

St Augustine's Gate, which once gave access to a large monastery, was badly scarred. In front, Lady Wootton's Green received direct hits from four high explosive bombs and a row of cottages to the left of this photograph were totally destroyed. Today, the magnificent St Augustine's Gate has been lovingly restored.

50 people were killed, or died later of their injuries, 400 buildings were destroyed and 1,500 damaged by fire.

The firewatchers were among the bravest on duty that night. Two of them were killed and Mr B. Wells, aged 70, whose job was to guard the Friars Theatre, single-handedly saved the building from destruction. He picked up unexploded incendiaries and carried them to safer areas and dealt with those which had fallen through the roof into the auditorium. As he worked he had no idea that his own house was burning down.

Mr George Marks, town clerk, was killed and six children died, including three from the same family.

A former mayor of Canterbury, Mrs Catherine Williamson later wrote about that night:

"By God's mercy the cathedral stood four-square, though vast craters gaped in its green precincts and the walls and windows bore grievous scars — a desecration as vile as when Becket fell beneath his murderers' swordblades. But the eastern half of the High Street was in a condition only comparable to that of Ypres during the previous war. It presented an almost unbroken vista of desolation and among the buildings battered into shapeless rubble-heaps or irreparably damaged were many hallowed by antiquity.

"Through that first day and the days that followed, Canterbury presented a picture which seemed fantastically unreal to anyone familiar with its normal aspect. Along its streets lay miles and miles of snakelike hosepipe. The gutters were full of sweeping glass and other debris. Over great mountains of wreckage climbed swarms of human figures, dimly to be seen through a curtain of fine dust and ash....Everywhere was the smell of burning."

As the great clean-up continued, scores and scores of Union Jacks were draped from the windows of damaged buildings. Historic Canterbury had died that night, but the message from its inhabitants was crystal clear.

Taken from the roof of Marks and Spencer's a few days after the raid, this photograph shows the traumatic sight of a totally flattened St George's Street. Incendiary bombs started fires which destroyed most buildings including St George's Church. The tower survived and can be seen here covered in scaffolding. There is plenty of activity in this sad scene — men with a horse and cart collecting useful pieces from the debris, cyclists dodging the stones and craters, men walking to work, two buses and a lorry. It is not impossible to imagine the despair of those who passed by every day. St George's Street was eventually rebuilt with a collection of typically fifties bland brick buildings, while those around the tower came later. The clock tower was restored and is perhaps the greatest reminder of the night that Canterbury will never forget.

This is one of the most depressing photographs that the Kent Messenger has ever taken. It shows the still-smouldering ruins of Canterbury from the Cathedral. The High Street runs left to right. Butchery Lane is on the right and the Longmarket, which housed the Corn Exchange is in the centre. This impressive building was built on three levels and ran from The Parade to the Burgate. One feature of the Parade frontage during the first two years of the war was a huge indicator which measured the amount of the city's war savings. The glow from the shattered windows on the left was caused by the fires that were still burning inside.

There were many heroes in Canterbury during the night of June 1st, 1942, and the days that followed. Among them were these eight ATS girls who took out their staff cars and conveyed casualties to hospital, while masonry was crashing around them. They were commended for their bravery.

The Duke of Kent visited Canterbury on June 4th, toured the blitzed city and chatted with many people including the girls from Marks and Spencer's. Their shop stood out like an island amid the sea of devastation.

*The real spirit of Kent was shown by this wayside refreshment stall
on the Harrietsham by-pass. Although bombed-out, the Union Jack
was flying and "business continued as usual" at Dickley Hill Wayfarers.*

The fishermen of Folkestone showed their gratitude to the British pilots by giving the best of their catch each day to the RAF Benevolent Fund, in thanks for the protection they were given.

Wellington bomber crash lands at Lydd

THE third raid involving more than 1,000 bombers came on June 26th when the Focke-Wulf works in Bremen were singled out. It was a night of tragedy for the RAF. Only 700 aircraft reached the city and, of those, 48 were lost. Because of this no further raids on this scale were attempted in 1942.

One of the pilots on that raid was a 19-year-old, flying a Wellington. The engine failed and he was forced to crash-land in a field near Lydd. The fact that his rear gunner's wife was expecting a baby gave an even greater urgency to the importance of a safe landing. The most welcome sound, he heard after coming to, was an English voice telling barking dogs to shut up.

Squadron Leader Hugh Kennard who had been on a bomber escort mission also crash-landed in East Kent — in July, 1942. Badly wounded, he brought the aircraft down on land belonging to Alderman Prior of Folkestone. He was pulled from the wreckage and taken to a first-aid post.

'We regret to inform you'... the tragic news came daily

POST OFFICE
TELEGRAM

THE morning post contained grim news for the people of Kent. Every day, somewhere in the county, came the news that a husband or son had been killed in action, or was lost, or was believed to be a prisoner of war.

With the desert war at its greatest, with bomber crews deep into enemy territory and competing daily against flak and fighters, with convoy patrols in the North Sea dodging U-Boats and mines, with submariners listening for the depth charges and with Kent's fighting men dispersed to hot spots all over the world, the post held terrible fears.

Take the month of July 1942. A Sevenoaks bank manager, Mr H.P. Archer received official notification that his son, Gunner Michael Archer was missing in Libya. Days later came the news that Michael was a PoW.

Mrs Elizabeth Cobb, of Brasted, daughter of the chairman of Kent County Council, Major Sir Charles Pym `was told that her husband, Lieutenant Patrick Cobb was missing after leading a gallant action in the Channel on the night of July 20th. An Admiralty communiqué later confirmed that Lt Cobb had been killed. They had been married for less than a year.

News came on July 15th that Brendan Finucane, the RAF's youngest wing commander had been shot down over the English Channel and drowned. Finucane had 32 confirmed "kills" but now joined the other 122 pilots "missing" since June.

The Norris family learned that their sons Reg and Jesse, serving with the Royal Artillery in a marine anti-aircraft unit, were missing after the ship had been torpedoed. Several weeks later the two boys walked through the door of Hazel Cottage, Wouldham and announced to their delighted family that they were in good health. They had clambered into a lifeboat after the ship went down and spent three days in the Atlantic baling out water as it was leaking. They were eventually rescued by cargo boat and taken to Havana.

Mr and Mrs Arthur Goodman of St Philip's Avenue, Maidstone received a telegram saying that their son Sergeant Pilot William Goodman had not returned from an operation over Emden. During the last week in July they learned that he was a prisoner in Germany.

Wing Commander Vernon Butter, son of the Chief Constable of Ramsgate, was another reported missing in July. He was leading a daylight attack on the Matford factory at Poissey and had been shot down on the homeward flight. Later came news that Vernon had been killed. He was buried in Beauvais.

The family of Brigadier J. Morley Stebbings from Ramsgate heard from the Vatican radio on July 17th that the officer was a prisoner in Italian hands — and they didn't even know he was missing. Brig. Stebbings, aged 53, who had been captured in Tobruk and housed in the Palace of the Bourbon King was well treated. In Ramsgate he had commanded the 236th Territorial Battery which was mobilised on the outbreak of war.

For more than eight months, Mrs L. Lenton of Hastings Avenue, Margate lived with the agonising news that her son, Flight Lieutenant Reginald Lenton was missing. Early in July, 1942 she heard he was in a European port, alive and very well. Captured in November in enemy territory the airman had escaped and made his way to the hills where he lived with bandits for several months so as to avoid recapture. Finally he stole a fishing boat and sailed for Europe. His mother was told that he was due to return home soon. Before the war Lenton played hockey for Kent.

While Mrs Lenton was rejoicing, the Bunting family of Woodside, Lenfield Avenue, Maidstone were mourning the death of their third daughter, Audrey. The 18-year-old who had joined the WAAFs in June, was killed during the last week in July following an accident with a barrage balloon at Chigwell. Audrey had previously been employed by Boots of Maidstone.

There had been sorrow, too, at 24 Mill Street, Milton Regis — the home of 35-year-old Private Sydney Fullager.

The Queen's Own Regiment soldier had been posted missing, believed killed after the fall of France. Private Fullager, was far from dead. He had spend two adventurous years in Occupied and Unoccupied France, first in Nazi hands and then, as an escapee, on a French farm.

On July 31st news came that he was on his way home with seven days escape leave, seven days privilege leave and 14 days disembarkation leave.

Home Guard battalions throughout Kent continued with their exercises. They displayed their skills in manoeuvres, with machine guns, experimented with explosives and even practised crossing the River Medway at Teston on a rope made of rifle slings (see picture). Unbeknown to all of them, the Kent Zone Commander, Brigadier-General H.S.E. Franklin was about to award a trophy to the most "efficient battalion in the county including operational training, shooting and general administration". The winners, announced during a parade at Knole Park in July 1942, were Sevenoaks Home Guard, whose O.C. Colonel G. Shaw received the coveted trophy.

For these ATS girls the best parade of the week was the Pay Parade! August 21st, 1942.

KENT TOWNS NOW 'ADOPT' A WARSHIP

THE astounding success of the *Spitfire Fund* in 1940, when Kent paid for a new squadron, and the *War Weapons Week* in 1941, was followed, in 1942, by the *Warship Week* in which each town was invited to collect enough money to equip a battleship or buy a smaller vessel. The results again were staggering. Here are some of the towns, the amount collected by each and the ship adopted.

Beckenham
(£600,000 for HMS Sikh)
Bromley
(£600,000 for HMS Broke)
Orpington
(£200,000 for HMS Columbine)
Penge
(£82,000 for HMS Parrell)
Sevenoaks
(£480,000 for HMS Gallant)
Faversham
(£190,000 for HMS Armeria)
Maidstone
(£1,036,000 for HMS (submarine) Maidstone)
Tenterden
(£50,000 for motor launches)
Herne Bay
(£70,000 for a torpedo boat)
Deal
(£89,000 for a minesweeper)

The ladies of Kent continued to be "fashion-conscious" in 1942 despite the fact that clothes made from "utility cloth" were now on sale in the shops. However, although there were fewer styles available, pleats were limited, hemlines rose and variety did not suffer. For the men, the summer of 1942 meant the end of turn-ups and double-breasted coats. Here are three fashionable models of the period who obviously found it impossible to dress smartly without a hat!

The Duke of Kent with members of the Civil Defence Services at Ashford on May 3rd, 1941.

Duke of Kent killed in flying accident

HIS Royal Highness, the Duke of Kent, who had succeeded in boosting the county's morale when it was so desperately needed and who gave comfort in times of great distress was killed on active service, in a flying accident, just before midnight on August 25th. The official statement read: "The Air Ministry deeply regrets to announce that Air Commodore HRH the Duke of Kent was killed this afternoon when a Sunderland flying boat crashed in the north of Scotland". Attached to the staff of the Inspector General of the RAF, he was on his way to Iceland when the accident occurred.

The Duke was Colonel-in-Chief of the Royal West Kent Regiment and patron of the Association of Men of Kent and Kentish Men. He frequently toured blitzed areas and was quickly on the scene after the Baedeker raid on Canterbury in June. During the same month he also visited the King's School, Canterbury at its wartime home in Cornwall and was a guest of honour at RAF Biggin Hill, where he

was greeted by the station commander Group Captain Dickie Barwell.

Ironically, Barwell also lost his life in a flying accident. On July 1st, shortly after the Duke of Kent's visit, the Group Captain took off on a patrol in a Spitfire V1, a new high altitude model. With Squadron Leader Bobby Oxspring he was on a mission to hunt down a lone reconnaissance aircraft. Unknown to Barwell two more Spitfires had taken off from Tangmere to find the same "bandit".

Over the Channel the Tangmere pilots spotted an unfamiliar fighter, opened fire and Barwell's Spitfire V1 spun down in flames. The Controller at Biggin Hill radioed Tangmere: "Your boys have shot down our station commander".

On August 20th, 1942, the Invicta Squadron, 131 (County of Kent), gave vital air cover during the Allied attempt to seize the French port of Dieppe and destroy its German defences. CO, Wing Commander Michael Pedley won the DFC for his

courage but the raid itself was a disaster and of the 6,100-strong force of British and Canadian commandos, more than 4,000 were reported killed, wounded or missing. Five squadrons of the Biggin Hill Wing also helped to maintain a fighter umbrella over Dieppe until the last soldier was re-embarked. On that day the RAF lost 106 aircraft, including six from Biggin Hill.

The tragedies continued to mount. The third American Eagle Squadron (133) had established themselves at Biggin Hill in May by unfurling the "Old Glory". The Yanks were longing for action — which came with a vengeance in September during a peaceful patrol. Twelve Eagle Spitfires were blown 100 miles off course by a vicious head wind and when the pilots emerged from the clouds they found themselves at Brest.

The flak defences in this heavily defended French port opened up and all 12 Spitfires were badly holed. Eleven force-landed and were taken prisoner. The twelfth was killed.

Daylight attack on Deal by low-flying pirates

THE Baedeker offensives declined in August but the daylight bombing and machine-gun attacks continued and the simplest target, in terms of flying time, was the town of Deal.

On Tuesday August 11th eight enemy aircraft suddenly appeared from over the sea at 6 pm when many people were returning from work. As the raiders flew low over the town with their machine guns crackling, people threw themselves to the ground or ran desperately for cover. A 16-year-old cyclist was killed as he pedalled over a bridge. The bombs followed; many houses were hit and the Odeon cinema badly damaged. Eight people died and six were seriously hurt.

Betteshanger was bombed again on September 29th and the colliery was out of action for several weeks. A month later came another, more serious, attack on Deal — and this time 16 died, many in the wreckage of their homes. It was the same formula with pirate raiders machine-gunning, then bombing the town in broad daylight.

Rescue squads, Civil Defence workers and the fire service worked all day to pull the injured from the debris, take them to the first-aid centres and find accommodation for those whose homes had been ruined.

Altogether 15 buildings were destroyed, 56 seriously damaged and 96 slightly damaged.

Although the famous Barbican was badly scarred in the autumn of 1942 and more than 50 high explosive bombs were dropped in the borough, Sandwich came through the war comparatively lightly considering its precarious position in Hellfire Corner. It was one of only three Kent local authority districts not to have any fatalities (the others were Southborough and Queensborough) and only seven properties were completely destroyed. Compare that to Dover — 199 killed and 2,998 properties severely damaged. This picture was taken on January 22nd, 1943.

A party of Canadian MPs inspected "Winnie".

Prime Minister, Winston Churchill was a regular visitor to Dover. On one occasion he sat on the clifftop and watched the dog fights over the Channel, on another he viewed the activity in Dover Harbour from the Royal Navy balcony outside the cliff casemates of Vice-Admiral Ramsey. He met the gunners, inspected the WRNS at Dover College and, on October 23, 1942 escorted General Smuts on a tour of the town and its defences.

A former Wren, later Mrs L.Crowther of Whitstable, recalled how she bumped into the official party when she was not in proper uniform. She stood to attention and saluted. Churchill gave a huge great wink, Smuts smiled but the other "brasshats" looked daggers drawn — she should not have saluted without her hat on!

One of the great Channel guns was called "Winnie" and Churchill, obviously delighted that his name had been adopted for this vast piece of artillery, once ordered it to be fired. Mrs Crowther remembered the incident. "Winnie, and the other gun 'Pooh' shelled France and the entourage had approximately 20 minutes to hustle Churchill out of town and onto a train before the Germans fired all their guns in reply."

The 18 inch Mobile Channel Gun on the Southern Railway at Dover.

Watching a demonstration at Chatham, these were Commanding Officers of the Southern Railway Home Guard unit who were responsible for four armoured patrol trains, based at Canterbury, Tonbridge, Barnstaple in Devon and Wadebridge in Cornwall. All the trains patrolled regularly and their armoured plating was made at the great railway works in Ashford which experienced its most productive days during the war. Working double shifts, the Ashford men and women made 75 ramp wagons to carry tanks, repaired and converted 43 3.7 Howitzers, produced bomb trolleys and tank fittings for the US Army and built one thousand open 12-ton freight wagons for Russia — and completed them in less than 10 weeks.

Ten killed at Ashford

WITH its involvement in such vital work, the Ashford railway works was obviously a prime target. In fact there were more than 4,000 alerts, and bombs fell in the vicinity regularly, but the most serious occurred on October 26th when a Dornier dropped two bombs and killed 10 men and a woman, many of whom had been sheltering under a wall which collapsed in the explosion. The machine shops were badly damaged but production continued.

A month later, on November 27th, two Focke-Wulf 190s attacked Ashford and killed George Barnes at the railway works. On their way back to France, the fighters spotted a train at the level crossing at Caldecot on the branch line to New Romney.

The aircraft bore down on the helpless tank engine, where driver Mr C.Gilbert and fireman, Albert Hills were cowering in the cab. The engine was hit by the first Focke-Wulf but the second, flying low behind, clipped the steam dome on the loco and lost control. The aircraft hit the ground and completely disintegrated. The pilot was thrown clear but drowned in a dyke.

Scalding steam from the ruptured engine poured down into the cab burning Mr Hills who was taken to hospital. The driver escaped with shock.

The engine, a Class D3 0-4-4 No. 2365 after collision with a Focke-Wulf 190.

Missing the thatched barn on the right which contained 40 cows, a Stirling bomber wrecked this farmhouse at Rye Street, Cliffe on October 20th, 1942. Mrs Lilian McPherson, aged 21, was killed.

People machine-gunned in the streets

THE boys and girls of Balloon Command (known at the time as "gas bag types") moved into Canterbury in the late summer of 1942 and, by the autumn, scores of these huge mini-airships were glowing in the southern sun with a great gaggle protecting the Cathedral. Around the city were the anti-aircraft guns and not far away, at Manston, the night fighters. The Canterbury defences were strong but many wondered just how effective they would be against another massive attack.

On Friday October 30th, Mrs Churchill and Mrs Roosevelt, wife of the American President, visited the town and saw that many traders had picked themselves up after the Baedeker raid and were now in business again. Later, the two ladies took a train to Barham to visit the Women's Institute, travelling along the Elham Valley Line.

The following day, a Saturday, the barrage balloons came down for essential repairs and this was the signal for the Luftwaffe to attack. At 5 pm, a force of about 20 Messerschmitt 109s screamed towards the city, skimming the rooftops before spraying the streets with machine-gun fire. A bus carrying eight passengers along the Sturry Road towards Herne Bay was strafed with bullets and all died except the driver. His colleague in another bus was shot through the heart by a bullet and the vehicle, out of control, crashed through a hedge and came to rest in a ploughed field. The raiders also took the Elham Valley Line and, just outside Barham, attacked a train, killing a fireman and a small boy.

The 109s machine-gunned the people in the main streets and dropped bombs in residential areas. Houses in Watling Street, Wincheap and Northgate were wrecked and people died as their homes caved in. Three more pubs were destroyed and the Regal Cinema was badly damaged. It was estimated that 50 high explosive and more than 400 incendiary bombs were dropped on Canterbury that evening.

But the raiders still hadn't finished. Shortly after 8 pm they returned to outlying areas and, in the early hours of November 1st, came back again, killing more people.

Thirty two died during the three raids, 55 were seriously injured and more than 250 people were made homeless. Again Canterbury people refused to give up. On that Sunday morning, troops joined Civil Defence workers to clear the streets of debris, help the homeless salvage what they could and place almost 1,000 tarpaulins over damaged roofs. The cheerful ladies of the WVS set up their incident posts, the two British Restaurants served food and the mayor and his wife, Alderman and Mrs Charles Lefevre toured the city offering what help they could.

Incredibly, the Cathedral survived all three raids. Windows had been blasted but the precious stained glass was safely in storage and the vast pile of sandbags in the crypt protected the great walls from blast. Canterbury author Paul Crampton later wrote: "The survival of the Cathedral was somehow symbolic of the spirit of the citizens of Canterbury. They, like the Cathedral, had endured the ordeal of bombs falling all around, and they, like the beautiful perpendicular towers, stood up proud, unshaken and unbroken".

The wartime caption on this photograph read: "Air raid alert — December 16th, 1942, somewhere in southern England". This was the Fiveways, Tunbridge Wells and, presumably, the inhabitants were hurrying for shelter. On that day bombs fell in the vicinity, killing three people and injuring 13 in neighbouring Tonbridge.

A marauding German bomber aiming for Tonbridge railway junction on December 16th, 1942, missed the target by a few yards and caused devastation in the adjoining Meadow Lawn residential area. People watched the bomb doors open as the plane swooped low over the town. Two bombs destroyed houses in Albert Road and Chichester Road, killing three people and injuring 30.

Canterbury welcomes Red Army assassins

CANTERBURY welcomed three special visitors to the town on November 9th, 1942 — Lieutenant Lyudmila Pavilchenka, Nicolai Krasavchenko and Lieutenant Vladimir Pchelintsev — heroes of the Russian Red Army, who had killed hundreds of Germans in defence of their homeland.

Nicolai was leader of the Moscow Youth, Lydudmila was a female sniper who had reputedly killed 309 in defence of Odessa and Sevastopol and Vladimir was said to have killed 152 Germans with 154 bullets and had received the Order of Lenin.

The Russians were welcomed by the mayor, Alderman Lefevre and were given a tour of the blitzed city.

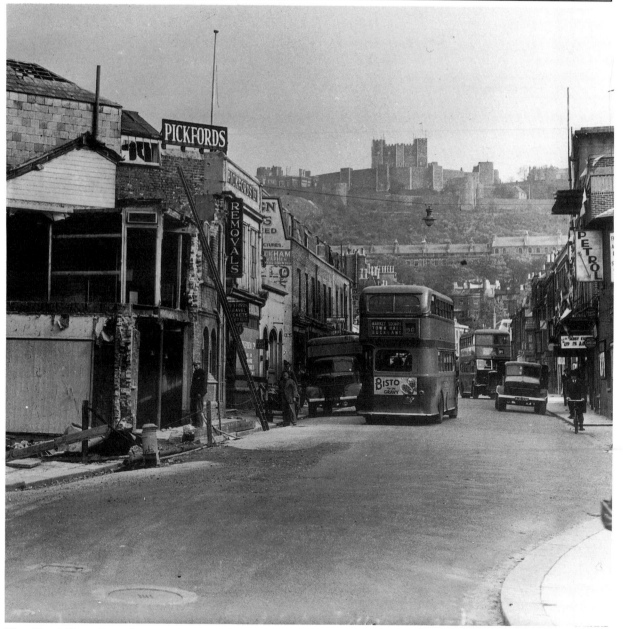

The East Kent bus drivers, conductors and their passengers had a harrowing time but they still carried on running their essential services. Here. another brave double-decker passes through a shell-damaged street in Dover in December 1942.

This jolly band, formed at the end of 1941, were always able to attract a sizeable audience, but not allowed to go on tour! According to the Kent Messenger caption, and no other details were given, they were prisoners in Stalag IX. Can anyone identify a father or husband or friend among this lot?

Kent club formed — in Stalag 383!

AS the fourth Christmas of the war approached, the people of the front-line county tried to put aside their grief and reflect on the good tidings that recent events had brought. The great talking point in Kent's pubs, offices and factories was Montgomery's victory at Alamein and the part the local boys had played in the "Torch" landings at Algiers, Oran and Casablanca two weeks later.

Many county newspapers, a little prematurely as it turned out, said that victory was in the air and the bells were ringing. Churchill, too, was optimistic. "Alamein", he said, "if not the beginning of the end, is at least the end of the beginning."

Members of the Association of Men of Kent and Kentish Men were delighted to hear that a new branch of the association had been formed — in Stalag 383! So many Kent men were being sent as prisoners-of-war to the camp in Austria that the organisers were able to hold an inaugural meeting with 40 members attending. By Christmas they had 161 members — all born in the county.

The secretary of the county association received this letter from the prison camp. "Please give our Christmas greetings to the British Red Cross and YMCA whose magnificent efforts on our behalf are greatly appreciated. I enclose a nominal roll of Kent men in the Stalag 383 branch. Their addresses will be the present home of their next of kin.

"Indoor activities at this branch consist of bridge, bridge, bridge and more bridge but we occasionally lapse into a game of crib. We have two theatres and we are staging some excellent productions including Merchant of Venice, Night Must Fall and the comedies George and Margaret and French Without Tears. Our leading light in the theatre is Colour Sergeant Moxon of Canterbury.

"We have a flourishing St John Ambulance Association and among the successful recent candidates is Albert Chambers of Ramsgate. Once more, on behalf of the Stalag 383 Branch of the Association of Men of Kent and Kentish Men, I extend cordial seasonal greetings to all Kent people all over the world. Next year, maybe, we'll be home."

(Signed) Norman Coates, Stalag 383.

Back at home, Kentish families tried to enjoy Christmas. Shells, or no shells, the Folkestone Garrison Theatre in the Pleasure Gardens was packed every night for the seasonal Ensa shows and troops and friends enjoyed the dancing at Maison Dieu, Dover. At Tunbridge Wells, the Assembly Rooms were used as the post office sorting house for the Christmas rush with schoolboys acting as willing postmen (above) on Christmas Day itself. This was the scene on December 25th.

Every morning, this ARP ambulance collected the babies of Maidstone's war-working mothers and took them to a nursery.

1943

Stalingrad, desert victory, Italy surrenders

January 14th: President Roosevelt and Mr Churchill met for talks in Casablanca.

January 23rd: Unemployment figures dropped to their lowest levels in British history.
British troops entered Tripoli.

January 31st: Germans surrendered in Stalingrad.

March 3rd: Tragedy at Bethnal Green tube station when people hurrying to shelter after an air-raid warning were crushed in the panic. 173 died of suffocation and 62 were badly injured.

March 5th: Britain's first jet fighter aircraft, the Gloster Meteor made its maiden flight.

March 7th: A "wings for victory" campaign was launched by National Savings. People were asked to stick savings stamps on to 500-pound bombs positioned in the streets to raise £150 million for building bombers.

April 12th: War costs for 1943 were estimated at £5,756 million. Purchase tax on luxury items was raised once more — on some goods to 100 per cent.

May 7th: Allied troops captured Tunis and Bizerta.

May 8th: Part-time war work became compulsory for women between the ages of 18 and 45, except for mothers looking after their own children under 14.

May 13th: General Alexander, Commander-in-Chief, reported that the Allies were now masters of all North African shores.

May 14th: Operation Mincemeat was confirmed a success by the intelligence service. This involved depositing a corpse off the coast of Spain, complete with briefcase and papers leading the Germans to think that the Allies intended to invade Greece.

May 16th: The Warsaw ghetto was finally destroyed by the Germans.

May 17th: The 617 "Dambuster" squadron led by Guy Gibson dropped the bouncing bombs designed by Dr Barnes Wallis on the Möhne and Eder dams. Gibson was subsequently awarded the Victoria Cross.

June 25th: RAF and USAAF bombers continued to bombard towns in the Ruhr valley; 870 acres of Wuppertal lay in ruins.

June 30th: An announcement was made that signposts were to be re-erected in rural areas of Britain now that the danger of invasion had receded.
Factory workers responded positively to Music While You Work and production increased by 15 per cent for the hour following the broadcast.

July 8th: French Resistance leader Jean Moulin, known as "Max" died after being tortured by the Germans.

July 10th: Allied troops landed on Sicily.

July 12th: The UK birthrate reached its highest level for 17 years in the first quarter of 1943, despite the fact that most men were away from home!

July 25th: Mussolini was dismissed from his post and arrested. Italy was in political chaos with strikes and riots.

July 31st: The city of Hamburg was razed to the ground by RAF bombers.

40,000 people were believed to have been killed, more than in the entire London Blitz.

August 18th: RAF bombers attacked the top-secret rocket and flying bomb site at Peenemunde on the Baltic coast.

September 3rd: Allied troops landed in Italy and the country surrendered.

October 13th: Italy declared war on Germany; only five weeks previously they had been allies.

November 6th: The Russians recaptured Kiev.

November 9th: The United Nations organisation signed an agreement to form an organisation for the Relief and Rehabilitation Administration to bring immediate relief to the populations of liberated countries.

November 20th: Amidst much protest from the general public, Sir Oswald Mosley was released from Holloway prison for health reasons.

December 2nd: It was announced by Ernest Bevin, Minister of Labour, that men would be conscripted to serve in the coal mines for reasons of "urgent national necessity".

December 24th: General Dwight Eisenhower was appointed supreme commander of the Allied Expeditionary Force being prepared for the cross-Channel invasion of France.

December 25th: It was estimated that only one family in ten would be able to enjoy a traditional Christmas dinner of turkey or goose. One butcher reported that he had only received 15 birds for 800 customers.

The Swastika on the wing of the Junkers which crashed at Brenzett was painted out so it could not be seen by the enemy. Some 40 years later the site was excavated by the Brenzett Aeronautical Museum and the tail fin is now on show at the Lashenden Air Warfare Museum, Headcorn.

Hat-trick for Beaufighter aces of 29 Squadron

FOR the first time since 1941 a large scale attack, in two phases, against London was mounted — and suddenly it was like the Battle of Britain all over again. This scrap, however, was at night, the aircraft in action were the Beaufighters of 29 Squadron, West Malling and the heroes of the hour were Wing Commander C.M. Wight-Boycott and his A1 operator Flying Officer E.A Sanders.

At 4am, in the dark hours of Monday January 18th, 40 German bombers crossed the South Coast while a cover attack by 10 aircraft came in from the east. 29 Squadron were immediately scrambled and met the raiders over the Weald of Kent.

First blood went to Wight-Boycott and Sanders when a Junkers 88 crashed to its destruction at King Street railway crossing, Brenzett. The crew were killed. A few minutes later the two airmen shot down a Dornier 217 which smashed into the chalk quarry of the North Downs, at Pilgrims House, Westerham, again killing the entire crew. By dawn on this incredible night the Beaufighter aces had achieved their hat-trick, although newspapers at

the time credited them with four victories. The third, another Junkers 88, fell at the Town End recreation ground, Caterham at 5.30 am. On this occasion one crew member baled out and was taken prisoner and the others died.

The fourth raider, credited at the time to Wight-Boycott and Sanders fell at Lovelace Place Farm, Bethersden.

The successful Wing Commander was awarded an immediate DSO for his bravery that night but, away from the exploits of 29 Squadron, there was much sadness. The enemy dropped 125 bombs on Lewisham, Wandsworth and Woolwich and 74 people died. The anti-aircraft guns were in action, of course, but some of the shells had been fitted with faulty fuses and they fell back to earth and exploded. Police Constable Robert Burns, of London Road, Bromley was struck by a piece of shrapnel and died and another policeman was wounded in Court Road, Orpington.

It was reported that more damage was caused in Orpington by "friendly" missiles, than by the Luftwaffe.

Another Wight-Boycott/Sanders kill. This aircraft completely disintegrated on impact and then burned furiously.

Good shooting sir! Wing Commander Wight-Boycott (left) with his Observer, Flying Officer Sanders and members of 29 Squadron at West Malling.

Kent's cricket captain killed in France

ONE week before the outbreak of war in 1939, Frederick Gerald Hudson Chalk, captain of Kent Cricket Club, scored 115 not out at Dover against Yorkshire. Almost four years later, on February 17th, 1943, Flight Lieutenant Chalk DFC, Spitfire pilot with 124 Squadron, was declared missing, presumed killed. It was thought at the time that he had come down in the Channel.

Gerry Chalk (second left) with Peter Foster, Leslie Ames, Brian Valentine, Hopper Levett and Alan Watt.

For Kent's cricket followers this was more than just another war statistic. He was one of the county's finest pre-war captains and the 1944 edition of Wisden stated: "Gerry Chalk's tragic death at the age of 32 was deplored by all who were interested in cricket. For Uppingham, Oxford and Kent he batted and fielded so brilliantly". During his short first class career he made 6,732 runs in 259 innings. His highest score of 198 was made against Sussex at Tonbridge in 1939.

Chalk joined the RAF at the outbreak of war and became a tail gunner on Wellingtons, flying over 30 sorties. At the age of 30, he became a Spitfire pilot. On February 17th, 1943, 124 (Baroda) Squadron were shepherding a bomber run from Harwich to Dunkirk. The raid was cancelled but the Squadron did not receive the call to return home. Instead, near St Omer, they were jumped by more than 40 Focke-Wulfs. Four aircraft were shot down and three pilots died. One of them was Chalk.

Forty six years later the last tragic day of Gerry Chalk took an astonishing twist. An excavation of a wartime site in Northern France recovered a Mark VI Spitfire — and there in the cockpit were the remains of the pilot.

He was finally laid to rest in a military cemetery near Boulogne, just a few miles across the water from the Crabble cricket ground where Chalk scored his final century. At the service were many of his former colleagues and his widow, Mrs Rosemary Taylor who flew in from New Zealand.

Catford children massacred at school

TWO days later the raiders were back — this time with an assault against the capital which came as such a surprise that the defences were unable to counter the attackers before they reached the city. On this day, January 20th, Focke-Wulf 190s and escorting Messerschmitt 109s bombed and strafed virtually at will. Four RAF balloon sites in Lewisham were destroyed, a gasholder at Sydenham was set alight, the President's House at the Royal Naval College, Greenwich was damaged and there were three direct hits on Deptford West Power Station. Worse, far worse, a 500 kg bomb fell on Sandhurst Road School, Catford, blowing out the whole central part of the LCC school where many children were taking their midday dinner break.

When the dust and the smoke subsided, the scene in the dining room was appalling. Twenty-four pupils and two teachers were dead. A further five died on the staircase and nine on the second floor. The blast reached the staff room where three teachers died and another was killed in the science room. The incident prompted enormous publicity from national and local newspapers who were certain the bomb had been deliberately dropped at a time when many of the pupils would be together. The *Kentish Mercury* described it as "the fiendish onslaught of a murderous foe".

Altogether 38 children were killed. Among them were sisters, Brenda and Lorina Allford, aged five and seven, who died with their friends Anne Biddle and her sister Judith. Nine-year-old Ronald Barnard and his brother Dennis, 10, were both killed. A police sergeant, Norman Greenstreet who had an eight-year-old at the school discovered the body of his son after searching through the

The frantic search for the children buried under the rubble of Sandhurst School, Catford continued both day and night as hundreds of rescue workers joined police and civil defence workers in pulling free huge pieces of masonry.

rubble. The six teachers who died were Mrs Ethel Betts, Mrs Virginia Carr, Miss Mary Jukes, Miss Gladys Knowelden, Miss Harriet Langdon and Mrs Connie Taylor.

Margaret Clarke, the headmistress said later that she was in her room on the top floor when she heard a distant siren. She went into the hall outside and the next thing she remembered was a tearing, rending sound and the hall, six yards from where she was standing, fell away. "I joined some children who were going down the stairs and on reaching the ground floor started to pull the injured children clear. Before the arrival of the rescue workers, soldiers on leave and civilians who were passing by came in to help us dig, among the stifling fumes of the fire, in the debris. It was not until later that I noticed my own injuries and I was taken to Farnborough Hospital.

"The only question the children were asking was 'How can I help, Miss?' They took home the younger ones, tore up their clothing to bind the injuries and even helped the rescue work — a grim job for youngsters of 14 and 15."

Many of the children were buried in a communal grave in nearby Hither Green Cemetery and the service, conducted by the Bishop of Southwark, was attended by 7,000 mourners.

The question that everyone asked after the raid was: "Why was there no warning?" Apparently there had been confusion among the Observer Corps plotters, and problems with some faulty equipment helped the raiders reach their target with complete surprise. The Alert did not sound until it was too late.

At an inquiry at Lewisham Town Hall, it was clear that the Civil Defence were quickly on the scene and there were congratulations for the volunteers, the heavy rescue squads, the mobile units, the REME soldiers stationed at St Dunstans and the Canadians at Bromley Wood. The meeting mildly criticised police for their inability to control parents but also agreed it would have been impossible to stop the frantic efforts of relatives in digging among debris to find their little ones.

Junkers jettisons bombs and crashes at Boxley

INCREASED activity by RAF Bomber Command over Germany prompted more hit and run reprisals and, at dawn, on February 3rd, four Focke-Wulf raiders swept in over the coast at little more than roof-top height and headed for Ashford. Within minutes six people had been killed and 11 seriously injured.

Bombs fell in St John's Lane, Birling Road and the Penlee Point area where people died in their homes. Another fell behind the High Street, shattering all the windows and badly damaging a Baptist chapel, hotel, bank and schoolrooms.

One month later, on March 4th, it was Chatham's turn to suffer again. A Junkers 88 on a bombing mission to London was attacked by Pilot Officer T.C.Wood and Sergeant L.Evans in a Beaufighter of the crack 29 Squadron. The raider, badly damaged and crashing, jettisoned its cargo over Chatham. Five people were killed, including one elderly couple and their grandaughter. Two were seriously injured and 98 people had to be accommodated in the rest centre.

The Junkers meanwhile tried to gain height and avoid the anti-aircraft fire but it was badly holed and crashed at Boxley Abbey, Maidstone. Two of the crew were killed and two, who baled out badly injured, were taken prisoner. Although this incident occurred at 4.25 am, scores of people heard the limping bomber and saw the huge flames on the horizon as the aircraft crashed.

A photograph of St John's Lane, Ashford after the dawn attack by four Focke-Wulfs on February 3rd. The notice on the middle window of the building on the right warns looters that they faced the death penalty or penal service for life should they be caught stealing from this or any damaged property. Sadly, despite the threats (and they were never carried out), looting became an unsavoury aspect of the Blitz.

Kent won its Wings in one hectic week

The Spitfire on view at Gravesend Clock Tower helped to swell the fund.

FOLLOWING the great success of the big appeals — in 1940 for the Spitfire Fund, in 1941 for War Weapons Week, in 1942 for Warship Week — the towns of Kent ambitiously named their target for the 1943 effort, Wings for Victory Week, held between March and June.

Bearing in mind the lack of ready cash and the demands placed on every individual from other charitable appeals such as Aid to China, Aid to Russia, the Red Cross, Salvation Army, National Savings, War Bonds, RAF Benevolent Fund, Prisoner of War Fund and many more, the results were extraordinary.

Sevenoaks was targeted for a mammoth £500,000 and announced the progress each day on a huge indicator on the Fountain in the High Street. The chairman of the council, Miss Maude Davis appealed to commuters each morning at Tubs Hill Station. "Hello, hello, this is Sevenoaks Wings for Victory news service. If your bank is in the city, please today arrange the maximum investment. Remember also that each member of your household must play a part. We are raising funds for Victory!"

Seven days later the *Sevenoaks News* proudly announced the result. "We've won our wings", they said. "£547,000."

Folkestone's target of £130,000 was doubled. Faversham set out to raise £100,000 for two Sunderland flying boats — they raised enough for three. Cranbrook ambitiously announced a target to buy 20 Typhoons, and easily succeeded. The Medway Towns hit the million pound mark and even little Eastry Rural achieved its promise of one Sunderland, one Mosquito and two Typhoons.

Throughout Kent, the villages made their handsome contributions by staging costume cricket matches, flower shows, fancy dress parades, whist drives, Victory dances, auction sales and street collections. It was hectic.

Fremlin's elephant chortled with delight as the contributions grew. This picture was taken the previous year, in May 1942.

A policeman stands on guard while Civil Defence workers and firemen survey the tragedy in this road at Newtown, Ashford.

50 killed in three minute raid

THE Catford bomb, which caused so much tragedy, had been dropped from a new Focke-Wulf 190-4 which had a special power boost system to improve low altitude performance. It belonged to the highly effective fighter-bomber Staffel of JG 26, later to become JG54, which was based at St Omer. The leading pilot was Staffelkapitan, Oberleutnant Paul Keller who, in a German broadcast, described how delighted he was with the success of this raid.

Keller, nicknamed the "Bombenkeller", had led a charmed life, but this was to end in the most dramatic fashion over Ashford on Wednesday March 24th when his FW 190 was hit by Ack-Ack fire and exploded in the air. Before he went, however, the "Bombenkeller of St Omer" and his unit dealt Kent its worst blow of the entire war exceeding, in terms of lives lost, the Baedeker raid on Canterbury.

On this day the Focke-Wulfs of JG54 came in over the rooftops in a copycat of the attack of February 3rd. The raid lasted just three minutes but in that time 50 people were killed and 77 seriously injured by bombs and machine guns which strafed the streets and exploded on buildings almost simultaneously.

In one way it was like Catford all over again, for a bomb fell on the 300-strong Victoria Road Primary School. Unlike Catford, however, the sirens sounded in time and the children were already in the playground shelters. Two classrooms which 80 girls had just vacated were completely wrecked. Parents and friends rushed to the school long before the All-Clear sounded and found the children unhurt.

The staff at the railway works had 25 seconds to find cover. Two spotters on duty on top of Newtown Bath House saw the aircraft flying from the Mersham direction directly out of the sun. They sounded the danger signal and dived for cover themselves as five bombs fell on the works. Five people were killed and 50-ton locomotives in the erecting shed were totally mangled.

The worst damage in Ashford occurred at Milton Road, New Street, where two died in Hayward's Garage, Dover Place, New Rents, Star Road, Hardinge Road and Kent Avenue, where five were killed in a baker's shop.

Paul Keller's 190 came down in pieces in Goddington Road, Keller himself being thrown out in flames. He died on the ground in a nearby playing field and his remains were taken for burial to Folkestone New Cemetery at Hawkinge.

The rescue work at Ashford went on all day and night with the Salvation Army and the WVS keeping everyone supplied with food and hot drinks.

Kent's worst raid of all in terms of lives lost. Top picture: A residential road in Ashford where every house was damaged. Left: Hayward's Garage, New Street, Ashford, where two people died.

Enemy invaders harrassed again by Home Guard

SOUTH-east England was "invaded" again on Sunday April 11th, 1943. On this occasion the enemy landed at "Goudhurst Harbour" where they established two bridgeheads. They then waited for support from the airborne troops who immediately seized airfields, attacked communications and prepared to deal with ambushers.

It was, of course, a convoy exercise in which the enemy were represented by regular soldiers and the defenders by members of the Home Guard from Tunbridge Wells, Maidstone and Hastings, split into three convoys.

After the wonderful parodies of television's Dad's Army, these exercises may appear, in retrospect, to be simple and crude but in April 1943 it was a deadly serious business. The Home Guard were proud of the fact that they escaped surprise attacks by the "enemy", adopted defensive measures, killed the ambushers, reached the harbour and saved the day for England.

It was, said a Home Guard officer, "a jolly good show".

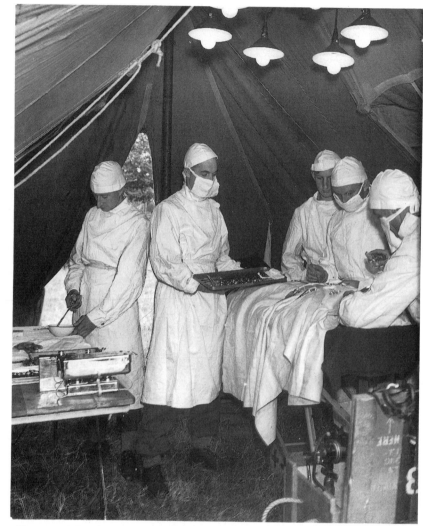

Above: An advanced Field Dressing Station on Tunbridge Wells Common. It was erected by 53rd Division RAMC with complete equipment for prompt aid for soldiers wounded in battle. Below: Members of the 28th (1st SR) Battalion of the Home Guard on the charge with fixed bayonets during an exercise at Chatham.

Above: An RAMC unit ferrying casualties across a river on improvised floats and
Below: A first-aid party dealing with casualties during an exercise.

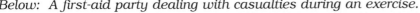

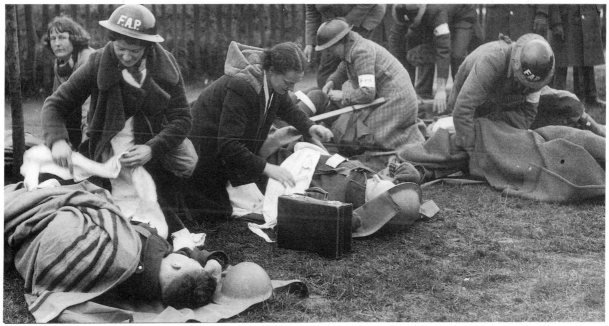

When the Luftwaffe landed at West Malling

This was the first FW 190 to arrive at West Malling, flown by Otto Bechtold.

THE fighter-bomber assault on London launched by 30 Focke-Wulfs on the night of April 16th-17th was not a great success. Only two bombs were dropped on the capital and a few Essex towns were hit on the way home. But four of the aircraft lost their way in the darkness bringing about one of the strangest episodes of the war.

The drama began when a searchlight beam at Sittingbourne picked out a lone aircraft, thought to be a Defiant in trouble. The beam of light was deflected in the direction of West Malling and, just past midnight, the duty controller at the airfield ordered the aerodrome beacon and runway light to be switched on. The pilot switched on his own navigation lights, fired a recognition flare and prepared to land on the grass runway.

To the surprise of the controller, the crew of the fire tender on standby, the men of the 4th (Ulster) Light AA Regiment on defence duties, the aircraft turned out to be an FW 190. As Gunner Lionel Barry rushed towards the pilot, Feldwebel Otto Bechtold raised his arms in surrender and he was taken into custody.

Minutes later a second aircraft entered the Malling circuit and commenced to land. This time the watch office duty crew were on a gun platform, having already identified another Focke Wulf. The pilot realised his mistake but as he gave his engine full throttle, a burst of fire from the Vickers gun mounted on the truck scored several hits. The fuel tanks burst into flames and the pilot fell out with his clothing on fire.

One of the duty crew tried to stop him running away and there was a struggle. The German pilot broke free, ran round the back of the tender straight into the arms of the CO, Wing Commander Peter Townsend. Leutnant Fritz Setzer surrendered and was taken to the sick bay.

The excitement continued as the third Focke-Wulf was heard circling West Malling. It was obvious that the German crews believed they had crossed the water and were back in France. This assumption also had dawned on the men of the Army units who were manning the gun emplacements and they opened fire. The aircraft crash-landed at Springetts Hill Farm, East Malling and Oberfeldwebel Otto Schulz escaped with concussion. The ambulancemen found him having a drink with a local who had seen him crash.

By this time the pilot of the fourth Focke-Wulf realised he was in hostile territory, abandoned his aircraft and jumped. He was unlucky. Too low for his parachute to deploy, Oberleutnant Kurt Khaln fell to his death some distance from the spot at Staplehurst where his aircraft crashed.

In trepidation West Malling waited for the entire German squadron to appear one by one in its circuit, but it was not to be. No further aircraft were spotted and the runway lights were switched off at 2.30 am.

The first intact FW190 caused much attention and West Malling was besieged later by representatives of the Air Ministry, newspaper reporters and other distinguished visitors including the CO at Biggin Hill, Sailor Malan. The aircraft was eventually taken to the Royal Aircraft Establishment at Farnborough for scientific inspection.

It later transpired that the four lost Focke-Wulfs had experienced navigation difficulties because of ground mist. They had spotted the searchlight beams and having heard no Ack-Ack guns assumed they were in France.

West Malling, in its operational life, had seen many astonishing things but this was the strangest of all.

The wreckage in Homefield Road, Bromley was carefully guarded.

Bomber disintegrates over Bromley

A LONE Junkers 88 which had been plotted by Observers almost aimlessly meandering over the south Midlands and then London for more than an hour, was eventually shot down by the pilots of a Mosquito night fighter. The action occurred over Bromley during the early hours of Sunday April 25th and the sky was lit up by brilliant flashes followed by a thunderous explosion as the aircraft disintegrated.

People below, who had watched the drama, heard the wreckage fall with a series of great thuds. Wheels, guns, engines and other parts of the Junkers were spread over a large area of the town including Homefield Road and Widmore Road, where two houses were virtually destroyed

by the ensuing fire. There was another blaze at Bromley cricket ground and the cockpit landed near the pavilion. The scout hall opposite was burnt down by one of the engines.

In his book "*Bromley in the Front Line* ", Lewis Blake tells of a small boy, Raymond Wattenbach, then a pupil of Bickley Hall School who cycled to the site the next morning and saw the body of one of the crew lying on the cricket ground. "There was no-one guarding the site so Raymond picked up one or two souvenirs which was standard practice among schoolboys at the time. Through the roof of a house near Holy Trinity Convent a wing tip pointed to the sky and a cannon lay in Homefield Road."

Dambuster trials at Reculver Bay

ON the night of May 16th, 1943, 19 Lancasters of 617 Squadron, led by Wing Commander Guy Gibson, set off from Scampton in Lincolnshire and attacked the heavily reinforced Möhne and Eder concrete dams sweeping more than 300 million tons of water into the western Ruhr valleys. The floods drowned 1,294 people, destroyed or damaged 125 factories, ruined nearly 3,000 hectares of arable land, destroyed 25 bridges and flooded many coalmines.

The raid was possible because of the specially developed "bouncing bomb" which had undergone a series of tests, in the utmost secrecy, at Reculver. In fact, the final successful trial took place at the Kent bay at 7am on the day of the Dambusters' famous "show".

It was at the end of March that Kent police were instructed to cordon off one square mile, east of the Reculver Towers. The Barnes Wallis "bouncing bomb" was

Guy Gibson with Roy Chadwick, designer of the Lancaster bomber.

at the prototype stage and plans were being made for a trial drop from a Lancaster bomber.

Gibson, formerly based at West Malling, had already been briefed on the raid he was to lead and he turned up for the first trial on Friday April 11th with Bob Hay, the bombing leader of 617 Squadron. They met Barnes Wallis on the beach where the whole area was surrounded by barbed wire and patrolled by special policemen. The twin towers of Reculver were chosen as the release point for the bombs, giving Gibson and Hay a flavour of what to expect at Möhne. It was the towers of the reservoir that gave valuable navigational aid during the final approach.

Dr Wallis, already famous for his Wellington bomber, had devised a bomb to skip along the surface of the water and then explode, but that first test was a disaster; the bomb broke up when it hit the water.

On their return journey to Scampton, the engine of their Miles Magister failed over Margate at a height of 300 feet. Gibson crash-landed, hitting a tree in doing so. Both he and Hay were unhurt, although the aircraft was a write-off. A local doctor, who went to the scene said: "It's a shame they make you fellow fly so young".

Back at Reculver Wallis had picked up fragments of the bomb from the water and taken them to Manston where engineers worked in a guarded hangar to strengthen the outside casing of the second bomb. He also decided to reduce the drop height from 150 feet to 60 feet. A second trial was held.

Two Lancasters made the second run from the east — one with the bomb and the other with a slow-motion camera. This test was better but fragments came off the bomb and Wallis was not satisfied. He went back to the drawing board and solved the problem by spinning the bomb as it left the aircraft.

The third trial at Reculver was on Thursday April 29th — just two weeks before the proposed raid. Vickers test pilot, "Shorty" Longbottom flew the Lancaster at 250 mph, dropped the bomb, watched it bounce on and on and then slide through the special marker buoys representing the base of the dam. As Longbottom banked round after the drop he could see Dr Wallis also bouncing in the dunes, waving his hat in the air.

It was now Gibson's turn to have a go. With two other pilots he flew to Manston and carried out a few more trials before Wallis was satisfied. On one occasion the 5lb bomb which was not charged, hit a breakwater and those watching had to dive to the ground as it bounced over their heads. It came to rest by the old Roman ruins.

The real raid took place as planned and was an enormous success. But only eight of the 19 Lancasters returned and 53 of the 133 crew were killed. Gibson survived the raid and continued to visit his old friends at Manston and West Malling from time to time.

In 1944 he lost his life when leading a bombing attack against a factory, near the Ruhr.

Squadron Leader Jack Charles of 611 Squadron chalks up the 1,000.

'1,000 Huns' — and the biggest party of all!

RAF Biggin Hill commemorated two important events in May 1943 — the 25th anniversary of the Royal Air Force on the 1st and the shooting down of the "1,000th Hun" on the 15th. The latter culminated in one of the biggest parties of the war and confirmed the station's status as "Britain's premier fighter station".

A mammoth sweepstake was organised at the station and whoever drew the winning ticket stood to collect £150 while the pilot making the vital "kill" would win £300. As the total neared the magic figure, pilots due for leave refused to go, the BBC sent Mr Gilbert Harding to cover the great occasion and Biggin Hill was besieged by journalists.

At 4.30 on May 15th, two squadrons were scrambled to accompany a formation of bombers in "a quickie over Caen". The Operations Room was packed as Wingco, Al Deere spoke to his pilots: "Brutus aircraft, look out! Bandits climbing at three o'clock". The total mounted to 999 and then, absolutely simultaneously, Frenchman,

René Mouchotte of 341 Squadron and Canadian Jack Charles of 611 Squadron fixed "two yellow bellies" in their sights and suddenly the score was 1,001.

As the two aces shared the prize money, the event was celebrated by the biggest party of the war. More than 1,000 guests were invited to Grosvenor House, London in the company of both Air Chief Marshals. The food was the most lavish known in wartime England. The bar was free, three RAF bands provided the music, the Windmill Theatre provided the cabaret and, as an extra bonus, the station commander, Sailor Malan heard that his wife had given birth to their second child.

Only one problem faced the pilots of Biggin Hill. How could they get back for dawn readiness? The answer was waiting in the foyer of the hotel. A motley group of London cabbies, ever grateful to the RAF, were elbowing their way into the dance hall past an astonished gold-braided officer. "Ere cock", said one. "Tell 'em inside that the boys 'ave arrived to take 'em back to Biggin".

10 died in Margate in one-minute raid

THE tenth, and last, attack on Margate which caused loss of life occurred on Tuesday June 1st, 1943 when 12 Focke-Wulfs came in low over the rooftops, dropped 14 high explosive bombs and then riddled the streets with machine gun bullets. It was a surprise attack with no air-raid warning.

The raid was carried out by SKG10, the Fourth Gruppe of Schnellkampfgeschwader (Fast Bomber Group), based at Amiens/Glisy which had already been involved in many daylight fighter bomber offensives, particularly against coastal shipping. SKG10 may well have been avenging an incident when, in the early hours of May 20th, one of their pilots landed at Manston believing it to be the airfield at St Omer. He was arrested and the brand new FW 190 was sent to Boscombe Down where it later joined the RAF's Enemy Aircraft Flight.

If this was an embarrassment for the Luftwaffe then it was a tragedy for Margate. The raid lasted only one minute but in that time 10 people were killed and four seriously hurt. Many houses and shops were badly damaged and the town's Holy Trinity Church was wrecked. An infants' school was also hit but, on this occasion, the children were having lunch elsewhere.

A man and his two sisters had a lucky escape when a bomb went through the upper storey of their house, brought the ceiling down, came out over the front door, bounced in the road and hit the house on the opposite side. Of those who were seriously wounded, 14-year-old Bernard Evans and firewatcher John Garland died later that day.

Troops joined in the rescue work which continued for more than 24 hours and a rest centre was set up in the Royal School.

The alert may not have sounded but both the anti-aircraft guns on the seafront and the Typhoons of 609 Squadron were quick off the mark. The Ack Ack boys scored the first hit and the aircraft roared over the town with smoke pouring from the fuselage before crashing near golf links behind Margate. The pilot was killed. Minutes later Flying Officer I.J. Davies brought a second plane down at Lydden. The pilot baled out but he also died.

A milliner's model surveys the wreckage of Margate after the hit and run raid of June 1st, 1943 Few towns of the same size suffered as badly as Margate. The population dropped from 40,000 (in 1939) to 9,000 as residents moved inland, shops closed and boarding houses pulled their blinds and locked their doors. The town certainly had its full share of hit and run daylight raiders. Many prominent buildings, including the Winter Gardens were damaged and two superb cinemas, the Regal and Astoria demolished. By the end of the war, Margate had received 83 enemy attacks, 9,170 of its 14,000 premises were damaged and 268 destroyed. In addition to 584 high explosive bombs, parachute mines and 2,489 incendiaries, five sea mines exploded close to the shore causing more damage to buildings on the sea front.

Holy Trinity Church, Margate was consecrated in 1829 and destroyed on June 1st, 1940.
The bomb was known as a "Bouncing Billy". It fell near Fort Paragon, bounced over some
cottages and landed in Canon Prior's Chapel where it exploded.

Signalman Len Bowley, who was taken prisoner after HMS Gloucester was sunk off Crete in 1941 meets his family at Wilson Avenue, Rochester.

Repatriation — the boys come home

GUY Gibson's success with the bouncing bomb was good news for Kent but it was nothing compared to the news that was coming from Rome. Italy, after a string of defeats, had been plunged into political chaos. Benito Mussolini had been sacked. Allied troops were on the toe of the country and the end of the Italian war was an increasing possibility. On September 3rd, the armistice was signed in Sicily and the immediate repatriation of prisoners of war was announced. Hundreds of Kentish families went wild with delight.

Two of the first to walk through the front doors of their homes in Kent were Marine Commando Eric Baldwin and Royal Marine Albert Crook of Sevenoaks, captured in Crete and Tobruk respectively. They spoke of the terrible conditions in Italian PoW camps, the lack of medical supplies, how they had been forced to eat nettles for a meal and the absolute delight when they received Red Cross parcels — their only link with the outside world.

There was also an exchange between Britain and Germany of sick and seriously wounded prisoners. Most of the British PoWs had been captured in 1940 in Dunkirk and others had been taken in the raid on Dieppe. This was the first PoW exchange and it involved 5,000 prisoners on either side.

Among them was Gunner Blackman of the Royal Artillery from Canterbury whose mother was evacuated to Sevenoaks when she was bombed out. Gunner Blackman was taken prisoner in France in June, 1940 and experienced many terrible German PoW camps living mainly on soup and looking forward to the Red Cross parcels.

Blackman eventually found himself in a camp in Poland and slept in a barn-like building with five-tier beds and a roof that leaked. He told his local newspaper that if they wanted to get to bed by 10 o'clock the man on the top tier had to start climbing at half past nine!

Another repatriated prisoner was Lieutenant Brewin, 11th Hussars of Tunbridge Wells who was wounded in Libya in 1942, taken prisoner, and travelled 600 miles to a hospital in Tripoli with his leg almost severed. The journey took six days. Brewin had his leg amputated and found himself in a room with an RAF pilot and a captain in the Artillery who both had amputations. For three months they all remained in bed in a small room without a book to read, eating macaroni and black bread.

Lieutenant Brewin also spoke of the delight in receiving a Red Cross parcel. It was not just the food but the fact that it was something from home with a British label on it. "All the men in his camp", he said, "would rush around swopping various items and then they would arrange an auction. It would keep the prisoners happy for days."

A rousing welcome from the neighbours to Private G.S. Gibson RAMC as he arrived home at Grecian Street, Maidstone.

The night the Frenchmen cried

HIGH summer 1943 was a hectic period for the Kent fighter squadrons. They were in action almost daily, pounding away at the Luftwaffe airfields, accompanying bombers and intercepting raiders. For the pilots the strain of long hours, particularly over enemy territory, became almost unbearable and frequently squadrons had to be withdrawn from the front line for a spell of well-deserved rest.

René Mouchotte's Alsace Squadron at Biggin Hill refused to take rest. Determined the *Boche* should be beaten they stubbornly continued with their everyday tasks although Mouchotte himself was among the weariest of all. "The sweeps go on at a terrible pace", he wrote in his diary. I am at the record figure of 140 and I feel my nerves wearing out."

On August 27th, 1943 the charismatic Frenchman, one of the most popular and respected pilots of the Biggin Hill wing, was given a different type of task. His Alsace Squadron (341) was to escort a big formation of American Flying Fortresses, 240 strong, on a bombing raid on a mystery construction hidden in a forest, north of St Omer.

The purpose of the construction was unknown at the time but it was highly suspicious and the instructions were to destroy it. (In fact it was the giant bomb-proof launch pad for the V2 rocket at Watten, scheduled to enter service in December.) The Flying Fortresses found the site, dropped their bombs, damaged the bunker and were ready to leave for home. As Mouchotte surveyed the scene of destruction he was suddenly attacked by a swarm of Focke-Wulfs which dived out of the sun. The Frenchmen were outnumbered; it was every man for himself in a bitter life-and-death struggle. Mouchotte found himself isolated and radioed back to Biggin Hill control: "I am alone with the bombers".

They were the last words he spoke. When the fighters straddled back one by one, Mouchotte was missing. Calls were made to other airfields, to the Air/Sea Rescue Service, to the Observer Corps. An almost uncanny silence fell on Biggin Hill.

Mouchotte's driver, Joy Neary, who lives today in Oxted, Surrey recalled the pain of that night. "The French pilots refused to go to bed. They waited and waited for news and most of them cried. He was the best of them all — a leader, a fighter and a gentleman."

This is what one ATS girl thought of the German hardware. She made a flower garden in an exploded sea mine, placed it outside the back door of an Ordnance Store in Appledore Road, Tenterden and looked after it with tender, loving care.

St James Church, Dover was frequently hit by shells as was the town museum. It was estimated that 3,000 to 4,000 shells fell on Dover and its neighbourhood and another 1,800 in the sea and Dover Harbour and, altogether, 148 people lost their lives from shell-fire during the war.

They downed their pints and dived for cover

MEANWHILE the shelling continued in Britain's front-line coastal towns. Dover endured a battering and lives were lost almost every month from May to December. Ramsgate was attacked in June, July, August, September and November. Folkestone suffered badly on September 25th and the gasholder in Deal was hit on December 11th.

The shells were fired by a network of batteries along the Pas de Calais coast and took, on average, about a minute to cross the Channel. There was no warning until after the first shell had fallen, but then came a double siren, indicating the guns were in action. "Just enough time", said one resident, "to down your pint and dive for cover."

The German batteries, under command of the Navy, totalled some 73 guns of all calibres. But 11 were long-range and it was these which persistently shelled the Kent coast. The largest was Batterie Lindemann whose three 406mm guns could reach out 34 miles.

One of the worst attacks of 1943 was on June 29th when only one of six shells fired landed on Dover. It exploded on Cannon Street and turned the peaceful thoroughfare into a battlefield. A child, a small girl, a Wren and 11 servicemen were killed.

The coastal guns in Hellfire Corner would often fire the first shots and that, almost certainly, meant a retaliation from the other side. In this situation, early warnings could be given as was the case on Monday October 25th when the Dover guns opened fire at a small convoy feeling its way along the French coast. The reply was devastating. Two fires were started in the Buckland area and six people were killed.

The little boy seemed quite unconcerned as he ate an ice-cream perched on a mine which had been washed up on a beach in Deal. Of course, the "sting" had been taken out of this mine.

This was Beach Street, Folkestone, badly damaged on October 3rd, 1943.

No wonder the children had everyday lessons in the air-raid shelters.   Here are the few pupils who were left in Dymchurch School in 1943. Despite the basic conditions, they seem to have their mind on the lesson — or were they listening to the bombs above?

Anti-Aircraft Command

provided cover against Air
Attacks in the Dover Area.

12th Army Corps

Worn by personnel of 519,
520 & 540 Regiments RA.

540 Regiment RA

Manned Wanstone, Fan Bay,
and South Foreland Btys.

Royal Air Force
had personnel in
the Dover Area, especially
for the Radar and the
Air Sea Rescue.

Royal Marines Siege Regiment
This Regiment manned Winnie & Pooh
and also the 13.5" Railway Guns
until November 1943, when they
were handed over to the Royal Artillery

The Railway Guns.
HMG Boche Buster. 18" Gun [Based at Bekesbourne]
  Wt. 250 tons. Range. 22,300yds. Shell 2,500lbs.
HMG Scene Shifter. [Based at Lydden]
HMG Gladiator. [Based at Martin Mill]
HMG Piecemaker. [Based in Guston Tunnel]
All 13.5" guns [originally from Iron Duke Class Battleship]
  Wt. 240 tons. Range. 40,000yds. Shell 1,250 lbs.

Wt 178,276 lbs.
Guns originally

'Winnie

Same type of gun as
First fired on 22nd August

Wansto

Wt 100 tons, Range 42
Guns originally built fo

Swingate Down.
There are 2 monuments here,
1, To the RFC from 14-18 War.
Other is the Anglo-American
Artillery Memorial of 39-45 War.

Radar Towers.

★Blériot Memorial

✦Langdon B.
Wt 16,575 lbs. Ro

The Town of D
12th August
buildings wer
AirRaids tota
216 Deaths, 3

Dover Castle
Control Centre of Hell Fire Corner [39-45]

These premises was also the
Command Centre for Operation
Dynamo. The Evacuation of the Forces from Dunkirk.
The Drop Redoubt. was used as a base for a
Commando Squad to destroy the
Harbour in the event of Attack.

Coast Artillery Ops Room.
Port War Signal Station.
Fire Command Post.

✦Eastern Arm
Turret Wt. 1,060 lb,

✦Knuckle B

Barrel Wt. 2,09

●Grand Shaft

St Martin's Battery. 6" guns.
Also known as Western Heights Battery

Breakwater Battery
Wt. 16,575 lbs. Range 14,000yds. S

Citadel Battery. 2x9.2 guns.
Wt 62,720 lbs. Range 36,700 yds.

Pier Extension Battery. 3x1
Wt. 1,395 lbs. Range. 10,100 yds. Shell 12

Turret Battery
Same guns as Fan Bay Battery.

Hougham Battery 3x8" guns.
Wt 38,528 lbs. Range 29,200yds. Shell 256 lbs
The Capel Battery was equipped with the same guns.

Lydden Spout Battery
Same guns as Fan Bay Battery.

HELLFIR
A MAP OF THE ARTILLERY DE

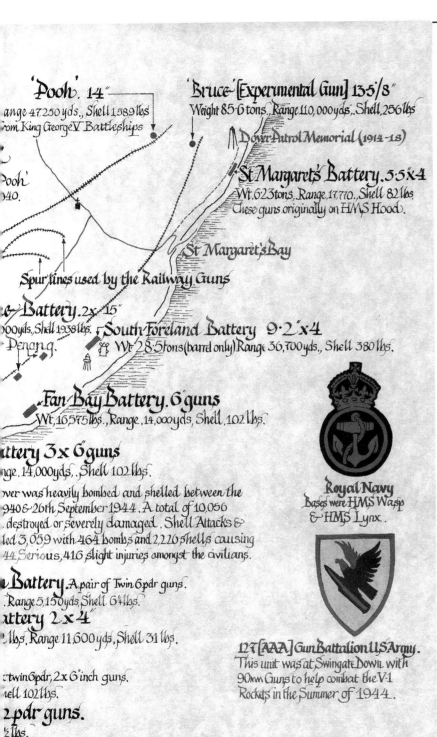

'Pooh'. 14"
ange 47,250 yds., Shell 1,589 lbs
rom King George V Battleships

'Bruce' [Experimental Gun] 13·5/8"
Weight 85·6 tons., Range 110,000 yds., Shell, 256 lbs

▲ Dover Patrol Memorial (1914-18)

St Margaret's Battery. 5·5"x4
Wt. 623 tons., Range, 17,770., Shell 82 lbs.
(These guns originally on HMS Hood).

St Margaret's Bay

Spur lines used by the Railway Guns

Pooh'
40.

&-Battery. 2 x 15"
00 yds., Shell 1,938 lbs. South Foreland Battery 9·2"x4
Penang. Wt 28·5 tons (barrel only) Range 36,700 yds., Shell 380 lbs.

Fan Bay Battery. 6 guns
Wt. 16,575 lbs., Range, 14,000 yds, Shell, 102 lbs.

attery 3 x 6 guns
nge, 14,000 yds., Shell 102 lbs.

wer was heavily bombed and shelled between the
940 & 26th September 1944. A total of 10,056
destroyed or severely damaged. Shell Attacks &
ed 3,059 with 464 bombs and 2,226 shells causing
44 serious, 416 slight injuries amongst the civilians.

Battery. A pair of Twin 6pdr guns.
Range 5,150 yds, Shell 6·4 lbs.

attery 2 x 4"
lbs, Range 11,600 yds, Shell 31 lbs.

twin 6pdr, 2 x 6 inch guns.
ell 102 lbs.

2 pdr guns.
2 lbs.

Royal Navy
Bases were HMS Wasp
& HMS Lynx.

127 [AAA] Gun Battalion US Army.
This unit was at Swingate Down with
90 mm Guns to help combat the V-1
Rockets in the Summer of 1944.

E CORNER
FENCES AROUND DOVER IN THE 1939-45 WAR

The hottest place in Hellfire Corner

GUN emplacements in Dover were established on the Downs, along the coast and on the ships. They were manned by men of the 12th Army Corps, the 519 and 520 Regiments of the Royal Artillery, Anti-Aircraft Command, the Royal Air Force, the Royal Marines Siege Regiment, the Royal Navy and the 127 (AAA) Gun Battalion of the US Army. This awesome array of firepower is clearly indicated on this map of the Dover defences. The two 15-inch guns were christened "Winnie" and "Pooh". They were later joined by railway-mounted pieces which could fire on enemy shipping in the Channel.

Apart from the Army, Navy and RAF personnel stationed in Dover, the town was host to overseas Allies from Norway, Canada, America, Holland, Poland and France. There were contingents from the ATS, WRNS and WAAF together with radio and radar operators, plotters, Air Sea Rescue, MTB, motor launches and barrage balloon handlers. Essential to Dover were the cheerful nurses of the military nursing staff, Queen Alexandra's and the Voluntary Aid Detachment (VAD). All of them played a vital part in the defence of this front-line town.

The troops escaped from the rigours of war in various ways. Cinemas were always popular and so were the pubs. The Prince Regent in particular became a firm favourite and here a room was provided for the boys and girls to show their various musical talents. The Hippodrome Theatre was world renowned but not so well known was the "Crypt" coffee bar, used by the Wrens. One hero of Dover's war was Freddie Overton, who ran the dances at the town hall. Here music was provided by the forces' own big bands, whose enthusiasm often drowned the sirens.

The population of Dover dropped dramatically as the war progressed — from 42,000 in 1939 to less than 16,000. There was accommodation for 5,000 in the tunnel caves. There were more than 1,000 siren warnings within the town between 1939 and 1945 and those people who weren't already in the caves (or in the dance hall) responded immediately.

Despite their care and vigilance, the civilian death toll in Dover was the highest in Kent. 199 people were killed, 307 seriously injured and 420 slightly injured. 910 buildings were totally wrecked and 2,998 severely damaged.

Drawing by Alex and Pamela Summers

Phoney invasion plans failed to fool the Germans

IN the autumn of 1943, shortly after the Allied invasion of Italy, plans were made for an "invasion" of Pas de Calais; at least that's what the enemy was meant to think. The mock attack was code-named *Operation Starkey* and the idea was to force the Germans to keep their troops in northern France, rather than send them to the aid of the Italians. The deception worked brilliantly as far as the inhabitants of Kent were concerned but there was no evidence to show that the Germans were fooled. People were told they could only stay in specific areas for a limited time and then only for certain specified purposes. Thousands of permits (or passes) were issued, many were refused entry and some were even prosecuted for contravening an order which was fake. Troops were moved to embarkation areas, there was phoney wireless traffic and a pretend armada was prepared. Although the deception must have been obvious, it was to prove good practice for Operation Fortitude, the great successful hoax, which preceded the invasion of Normandy in June 1944..

Five injured people were rescued from this bungalow and a baby boy was killed.

Two-year reprieve ends for Sevenoaks

ALTHOUGH Sevenoaks and its villages had been peppered with bombs of all sizes, there had been no loss of life in the town since November 1940 — and that, considering the activity overhead, was a remarkable fact. However, on November 18th, 1943 the two-year reprieve ended with a raid that left six people injured and an infant of 17 months dead on his mother's lap.

Five of those who were hurt lived in a bungalow in Sevenoaks. With them was a neighbour, Mrs Lott and her son, John who were just leaving when the ceiling collapsed. Rescuers spent some time pulling the people from the wreckage.

The incident renewed fears that the return of the darker nights would give the enemy bombers more opportunities for operations. That, in fact, was the case and there were some tragic scenes in south-east London in the run up to Christmas. In Bromley 30 shops were damaged and five people killed and in St Mary Cray a bomb fell in Anglesea Road, killing seven people. Apart from those in Metropolitan Kent, however, there was only one more civilian fatality in the county in 1943 — and that was in Northfleet on December 21st.

1944

D-Day, doodlebugs, Arnhem

January 4th: *Operation Carpetbagger* began, whereby American and British bombers dropped supplies to the resistance movements of Europe to arm them for the forthcoming invasion.

January 27th: Leningrad was freed by the Red Army after a German siege lasting 872 days with more than a million deaths.

February 1st: In an about-turn decision, men's suits could once again have pockets and trousers with turn-ups. Restrictions on pleats and buttons on women's clothes were also lifted.

February 5th: Michel Hollard, the French resistance leader who spied for the British on the development of launching sites for the V1 flying bomb, was arrested by the Gestapo.

February 12th: Residents of the occupied Channel Islands were near to starvation, existing on a diet of mostly root vegetables.

March 8th: A faster Spitfire model, the Mark XIV came into service, able to compete more equally with the German Focke-Wulf 190.

March 19th: Hungary was occupied by the Germans.

March 24th-25th: A total of 76 Allied PoWs escaped through a tunnel from Stalag Luft III after two years of preparation and digging. Only three, two Norwegians and a Dutchman, reached England; the rest were recaptured and many of them shot.

March 31st: The Battle of Berlin was finally called to a halt. Since November 18th, 1943 a total of 1,117 bombers had been lost.

April 27th: As part of the preparations

Home on leave — a precious time for families all over Kent. Here, little Fern is reunited with her actor father, Richard Warner, of Sevenoaks.

for *Operation Overlord*, all foreign travel from Britain was banned and civilians prohibited from coastal areas.

April 30th: The first pre-fab house was erected in three days in London. The two-bedroom single storey factory-made house cost £550.

May 2nd: The compiler of the *Daily Telegraph* crossword, a teacher from Leatherhead, was investigated after answers to the clues were spotted as being important code words for D-Day — Utah, Omaha and Overlord.

May 18th: Monte Cassino in Italy finally fell to the Allies after a long battle and American troops entered Rome.

June 6th: The historic and heroic D-Day landings took place after a postponement of 24 hours due to bad weather.

June 13th: Hitler's secret weapons made their appearance over England with the first of the V1 flying bombs.

July 20th: There was an unsuccessful attempt to assassinate Hitler with a bomb at his "Wolf's Lair" headquarters.

August 25th: Paris was liberated by the Allies and General de Gaulle returned to the French capital.

September 8th: Brussels was liberated.

September 8th: The first V2 rocket fell in Chiswick, West London killing three people.

September 19th-20th: Wing Commander Guy Gibson, VC, hero of the dambusters was killed when his Mosquito crashed in Holland.

September 27th: Allied troops failed in their attempt to capture Arnhem.

October 14th: Athens was liberated by the Allies.

November 12th: The last remaining German battleship, the *Tirpitz*, was sunk by RAF bombers in a Norwegian fjord.

November 28th: It was revealed that during the previous five years war output in Britain included 102,600 warplanes, 25,000 tanks, 722 warships and 4,5000,000 tons of new ships. One civilian had been killed for every three servicemen and one in three British homes had been damaged or destroyed.

December 3rd: The last parade of the Home Guard was held in London. The stand-down in Kent had been in June.

December 16th: The bandleader Glenn Miller was reported missing when his plane disappeared en route from England to Paris.

December 22nd: The Battle of the Bulge raged in the Ardennes between German and Allied troops.

The crew of the submarine Thrasher, captained by Lieutenant H.S.McKenzie, came ashore at Dover to an heroic welcome. Since she was commissioned for service in 1941, Thrasher had torpedoed 11 merchant vessels, four small supply ships and one tug totalling 40,000 tons in all. Among her crew were two VCs, one DSO, two DSCs, six DSMs and 13 mentions in despatches. One VC was Petty Officer T.W.Gould of Dover who removed a live bomb which had entered the outer casing of the sub during a dramatic incident in the Mediterranean. See page 220.

Enemy shell damage in the foreground reveals a Christian message on the Central Hall Chapel at Deal. There is a great touch of irony here for the people of Deal believed that the only way they could be saved was by making a rapid dash for the shelters and that's just what they did on the morning of Thursday January 20th, 1944 as the shelling began again. Sadly, one exploded on the surface shelter in Robert Street and eight people were killed. Two more were killed on the road outside and, in Park Street, the landlord of the Park Tavern and his wife also died. They had taken refuge in a Morrison shelter!

Kent towns suffer in the Baby Blitz

THE Luftwaffe had been quiet for many months, but the concentrated bombing of German cities by the RAF invited retaliation and they finally managed to appear in some strength at the end of January, 1944. The target was London.

For this offensive the German bomber force had been re-equipped and new pilots had been trained. It was code-named *Operation Steinbock* and was to last until March 31st. In that time the Luftwaffe carried out large-scale operations on 15 nights with smaller attacks on seven. Many Kent towns, including Sevenoaks, Gravesend, Rochester, Bexley and Dartford were badly damaged and there was considerable loss of life. It came to be known as "The Baby Blitz".

The Luftwaffe, however, also suffered grievous setbacks —300 aircraft in five months— and a crew loss almost equalled by civilians killed. In fact the Luftwaffe was so badly mauled and morale so completely shattered that all manned bomber operations over Britain virtually ceased by June.

The first night of the assault, which came in two phases, was January 21st/22nd. Bexley Mental Hospital, near Dartford was hit and 13 people, 12 of whom were patients, were killed when two wards collapsed. The Town Hall and a fire station at Erith were also destroyed.

During that eventful night 21 aircraft were lost. The first to fall was a Dornier 217, shot down by Mosquito pilots of 488 Squadron. It crashed south of Dungeness. Others to fall in Kent were a Junkers which crashed on the physical training gym at Western Heights, Dover (AA fire), a Junkers on Horton Priory, Sellinge (488 Squadron), a Messerschmitt on the Lydd Ranges (AA fire), a Junkers on the railway embankment opposite the Hop Pocket pub in Paddock Wood (96 Squadron) and a Junkers on Lower Chantry Lane, Canterbury (AA fire).

Before the end of January there were fatalities in Crockham Hill, Gravesend, Sittingbourne, Sevenoaks, Northfleet, Gillingham and Dartford again. Gravesend suffered on Friday February 4th when a bomb fell at the junction of Wrotham Road and Cross Lane West and made an enormous crater which caused nearby buildings to collapse. Thirty-eight shops and buildings were wrecked and many people trapped in their shelters. Eight died.

Before the end of March, more German bombers came down at Biddenden, Whitstable, Willesborough, Shorne, Lamberhurst and Hollanden Park, Hildenborough.

As the summer of 1944 progressed the bomber offensive gradually fell away and, with the Allied invasion expected, there was cautious optimism in the air. However, morale was soon to be sent plunging by the advent of the terrible new weapons which were to devastate Kent. The age of the missile had almost arrived.

Wrotham Road, Gravesend, bombed February 4th, 1944.

It wasn't only the Luftwaffe who suffered losses. This is the wreckage of an American Thunderbolt which crashed at Shorne on January 7th, 1944.

Decoy airfields to fool the Luftwaffe

IN order to mislead the Luftwaffe, the Nazis were led to believe that the RAF was growing so rapidly in strength that more than 50 squadrons alone were based in Kent. It was, of course, bunkum!

There was room for 50 squadrons, for small airfields had been constructed, known as advanced landing grounds. These existed at Ashford, Kingsnorth, Brenzett, Egerton, High Halden, Newchurch, New Romney, Woodchurch and Headcorn. Some had been built with the rubble from the bombed streets of Birmingham, carried south on freight trains.

The airfields contained dummy buildings, dummy aircraft, such as gliders and, knowing the Germans would intercept, there were deceptive wireless messages. It was all part of an elaborate plan that had expanded since the early days of the war.

Decoy airfields also existed in Kent and these added

to the deceit. The idea was to produce fake targets and make them so convincing that the enemy would be lured away from the real ones and bomb them instead. On the airfields were real-life models of aircraft, fighters and bombers, and there were accessories such as old cars, bicycles and oil drums. For deception purposes the Vauxhall motor company produced an inflatable version of their Bedford truck.

The biggest site was at Lullingstone, near Eynsford and this was known as a Starfish site. It contained a metal building covered in hessian and inside were drums packed with highly combustible materal and the whole was clad in asbestos sheeting. Whenever nearby Biggin Hill came under attack, the building at Lullingstone was ignited to give follow-up raiders the impression that this was the real airfield.

Monty came to Maidstone on February 3rd, 1944. The Field Marshal, fresh from his great victory at Alamein, stood on top of his jeep in Mote Park, Maidstone and spoke to the 53rd Division. "I want you to know", he said, "that I never send men into battle unless it is a good show; you can rely on that and you can rely on me. I'm tired of this war. It is time it was ended. We can end it together this year." Field Marshal Montgomery went on to inspect the troops at Sittingbourne, giving individual men pep talks about the Second Front. There was another event of military importance in Kent that month — the Queen's Own Royal West Kent Regiment received the Freedom of the Borough of Maidstone.

Monty had said that the Second Front was imminent; now there were to be essential manoeuvres all over the county and more tanks were required urgently. Here, the Churchill's go steaming through the Kent countryside to the "battleground". Below: lunchtime in Headcorn — it was not an unusual sight to see tanks during the days before the invasion.

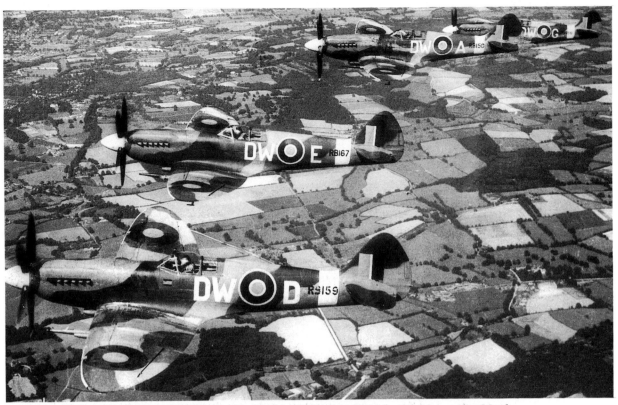

A new type of Spitfire was seen in the skies of Kent in March, 1944 — the Mark XIV. The Merlin engine had been replaced by the 2,050hp two-stage Griffon, enabling the aircraft to reach speeds of almost 450mph as well as improving the rate of climb. The new model was now a match for the Focke-Wulf 190 and was to prove invaluable in the battle against the flying bombs.

Bevin boys are sent to the mines

BY March, 1944 the first batch of young recruits to the mines had started work. These were known as "Bevin Boys", after the labour minister, Ernest Bevin and their names were picked by ballot. They spend a few weeks training under experienced miners and were paid a weekly wage of £2 10s 6d.

Many Kentish lads had volunteered for the Services and were rather stunned to be picked out of the "Bevin hat". One of them was Fred Rickett of St James Road, Sevenoaks who had wanted to join the Royal Navy but was directed instead to the Chislet Colliery, near Canterbury and issued with boiler suits and steel-toed boots. Fred found his height (over six feet) a slight disadvantage on the coal face but said at the time that he was determined the make the best of his new bleak life underground.

Two 18-year-old Birchington "Bevin Boys" also tried to make their best of it, but after five days on the coal face at Chislet they walked out. Kennety Field of Canterbury Road and George Buckman of King's Road said they were both willing to go into any of the Services but objected to going down the mines. They said it made them feel bad.

Kennety Field had actually passed Grade A for the Royal Marines and George Buckman had planned to be an air-gunner with Bomber Command and when their names came out of the Bevin ballot they were distraught. They appeared at Margate police court for failing to comply with the direction of a National Service officer.

Inebriated cockatoos

Vera Lynn, the darling of the troops, and her fellow crooners were attacked in the House of Commons in March when Lord Winterton claimed: "They remind one of the caterwauling of an inebriated cockatoo. I cannot believe that all this wailing can possibly have a good effect on troops who are about to endanger their lives".

The Steinbeck raiders dropped scores of bombs on Strood on March 2nd, 1944. A terrace of six houses was wrecked in Grove Road, on the corner of Station Road, burying victims under tons of debris. Of the many families who lived in these homes only three people escaped unhurt and they had taken refuge in their Anderson shelter five minutes before the attack. Mr and Mrs Bevan and their son Ronald were rescued two hours later from their shelter which was right on the edge of the bomb crater. Apparently it had lifted in the blast and its exit was jammed by tons of rubble. Their lodger had been killed in his bed. Eighteen people died, eight were seriously injured and more than 300 people were left homeless. 1,000 buildings were damaged, including 74 shops. It was the worst attack of all on the Rochester area.

This oast house at Staplehurst became headquarters of the 363rd Fighter Group. They were involved in pre-D-Day operations.

Gum-chewing newcomers delighted the girls

A NEW culture shock began to hit Kent — particularly south and east Kent — in the spring of 1944. Suddenly there were new dances, new fashions, new words and a strange new substance called chewing gum. It was the arrival, in some force, of the American troops whose brash way of life intrigued, annoyed and, in many cases absolutely thrilled, the locals.

American anti-aircraft batteries dug themselves in right along the coast. They set up tented villages, took over oast houses and built themselves corrugated fortresses. They were joined by fighter pilots on the advanced landing grounds and Ordnance crews and became affectionately known as GIs after the words "Government Issue" on their equipment. By April a coastal belt 10 miles deep, from the Wash to Lands End, was out of bounds to any but those who lived there. This new security law together with the

arrival of the Yanks led to the suspicion that an invasion force was being prepared.

The local girls were delighted by their arrival but the British soldiers were not so keen on these "overpaid, oversexed" newcomers. There were disputes, fights and many jealousies and the situation became so bad that six American and six English soldiers held a meeting in Ashford to thrash out their differences.

The Americans complained about the lack of showers and the old fashioned automobiles. They were surprised that there were no refrigerators and spoke about the lack of progress made during the century. The English replied that there had been two world wars and one complained how he had been "cut out" when chatting up the girls. The meeting ended, the soldiers shook hands and decided they had one common purpose — to defeat Jerry!

Biggin Hill pilot masterminded the "Great Escape"

HUNDREDS of Allied airmen, many from Kent, were prisoners of war at Stalag Luft III, the infamous camp near Sagan in Silesia. Among them was Flight Lieutenant Roger Bushell who flew with 601 Squadron from Biggin Hill and was shot down over Dunkirk during the evacuation. Bushell became "OC Escaping" at Sagan and, in the spring of 1944, was ambitiously masterminding the "Great Escape".

He had plenty of time to plan the break-out and considerable help. Bob Stanford Tuck was at Stalag Luft III until his transfer to another "escape-proof" prison. Squadron Leader Ken Campbell, of Sevenoaks, who was shot down in 1941, was another colleague.

Although he was on the escape committee, his injuries were to prevent him taking part.

On May 19th, 50 airmen crawled through the tunnel, one by one, and attempted to make their own way back to England. Only three succeeded. The others were captured, handed over to the Gestapo, instead of the Luftwaffe as required by the Geneva Convention, and shot.

Bob Tuck also managed to escape and was found by the Russians. He spent some weeks fighting alongside them, eventually reached the British Embassy in Moscow and was put on a ship for Southampton.

Kent helped to open the road to Rome

FOR several weeks in the spring of 1944, units of the Buffs and the Royal West Kents, fighting with the British Eighth Army, helped to repel the full force of German resistance at Monte Cassino. Above them, high on the mountainside, stood the smouldering remains of the historic monastery of St Benedict which was to symbolise one of the toughest battles of the war.

News of how the county regiments held vital positions under a hail of fire, helped to breach the German line and open the road to Rome was reported in the *Kent Messenger* on May 5th. "The county will be prouder still of the Buffs and the Royal West Kents", said the newspaper.

"On Castle Hill the West Kents dug in, holding their position until relieved. It was incredible that they were able to reach their objective with the full might of the enemy's fire power ceaselessly directed upon them. Yet they not only ran the gauntlet of shells and mortar-bombs but they remained on Castle Hill until their job was done.

"Meanwhile three companies of the famous East Kent Regiment, the Buffs, were in the Cassino railway area. One company covered a prominent road junction, another the area south of the town and the third was in reserve. The locomotives in the station became armoured cars and the tenders were ideal as machine gun posts but so intense was the barrage of fire from the enemy that they counted 1,890 German shells on a position 600 yards long by 300 yards

wide. In one day, there were 30 direct hits on one house alone. But the Buffs held their positions."

There were many casualties but the tenacity of the two regiments gave other units the opportunity to advance in numbers along the Liri valley and for the indomitable Polish Corps to attack in waves and take the town of Monte Cassino. It was a brilliant action. The German divisions were scattered with 2,000 men taken prisoners and many killed and injured.

"The Kent warriors", said the *Kent Messenger,* "born east and west of the Medway were banded together in a common cause. It was through a maze of roads, ancient and new, over mule tracks and mountain paths, through rivers heavy in spate that the Kent men and their vital supplies went into the forward positions. But there were Kent men from other regiments on the Cassino front; they were the gunners, the tank men, the sappers and the signals and, above all, the infantrymen, for they had the most vital job of all in this famous battle".

A tank, semi-camouflaged waits in a Kentish wood for invasion orders. But this impressive monster would have been little use against German Panzers. It was a dummy, made by Dunlop and inflated in the same way as a barrage balloon.

How Kent fooled Rommel's great army

UNDER the branches of oak trees, around the farmyards, in the fields and copses — in fact everywhere in the Kentish countryside from Westerham to Wye and beyond — stood equipment and stores for the Second Front. There were guns, tanks, landing barges, bulldozers, cranes, pontoons and gliders. The invasion force, when ready, would sail and fly from the Channel ports and crack open Hitler's European fortress in the Pas de Calais area. The planned assault was called *Operation Fortitude*.

But Fortitude was a giant hoax, designed to make the Germans think that the Allied force would take the shortest route to France. Mingled with the real equipment for the real invasion were elaborate clues designed to mislead the enemy. They were strewn all over the county.

As Field Marshal Rommel's army began to assemble in strength in northern France ready to repel the invaders from Kent, the assault force proper was secretly gathering along the southern coast. Two battalions were missing — the Canadian 2nd Corps and the British 12th Corps — for they were part of the great deception.

The planners of *Operation Fortitude* went to enormous lengths to give authenticity to the hoax. Roads were built on the beaches at Greenhithe, Northfleet, Shorne marshes, Lower Upnor, Hythe, Folkestone, Dover, Deal and Walmer. Some were lit up at night and boats were moored nearby to indicate great activity. There was a fake oil-deck and pumping head HQ on the cliffs at Dover, made entirely of old sewage pipes and scaffolding. Military police guarded the area and wind machines were used to create constant dust storms to hide the fact that there were few people about. Monty inspected the dock, the King visited the area and General Eisenhower spoke to the construction workers at a dinner.

The installations at Dover were shelled frequently. When this happened false fires were created from sodium flares to give the Germans the impression they had scored a hit. Army manoeuvres were held all over Kent, the RAF flew fighter patrols along the coast to "protect" the installations, additional bridges were built over the River Stour and Medway, roads were strengthened to cope with the weight of heavy tanks and the entrances to all coastal towns were heavily guarded by police.

The scene designers at Shepperton film studios played their part in the hoax by making more than 400 dummy landing craft with funnels that smoked and laundry that draped from the "rigging". They were placed in river mouths, creeks and harbours.

All this, of course, was mixed up with the real thing for the vast range of equipment and stores were eventually to accompany the Allied army at Portsmouth. And so were the troops encamped all over the county with embarkation headquarters at Wrotham and Frindsbury.

May 12th, 1944. As D-Day grew nearer, security police and civil police played their part in the great deception. Here, in Chatham identity cards were checked.

POLICE BARRIER
STOP

Police set up barriers all over the county. No-one was allowed to go within 10 miles of the Kent coast unless they were residents in the area. The number plate had been removed from this car.

The Royal Engineers worked among the camouflage of cherry orchards during the early summer of 1944. They gave good protection from tip and run raiders.

KENT MESSENGER, JUNE 9th, 1944.

The Original Blood Purifying Medicine for BLOOD and SKIN COMPLAINTS — CLARKE'S BLOOD MIXTURE

Kent ✠ Messenger
THE COUNTY PAPER OF KENT

Still the Best! BIRD'S CUSTARD

Head Offices: Maidstone (Phone Maidstone 3388). Branch Offices: Ashford, Canterbury, Chatham, Gravesend, Sevenoaks, Tunbridge Wells, and 80, Fleet Street.

THREE PENCE No. 7,210   INLAND POSTAGE 1½d.   FRIDAY, JUNE 9, 1944   Subscription inland 6s. per quarter in advance.   THREE PENCE

A Strip Of The French Coast As Seen From Dover And Where Jittery Germans Await Fresh Landings

THE FRENCH COAST AS SEEN FROM DOVER.—The scene above is Calais. On the far left (1) is the entrance to Calais harbour, familiar to thousands of peace-time travellers. Past the dock cranes you can see (2) the lighthouse. An outsize crane (3) shows up left of (4) the Notre Dame Church. Next you can see clearly the (5) Hotel de Ville (Calais Town Hall) with its clock tower. The other outstanding buildings are in order (6) church, (7) gasworks, (8) the chimney stacks of Courtaulds, and (9) the rising ground which ends in the Dover Memorial (off the picture).

Kent sacrificed her blood and beauty for this glorious moment

AT midnight on June 5th, six motor launches of the Dover Command and a squadron of Bomber Command launched a dramatic attack against the beach defences at Boulogne. The launches carried equipment that included balloons, reflectors and smoke and the aircraft dropped strips of foil. It was all part of *Deception Fortitude*; to give the impression to the massed armies in Pas de Calais and the large German fleet in the Channel that a huge convoy of ships was approaching the French coast.

At the same time British army gliders were on their way to the Caen Canal to secure vital bridges in preparation for the infantry landings in Normandy. Two hours later, as British paratroopers dropped east of the Orne River and US "floating headquarters" anchored off Utah and Omaha Beaches, the German General, von Rundstedt decided it was all a feint to cover the real invasion force about to land near Calais. The news also reached Hitler's headquarters but no-one wanted to wake him.

As the Führer slept, a vast armada of more than 6,000 ships was on its way to Normandy. Fifty miles wide and protected by scores of fast-moving torpedo boats, the invasion fleet carried 185,000 men and 20,000 vehicles. Each man and each landing craft was timed to arrive at a precisely-chosen place at a specific time.

Operation Overlord owed much to *Operation Fortitude*. Vast German divisions had remained in Pas de Calais for the invasion that never took place and, because of this, Kent had played a vital part in the greatest seaborne invasion in world history. Little wonder that the *Kent Messenger* report of the Allied landings was written with such verve.

"It was with a long, pent-up sigh of relief that Kent, proud, dauntless bastion of England, heard on Tuesday morning that the Allied invasion for the liberation of Europe had been launched. For months, for years — ever since Dunkirk, in fact — Kent has yearned for this glorious moment, prayed for it, toiled for it, sacrificed her blood and beauty for it.

"News of the landings and the securing of substantial bridgeheads excited tremendous elation. People shook each other's hand. Members of the forces became objects of hero-worship. Women wept with joy.

"But there was no exultation. Kent, as England's front-line county has witnessed too much of the grimness of war to exult — yet. Memories were too fresh of the wearisome blackouts, the thousands of air raids and shell warnings, the whistling shrieks of bombs and the crump, crump, crump of desolating explosions.

"No, the temper of Kent was not only one of subdued optimism but also one of stern resolve to see the invasion through to a triumphant end and, above all, to avenge Dunkirk."

Daily bulletins about the progress of *Operation Overlord* were followed in Kent with the greatest possible interest for the feeling of tension that had existed in the county for weeks had suddenly been lifted. There was an unprecedented demand for newspapers. Wireless reports were relayed to factory workers and spurred them on to greater efforts.

News of the landings was given to the world by nine ATS signals operators on duty at the Supreme Headquarters in Portsmouth — and one of them was Private Betty Drewell from Gravesend. Soon after the girls came on duty at dawn on June 6th a message was handed to them from General Eisenhower. This was taken to the teleprinter room where Private Drewell and her colleagues simultaneously transmitted it to the War Cabinet and Allied HQs all over the world.

Guns for the Second Front were stored in Northfleet Paper Mills. The Mills had been badly damaged by a bomb that destroyed most of the paper-making machines.

Part of the D-Day Armada did sail from Kent. They gathered in twos and threes outside the Thames Boom and then set off on the long, lonely crossing. Among them was Frank Wright of Park Avenue, Northfleet who had joined the Navy four days before the Armada sailed.

Many of the bombs that destroyed Berlin and other German cities were stored in this wood at Egerton, near Pluckley. There were 13 miles of roadway containing row after row of bomb bays which were used by the US heavy bombers when they infiltrated the heart of Germany. They were accompanied by long-range Mustang fighters which were able to escort the bombers all the way to their targets and proved to be superior in every respect to the Messerschmitt 109 and the Focke-Wulf 190. As the Allies advanced towards Berlin the bombers "softened up" the area ahead of them with heavy raids.

Bombing up "Little Chris 11" before a raid. The Mustang of US Group 373 was based at Woodchurch. The bomb markings on the aircraft show the number of missions undertaken.

Planes on the airstrips in Romney Marsh were fuelled by American tankers whose drivers were stationed at Wye. The huge tankers and trailers carried 4,000 gallons of aviation fuel.

As the Allies pushed their way across France, the Americans on the anti-aircraft batteries were left behind in Kent to face the new foe — the V1s, or doodlebugs. Top picture shows a 90mm emplacement at New Romney. Below: The tented accommodation of 125 AAA, near Hythe. These pictures were taken in August 1944.

The battle of the doodlebug — Kent in the front line once more

THE joyful scenes in Kent were short-lived. On June 13th, shortly after midnight, Folkestone was heavily shelled and, incredibly, so was the little village of Otham — and Maidstone where a woman in Hayle Road was killed. The Observers on duty in their lonely observation post at Dymchurch heard the chilling sound of the German guns and must have been surprised at the distance gained. But it was nothing to the surprise that came rattling towards them a few hours later.

Above the murky waters of the Channel it looked like a fighter on fire. Red flames were spurting from the rear end and it was making a noise "like a Model T Ford going up a hill". As it approached their Martello Tower, the Observers, E.E. Woodland and A.M.Wraight instinctively knew that this was Hitler's much-vaunted pilotless plane or flying bomb — one of the V1 vengeance weapons which they had been told to look out for.

Woodland seized the telephone, remembered the codeword and passed the message to Maidstone headquarters. "Diver, diver, diver", he shouted "on north-west one-o-one." The sirens sounded. The new Battle of Britain, which was to bring so much more damage and tragedy in Kent, was about to begin.

That first flying bomb, later christened 'doodlebug', crashed harmlessly in a field at Swanscombe. It was one of four — range-finding affairs — and it was followed by a bombardment that was to last, unbroken, until September, by which time the launching sites had been overrun by the Allies in northern France.

The doodlebug came directly after D-Day when everyone in Kent thought the war was almost won and had a devastating effect on morale. Day after day, night after night these novel weapons, armed with an explosive nose and propelled by a pulse-jet engine would speed across the sky just above roof-top height. When the engine cut out it would fall silently to ground, followed by an enormous explosion.

The loss of life in Kent was considerable. 47 soldiers died when a flying bomb was shot down onto Newlands Military Camp at Charing Heath, 22 children and eight domestic staff at an LCC nursery school at Crockham Hill were slaughtered in June, 11 were killed when one fell on the Army camp at Pattenden Lane, Marden, seven died at Dartford, 12 at Snodland and 13 at Swanscombe. By the end of the war 1,444 doodlebugs had fallen in Kent, 152 people had died and 1,716 were injured.

There were three groups of defenders in the battle against the flying bomb — gunners, fighter planes and barrage balloons. But they frequently got in each other's way in their bid to shoot, tip or blast the missile out of the sky so a new defence plan was put into action — and it was all deployed in less than a week.

Daylight patrols of fighters which flew above the Channel between Dover and Beachy Head were the first line of defence. The second was an enormous barrage of anti-aircraft guns ranged along the coast and on the coastal slopes of the North Downs. The third was more fighters which roamed inland in mid-Kent. Goalkeepers were the fourth — 480 balloons anchored on the higher ground of the Downs between Redhill and the Thames Estuary. At night radar-controlled fighters took over, brilliantly aided by the searchlight units sited along the coast between the South Foreland and Seaford in Sussex.

As the campaign continued, more fighters, more gunners and more balloons were distributed to mass their strength against the approach route of the bombs across Kent. As Number 11 Group Operations Room was fully engaged in controlling operations over France, control of all "Diver" defences was given to RAF Biggin Hill. The airfield became Balloon Headquarters and Operations was situated in a large house called Towerfields at Keston.

The doodlebugs were launched from mobile ramps in Pas de Calais and Picardy, set up in woods, roads and even in villages. The busiest route was between Dungeness and Hythe so the greatest emphasis on air defence was placed there. A Tempest Wing, established on the landing strip at Newchurch on Romney Marsh and commanded by Wing Commander Roland Beamont led the battle in the air destroying an incredible 632. The Mustangs of 129 Squadron and 315 (Polish) Squadron operated from Brenzett and the night-fighting Mosquitos of 96 Squadron from another landing strip at Ford. Further inland at West Malling, 316 Squadron flew the Mustang alongside the Spitfires of 91 and 96. Other Squadrons came and went on brief, but hectic courses of duty.

An Australian pilot, Flying Officer Ken Collier, flying the new Spitfire XIV from West Malling discovered a method of destroying a flying bomb that became part of aviation folklore. Having run out of ammunition he caught up with his prey, flew alongside and tipped the missile over with the wing of his Spitfire. Other pilots found this a satisfactory way of defeating them.

The heavy guns on the coast provided a formidable battery. There were 412 heavy guns and 572 light guns of the Royal Artillery and US Army. They were supplemented by 168 light guns and 416 20mm guns manned by

Primary schools in Kent nominated children to take their turn at "doodlebug spotting". They would go into the playground wearing their tin hats and shout "doodlebug" whenever one appeared. The class would then hurry into the air raid shelter.

the RAF Regiment and 200 rocket launchers and 28 light guns of the RAC. Warning of the doodlebugs came from the radar stations at West Hythe, Fairlight, Swingate and Beachy Head where they were plotted as they flew over the Channel. The radar-controlled guns went into action as the missiles came in sight. Those which managed to escape the shooting gallery were then faced with the fastest fighters over Tenterden.

The men manning the guns became more accurate as the campaign continued but to those who lived in this part of Kent, the Ack-ack guns became as great a trial as the doodlebugs themselves. The jagged fragments of shrapnel rained down, ruining many houses.

Inland, one dramatic moment followed another. One pilot shot down a flying bomb which exploded and blew up a railway bridge at Newington, near Sittingbourne. To his horror the Margate Express came round the corner. The engine and tender jumped the gap but the first two carriages plunged into the chasm.

A doodlebug crashed on top of the village church at Little Chart and the impact brought down the walls. No-one was killed but the villagers campaigned to keep the ruins as a symbol of Kent's ordeal in the summer of 1944.

There was a tragic incident at Beckenham in August 1944 when a flying bomb crashed onto a restaurant, killing 44 and injuring many more. It was lunchtime and the restaurant was full of customers and many died instantly. South-east London's worst incident occurred on July 28th when a doodlebug exploded on the roof of a shelter at Lewisham, demolishing shops on both sides of the street. 59 people were killed.

The onslaught ended in September when the Allied armies overran the launching sites. There was a brief respite before they appeared again, this time fixed to Heinkel aircraft.

A flying bomb was shot down by a fighter and destroyed a house in Rolvenden on July 19th, 1944. Two people were killed and one seriously injured.

The village centre at Pluckley was hit by a doodlebug in July, 1944 and several buildings were destroyed. During the flying bomb campaign, more than 80 Kentish oast houses were damaged. 1944 was not a vintage year for beer!

A doodlebug, shot down by a fighter, crashed at Newington, near Sittingbourne on August 16th and exploded under the railway line over Oak Lane. Seconds after the incident the Margate Express plunged into the chasm, killing eight people and seriously injuring 33. Photograph shows the damaged locomotive being lifted back onto the rails.

Flying bomb damage at Grafton Avenue, Rochester where eight were killed and 17 badly hurt on November 8th, 1944. Fourteen houses were demolished and 573 were damaged.

Victoria Cross for Arnhem heroes

THE Victoria Cross was awarded to two Kent soldiers who lost their lives in extraordinary acts of courage in Operation Market Garden — the attempt to capture two bridges over the Rhine near the German border.

It was on September 17th that British paratroopers and glider pilots were dropped at Arnhem to seize the bridges. The plan was to bypass the fortified Siegfried Line and push into Germany by the lightly defended "back door". It was an operation dogged by misfortune.

One parachute squadron came down without opposition but were nearly an hour ahead of the main force. By the time they reached the bridge at Arnhem it was being blown up. Other groups came face to face with strong German forces and, worst of all, discovered they had landed within two miles of two German panzer divisions. The British battle plan was found by the enemy in a crashed glider so when the 4th Parachute Brigade arrived the men were picked off as they hung helplessly beneath their parachutes.

Among those trapped on the ground was a unit of the Royal Sussex Regiment, whose captain was Lionel Ernest Queripel of Warwick Place, Tunbridge Wells. For nine hours the men were involved in a bitter battle and Captain Queripel was wounded on three occasions. Eventually he decided to cover his men's withdrawal and he was last seen facing the enemy alone with a pistol in one hand and a hand grenade in the other. He was posthumously awarded the Victoria Cross.

The men holding the bridgehead against overwhelming odds remained there for nine days — the last three without water and little food. The order to abandon the operation was given by Montgomery and the withdrawal took place on the night of September 25th-26th. Of the 10,000 who took part in the operation, 1,200 were killed and 6,642 taken prisoner.

Among the dead was Lance Corporal Eric Harden, aged 33, of Colyer Road, Northfleet. He was with the Royal Army Medical Corps. On two occasions he risked enemy fire to bring in wounded colleagues, ordering a Bren gun to give cover. He was wounded and his smock was ripped to pieces but he took no notice and carried on. On the third occasion he attempted to bring in a wounded officer who was fully exposed to enemy fire. He reached the man but then fell with a sniper's bullet through his head. Harden was also awarded a posthumous VC.

Time bomb in the Thames Estuary

THERE was high drama in the Thames Estuary during the night of Sunday August 20th, 1944 that had nothing to do with the Luftwaffe or the flying bomb. An American Liberty ship, the *Richard Montgomery*, sailed into the Estuary with a load of bombs for the US Air Force and anchored off Sheerness. She was waiting for a convoy to lead her to Cherbourg. In the night the ship swung violently into a sandbank, broke in half and sank with thousands of bombs of all sizes inside her hold.

In 1994, the *Richard Montgomery* was still in the Thames Estuary and her masts could be seen sticking out of the water. Below the surface, inside the hold is the lethal cargo. There is an order that the wreck should not be disturbed — should the bombs explode, Sheerness could be wiped off the map!

Shelling begins again as troops advance

AS the first wave in the battle of the doodlebugs drew to a conclusion, so the shelling of the coastal towns began with a new intensity. Just after midnight on Friday September 1st the German batteries at Cap Gris Nez and Calais carried out an attack under a full moon. For more than two hours the assault continued without respite and it was estimated that more than 100 shells were fired on Dover and the harbour.

This was the start of the final fling. The Allies were advancing rapidly through northern France towards Pas de Calais and there was little doubt that the Nazis would soon have to abandon their batteries, just as their colleagues on the flying bomb launching sites had done.

A few miles east, on the English shore, the Americans ,who had played a major part in shooting flying bombs out of the sky, were still encamped at Langton Bay with their 90mm guns and equipment. From the bay, with binoculars, they could tell the time by Calais town hall clock. It was always an hour fast!

They knew that time was running out for the Germans. But the shells kept coming. Four people were killed when one hit the Lagoon Cave shelter in the High Street and two died near Tower Hamlets, Dover. There was a direct hit on Woolworths store, several building firms were damaged and gas and water mains fractured.

At 11.45 pm on September 1st, a Junkers 88, presumably attacking coastal shipping, was shot down and crashed at Hothfield, near Ashford. The explosion made a crater 12 feet deep and 40 feet across.

This was the last enemy aircraft to crash on Kentish soil.

Brighter days in the west — but not in the east!

A decision made by the Government on September 17th, 1944 gave the people of West Kent every reason to believe that the war was ending, while those in the east of the county knew there was still a long way to go. For Westerham, Sevenoaks, Edenbridge, Tonbridge, Tunbridge Wells, Tenterden, Dartford, Rochester, Gravesend etc the black-out was replaced with a dim-out while, in Hellfire Corner, the blackout continued.

Now some housewives could abandon the great wooden black-out board which had been a feature of evening life for almost five years and put back those old curtains and blinds — a real reminder of happier days. Skylights had to continue to be fully blacked out.

No more attacks from the air and soon, no more attacks from the shells. Britain almost had control of the Channel where the war had been relentlessly fought since the first attack on a British merchant ship back in March 1940. In those years hundreds of lives had been lost but the gallantry of merchant seamen knew no bounds. The part played by the Royal National Lifeboat Service was also legendary for these men, all volunteers, saved hundreds of lives, rescuing seamen and airmen, often under enemy fire and in appalling conditions. They also rescued the foe and, although this picture is not of the RNLI it serves as a reminder of the Channel war as Nazi seamen climb upon a British warship.

Former Judd schoolboy is a new Kent hero

A new name began to hit the headlines in 1944 because of his incredible feats in the "Mediterranean Theatre". This was former Judd schoolboy, Squadron Leader Neville Duke, the pride of Tonbridge, whose home was in the Hadlow Road.

Duke joined the RAF in 1940, aged 19, and was one of the first pilots to be trained in wartime. He joined 92 Squadron at Biggin Hill and when Winston Churchill paid a visit to the station, Duke tipped a Spitfire on to its nose — a *faux pas* that the PM chose to ignore.

Constantly in action in Britain and the Middle East, he then took part in more than 60 sweeps over the English Channel. On one occasion he was pounced on by seven Messerschmitts but frustrated his opponents by playing hide and seek in the clouds. In the summer of 1944, Duke bagged his 24th victim — an Me 109.

He was later to become even more famous for his feats as a Test Pilot.

Guns are silenced: the church bells peal

THE bombardment from Calais was stepped up a gear as the Allies moved even closer to the German stronghold. The battery men did not want to leave any ammunition behind and they certainly had no intention of taking it with them. The 406mm guns of Batterie Lindemann and the 380mm guns of Batterie Todt swung menacingly in an arc from Ramsgate to Hythe but it was Dover, as always, which received the most attention.

Between September 1st and 26th, 54 people were killed in this final blitz on Hellfire Corner and, of that total, Dover's toll was 40. The town was shattered and desolate with many buildings completely wrecked and others in a state of collapse. Fires burned from the rubble in Dover's streets, unexploded bombs littered the town, possessions were lost and hundreds of people bore the scars of terrible injury.

One of the worst attacks was on September 13th when a shell exploded outside Priory Station where the 1.15 train from Charing Cross had just arrived. Five passengers died in the booking hall and 20 were injured. Folkestone's turn came the following day. The shell warning lasted for more than 11 hours — the longest yet known. Not surprisingly the town was deserted. Cinemas, shops and pubs closed but bus companies continued to run limited services. On this day six people were killed and more than 30 injured.

The work of the wardens, off-duty service personnel, civilian helpers, balloon crews and all those who mounted intense rescue operations time and time again was amazing. Among those who gave comfort and practical help were the soldiers of the Salvation Army and it was a particular tragedy when a shell fell on their Red Shield canteen at Snargate Street, Dover on September 23rd. The building completely collapsed and rescue workers searched among the debris for more than 36 hours without

A Canadian soldier in the barrel of a captured gun.

break to find the dead and injured.

If it were possible to relax in Dover, then the Hippodrome was still the great favourite. The musical comedy star, Evelyn Laye was among the ENSA entertainers and so was Drina, who performed a striptease act. On one occasion in the middle of her show the scenery collapsed and many soldiers clambered on stage to pull the embarrassed artiste from the wreckage. The guns of Calais had the last word as far as the Hipprodrome was concerned. On September 15th, 1944 a shell smashed through the roof and wrecked the stage. The Forces' Theatre was closed and eventually pulled down.

On September 26th, 50 shells — the greatest number received by one town in a single salvo — fell among Dover's ruins. But this was the last desperate gesture by the enemy. The USAF dropped more than 5,600 bombs on the Lindemann Battery and a few hours later Canadian and British troops led by the Buffs closed in completely.

Nearest to the enemy and long abandoned. The hotel and houses under the white cliffs at St Margaret's Bay were repeatedly hit by German shells.

At 10.45 on the evening of September 30th, the mayor of Dover, Alderman Cairns received this telegram from the commander of the 9th Canadian Infantry Regiment.

" "To the Citizens of Dover. Greetings from the Brigade and may you enjoy your pint of beer and stroll on the front in peace from now on. We have all of Jerry's Big Berthas".

Dover's reply came immediately:

"Thank you for your message just received and most grateful appreciation of the gallantry and skill of you and your officers and men in capture of Jerry's Big Berthas. We shall not enjoy our beer and stroll on the front to the full until you all can join us in it. We wish you God Speed".

The shelling has ended. Within minutes loudspeakers were relaying the good news. The few flags that were not buried under the rubble began to appear and thanksgiving services were held in churches. More than 100 children from families which had suffered most were given a week's holiday in Brighton as a guest of the mayor.

The bells of St Mary's had survived the years of shelling. As a special salute, simple but effective, they pealed out five slow notes and two quick ones.

It represented the initials of Britain's front-line town — DOVER.

Members of the Tonbridge Home Guard marched through the High Street in the Salute the Soldier parade.

Kent's farewell to its Citizens' Army

THREE thousand officers and members of Home Guard units throughout Kent gathered in Canterbury on Sunday October 15th, 1944 — not to take part in more manoeuvres or to receive any new orders. On the contrary; they were attending a stand-down service in the Cathedral.

When they were formed in 1940, the future of England was in the balance and the invasion was imminent. Their skill and expertise were never tested thanks to Hitler's indecisions and then to the pilots of the RAF.

By October, 1944 the threat of an invasion had disappeared so the Home Guard was no longer needed, but how they enjoyed their final triumphant parade. The men, accompanied by their own bands of Ashford and Dartford battalions fell in at the Chaucer Barracks and marched through the city, past cheering crowds to the Cathedral.

After the service the men reformed and Lord Cornwallis took the salute outside the city walls. The 3,000 men, representing more than 60,000 colleagues, drawn from three transport columns and two AA batteries, heard Lord Cornwallis pay the final tribute:

"There is one thing of which I wish to remind you today — when we in deep anguish received into our little Kentish ports our hard-pressed Armies retreating from Dunkirk — when we saw endless train-loads being taken back to the west through our county for rest and refitting — we might have thought that there was little hope — but always remember with pride that when those tired Armies were going back west, a citizens' army was rising in the south-east, ready to fight on the beaches, in the fields and in the streets to secure the breathing space the nation so urgently required. That citizens' army was you — the Home Guard of Kent — and today I give to you all the humble and completely sincere thanks of the people of your county."

A few days later came the news that Hitler, preparing to mount his final defence, had formed the Volkssturm, a "home guard".

The boot, if you like, was on the other foot!

"Go into action — with your savings." This was the headline which appeared in Kent newspapers during the summer and autumn of 1944. For Salute the Soldier Week Kent towns and villages were invited to name an ambitious target and then try to break all previous records with the final total. It was, of course, another huge success. To help with their appeal Gravesend had a unique event — a display of Russian and Japanese guns by the Clock Tower.

Hellfire Corner had been out of bounds for the Royal family but soon after the capture of the Calais guns, the King and Queen visited the town and paid tribute to all those who refused to be beaten during their terrible ordeal. Here, outside the Maison Dieu, the Queen inspects those who knew more about the front-line than most — Dover's wonderful Civil Defence Services.

The V2 rocket (left) and the V1 (flying bomb), christened doodlebug by the people of Kent.

As the second phase of the flying bomb campaign began, a new defence strip was created between the Thames Estuary and Norfolk. The guns were moved from Kent in a deployment that was considered to be a great military achievement — the equivalent, it was said, of building two towns the size of Windsor. For this stage of the assault the doodlebugs were fixed to the bellies of Heinkels and in this way more than 1,000 were launched. The fighters and the men on the anti-aircraft batteries were by now formidable opponents and only 66 reached London.

Double thunderclap as the rocket arrives

WINSTON Churchill admitted in the House of Commons on November 10th, 1944 that Britain was under attack by another of Hitler's secret weapons, the German long-range rocket, the V2. It may have been news to some but for the people of Lullingstone, Knockholt, Eastchurch, Chislet, Borough Green, Bexleyheath, Orpington, Ditton, Lewisham, Penshurst, Yalding and many south-east London boroughs it was just confirmation that the ballistic missile, the most sadistic weapon of all, was causing more tragedy in the county of Kent.

The people in these towns and villages had already experienced that thunderous explosion as the rocket hit the earth, followed by another thunderclap as it broke the sound barrier. They already knew that it came from the stratosphere, at a height and speed that revolutionised military stategy but they also knew that this was not a weapon that would win the war for Hitler, despite the Führer's rantings.

German radio claimed that south-east England had been "devastated" by the V2 rocket but Churchill denied this. "The casualties and damage have not, so far, been heavy", he told Parliament. No single weapon, however, had ever been more destructive. The rocket rose to a height of 60-70 miles and travelled at 3,500 mph, carrying a ton of explosive in its nose. The first had crashed at Chiswick, South London killing three people and there had been

serious incidents in Southgate, north London and Croydon.

They were launched from mobile launching machines in The Hague — for thanks to the Allied troops the rocket sites in Pas de Calais and Belgium had been captured and many of the construction sites, including the rocket research centre at Peenemunde, had been heavily bombed.

But the people of Kent who experienced those first early shots were under no illusion but that this was another Revenge Weapon. They certainly did not believe the "gasworks explosions" which were the official explanation for the first few blasts.

It was in an effort to still the rumours of a secret weapon and to counter Nazi propaganda that Mr Churchill lifted the official silence. "Although there has been no panic", he said, "action against the V2s depends upon Allied forces destroying the rocket bases in the Netherlands." He was right. There was no other defence against the V2 for they took just five minutes from launch to impact and travelled too high and too fast to be tracked down.

Between September 1944 and March 1945, 1,115 rockets were fired at Britain, killing 2,612 people in London and 212 elsewhere. 64 fell in Kent and caused death and destruction in many communities. Hundreds more were destined to land on British soil but the Allied armies gained the initiative and the rocket pads were overrun.

On November 13th, three days after Churchill's statement, Gravesend suffered Kent's first serious V2 incident when a rocket exploded in Portland Avenue, damaging the town's Co-op stores. Five were killed and 16 seriously injured.

Gravesend was the unlucky recipient of a second rocket — this one near the town centre. Six died when a missile crashed at Milton Place on November 29th at 10.38pm.

This was one of PLUTO's "conundrums" — 30 miles of three inch steel pipe wound round and round the drum. This one broke loose during a storm and stuck on the sands off Greatstone.

The great pipeline under the ocean

DURING the invasion preparations, Lord Louis Mountbatten had an idea which was to contribute significantly to the ultimate victory in Europe. He suggested building a pipeline under the Channel to carry the petrol desperately needed by the Allied forces. PLUTO (Pipe Line Under The Ocean) became a reality in 1944 and by the end of the war had delivered 172 million gallons to the armies on the continent.

Following successful trials, first in the Thames, then the Medway and Bristol Channel, top secret installations were established at Dungeness and Sandown Bay on the Isle of Wight.

In order not to arouse suspicion, harmless-looking "holiday bungalows" were built to conceal some of the pumping plant, while high pressure pumps, which maintained the supply, were hidden in the sand dunes at Dungeness. A network of pipes a thousand miles long linked both pumping stations to ports in the West of England and oil-refineries such as the one at Grain. Tanks of petrol were also concealed on the Kent coast in case the supply broke down.

Two months after D Day, when the Cherbourg Peninsula was in Allied hands, the first PLUTO pipeline was laid between the Isle of Wight and Cherbourg. As the armies advanced through northern France that was abandoned in favour of the shorter route from Dungeness to Boulogne, where the first connection was made in October enabling 3,500 gallons of petrol a day to be pumped under the ocean. This was followed by 16 more pipe lines.

The tubes which carried the petrol beneath the Channel were manufactured in 72 yard lengths and each weighed 15 tons. They were made at Henley's, Gravesend and welded together at Littlestone where a special technique enabled them to withstand the enormous pressure of the water. These continuous pipes, by then about 30 miles long, were then wound on massive drums, known as "conundrums" and towed out to sea by tugs.

By February 1945, one million gallons of petrol a day were flowing beneath the English Channel — enough to quench the thirst of the Allied vehicles moving steadily towards the German border.

1945

Dresden, Hitler's suicide and victory

January 17th: Russia's Red Army defeated the Germans and marched into Warsaw.

January 27th: The Russians entered Auschwitz and discovered the horrors of the Nazi's biggest extermination camp.

January 31st: The Red Army crossed the German frontier and captured Driesen, 95 miles from Berlin. The Burma Road, from India to China, reopened, allowing supplies through to Nationalist China.

February 11th: The Yalta conference took place when Roosevelt, Stalin and Churchill met to discuss the future of post-war Europe.

February 14th: The city of Dresden in Germany was devastated by RAF bombers amid much criticism.

February 23rd: US Forces captured the island of Iwo Jima after four days of fierce battle.

March 10th: Massive US firebomb attack on Tokyo killed more than 80,000.

April 6th: US Forces landed in Okinawa.

April 12th: President Franklin D.Roosevelt died suddenly aged 63. He was succeeded by Harry S. Truman.

April 28th: Mussolini killed by partisans in Italy.

VJ party on Foster Clarke Estate, Maidstone in August, 1945. Star of the show was the little boy with the famous cigar!

April 30th: After a nine-day battle, the Red Army captured Berlin. Hitler and his mistress Eva Braun were reported to have committed suicide in Berlin. This marked the end of the Third Reich.

May 3rd: The Burmese capital of Rangoon was captured by the Allies.

May 8th: VE Day. The war was declared to be over in a broadcast by Mr Churchill from 10 Downing Street at 3pm. However, the war in the Far East continued.

May 9th: Prague was liberated, the last of Europe's capitals to be freed. The Channel Islands also surrendered, after five years of occupation.

May 28th: Lord Haw Haw (William Joyce) was captured near Hamburg.

June 18th: The demobilisation of British troops began, each man was entitled to a 'demob suit' and other civilian clothing.

July 16th: The US carried out the first testing of the atom bomb in New Mexico.

July 26th: The Labour party won a sensational victory in the general election. Winston Churchill resigned and Clement Attlee moved into Number 10.

August 6th: The Americans dropped the Atomic bomb on Hiroshima causing devastation and loss of life on a scale the world had never known.

August 14th: Japan surrendered, bringing the second world war to an end.

August 15th: The Allied nations celebrated VJ Day.

August 31st: Harrowing tales emerged of cruelty suffered by Allied PoWs in Japanese camps.

Troops who had enjoyed Christmas with their families in Kent returned to the Continent from Dover on January 4th, 1945. This was the first sailing of a leave-party from a Channel Port for many years and the men reached Calais without incident. No Stuka dive-bombers, no doodlebugs, no shells — just a few mines to dodge on the way.

Four days later another leave-party returned to the battleground from Folkestone. The Channel Ports had almost returned to life. Already coasters, carrying ammunition and stores had left for Ostend, army mail was being shipped across and ferries were crossing to Calais.

In Hellfire Corner, the battle of the beaches was over.

Well-earned leave. Victorious troops came ashore

Six of the best. Civil Defence wardens at Ramsgate stand outside one of the many blitzed houses in the town. More than 1,100 bombs had fallen on Ramsgate, killing 84 people and injuring 228.

Barbed wire was a painful feature of the war years. It was everywhere — especially in places where children played. Miles and miles of it stretched along the coast and it was with great satisfaction that Civil Defence wardens pulled it down during the winter. This was Margate's seafront where there would soon be access to those golden sands.

Whitstable children dived under their desks

ATTACKS by V2s continued to cause heavy damage and many casualties. One fell near All Saints Church, Whitstable and killed 57-year-old Mrs Snell who was walking along the road. Children at nearby Meadow Croft School dived under their desks as they heard the missile explode after its supersonic descent. On February 18th Charles Huckstepp, aged 19, and Isabel Gladish, 75, died when a V2 fell at Rede Court, Strood.

The church at Stoke, on the Isle of Grain, was damaged when a rocket fell on February 19th. Mrs Irene Dodd was killed in her bedroom but her husband escaped injury. A gardener at Ash Platt on the Seal Road, Sevenoaks died on February 23rd. A number of girls were in the greenhouse when the bomb exploded, shattering the glass in thousands of tiny fragments.

Kentish farms suffered badly from doodlebugs and rockets. A V2 fell on Larkins Farm, Penshurst (famous today for Larkins beer). Buildings blazed and many cattle had to be rescued. In the same month, March, Mr Turk who farmed the lonely Coles Farm at Bough Beech had a shock when a rocket fell out of the pitch-black sky into his orchard. Farm buildings were completely wrecked.

One of the worst incidents occurred at Sidcup when a V2 fell in Day's Lane at teatime. Among those buried by many tons of rubble were Mrs Macdonald and her twin daughters, Beryl and Josephine.

Only Josephine was found alive and six other people in the road were killed.

Two people died in this house in Wickenden Road, Sevenoaks and, next door, a family of four were killed. More than 500 homes in all were badly damaged.

Nine die as a second rocket hits Sevenoaks

THE V2 rockets, destined for London, continued to go badly off course and crash in Kent. On Tuesday February 27th one exploded near the centre of Swanscombe and the town shops had every window blown out.

This small town had already had its share of tragedy on numerous occasions. Now, eight people were dead, including two men who were repairing a "doodlebugged" house at the time. A baby, found in a cot buried by debris, was miraculously still alive.

A few days later, on Saturday March 3rd, a missile struck a housing estate at Wickenden Road, Sevenoaks killing nine people. The rocket impacted on a semi-detached house which was blown to pieces in the explosion. Three adjoining houses collapsed and two complete blocks of semi-detached houses were devastated.

Those who died were Leonard and Gladys Webb and their two young children, David and Deidre, Mr and Mrs Bereford Moyce, Mrs Frances Kidd, Mrs Hilda Tomlin and Rosemary Tomlin, aged six. This was the second rocket to land in Sevenoaks.

Between September 17th and March 25th, rockets peppered the Sevenoaks area. There were explosions at Knockholt, Borough Green, Penshurst (twice), Ide Hill, Chevening, Riverhead, Plaxtol, Platt, Farningham, Shoreham, Eynsford and Ightham.

The Dartford area was again in the firing line when, on March 14th a rocket came down in front of a bootmakers shop in Sutton-at-Hone, killing 10 people.

A Flying Fortress, returning from a raid on Northern Europe, crash-landed among the haystacks on a farm at St Margarets Bay in February 1945.

Lord Haw Haw lived in Chatham before the war

WILLIAM Joyce, a former member of the British Union of Fascists who won the sobriquet of "Lord Haw Haw" because of his superior drawl and sneering propaganda broadcasts from Hamburg was arrested in Germany on May 28th, 1945 and brought to England where he was charged with high treason.

Joyce lived at Chatham before the war and used to drink in the Old Lord Raglan on Chatham Hill, where he had many friends. The landlord of the pub at the time was Mr E.G.Maynard who later recalled how Joyce once asked if he could distribute (fascist) leaflets. He was refused.

Many meetings on the subject of National Socialism were held in Chatham with Joyce making dramatic speeches. One such gathering was in Batchelor Street where many of Chatham's pugilists wore their famous blue jerseys. Joyce, of course, whipped them up into a frenzy of patriotism, spurred on by his wife who once lived near Chatham Hill.

Joyce went to Germany at the outbreak of war and because he "was greatly impressed with the work of Hitler", adopted German nationality. His broadcasts from Hamburg in which he sneered, taunted and threatened, attracted some 16 million British listeners who switched over to him every night after the nine o'clock news.

He was arrested on May 28th after accosting two British army officers who were suspicious of him. On challenge he admitted his identity and went to draw a pistol. One of the officers shot first and wounded Joyce in the thigh. He was taken into custody and charged with high treason at Bow Street.

On January 3rd, 1946 William Joyce was hanged in Wandsworth Jail, aged 39.

George Blake was the only victim of a rocket which exploded in the garden of a house in Madan Road, Westerham on March 11th — but seven people were seriously injured and scores had lucky escapes. The blast, which could be heard for miles around, caused damage to more than 300 homes. The WVS provided comfort and cups of tea for the residents.

More than 8,000 New Zealanders from German PoW camps arrived in Margate in the hope that the town's bracing sea air could help restore them to full health. The men, who belonged to the second New Zealand Expeditionary Force (Anzacs) captured in the Middle East and Italy, were suffering from malnutrition and the effects of a forced march across Germany. They took over the best 30 hotels in Cliftonville, including the Norfolk Hotel (above).

The gardens behind No 88 Kynaston Road, Orpington where the final V2 rocket fell.

Parting shot exploded in Orpington

TOWARDS the end of March, 1945, the rocket troops in The Hague found themselves virtually cornered. Paris and Brussels had long been liberated and the Allies were advancing across the Rhine. The disaster at Arnhem the previous year, where beleaguered forces had been trapped after failing to take the Rhine crossings, had lengthened the duration of the war, but that was in the past. Cologne had now fallen and the Reich was being attacked from all sides. Time was certainly running out.

On March 27th, SS Gruppenführer Klammer in charge of the rocket battery ordered the men to fire two further missiles and then leave. The first landed in Antwerp and killed 27 people. The second fell short of Central London and exploded on a small estate at Orpington between Kynaston Road and Court Road. People for miles around heard the explosion. Buildings shook, windows shattered and paving stones were blown into the air.

In that final attack, 23 people were injured and one killed. Housewife, Mrs Ivy Millichamp was in her kitchen at 88 Kynaston Road when the rocket fell. She was pulled clear by her husband Eric but she had caught the full force of the blast and was already dead.

Ivy Millichamp, aged 34 was the youngest of seven daughters. She was buried in All Saints Churchyard, Orpington and, today, a headstone records the fact that she was the last person in Britain to be killed by enemy action.

The days of the V2 rocket were over but not the V1 flying bomb. The

Mrs Ivy Millichamp

third and last phase had begun on March 3rd when several salvos were launched from ramps near Delft. On March 26th, Flight Lieutenant James Grottick of 501 Squadron shot down a doodlebug which crashed on the Essex side of the Thames Estuary — it was the last intruder of the war to be toppled by a fighter. Three days later, on March 29th, anti-aircraft gunners in North Kent triumphantly claimed what was to be the last V1 to land on British soil. It exploded in open country at Iwade, near Sittingbourne.

Hitler committed suicide on April 30th and his body was doused with petrol and set alight. A few days later, Germany surrendered. Effigies of Hitler were burned on bonfires all over the county. This one was at Milton Place, Gravesend where a rocket had killed eight people a few months earlier.

Germany surrenders and Hitler is dead

HITLER'S vengeance weapons, ghastly though they were, had arrived too late to save Germany. By April 1945 the Nazi retreat was becoming a rout as the Allied armies advanced. President Roosevelt died on April 12th and the next day the concentration camps at Belsen and Buchenwald were taken by the British. The Russian stranglehold tightened on Berlin. Mussolini was executed on April 28th. The survivors of the Dachau death camp were liberated and the SS guards condemned to death. German forces in Italy surrendered on April 29th, many thousands of prisoners were taken in The Ruhr and Hitler retreated to his bunker, to be joined by Eva Braun.

On April 30th, 36 hours after marrying Miss Braun, Hitler dined with his secretaries and then retired to his quarters. A single shot rang out. The body of Hitler, dripping blood was found slumped on a couch. He had shot himself in the mouth. Beside him was Eva Braun; she

had taken poison. With Russian shells exploding all around, the bodies were doused with petrol and set alight.

Four days later, on May 4th, the German forces in western Europe surrendered. General Montgomery read the capitulation terms which were to take effect from 8 am the following day. The Third Reich, which Hitler said would last 1,000 years was dead. The official announcement came on May 8th when Churchill, from 10 Downing Street, said: "The German war is at an end. Advance Britannia, Long live the cause of freedom".

Right across the front-line county of Kent enthusiastic bands of revellers lit bonfires, danced and sang. Some people climbed lamp-posts and jubilantly draped their Union Jacks out of windows. By Tuesday night (May 8th) this had grown into a striking display, particularly in High Streets and residential areas. There were fireworks, private parties, thanksgiving services and, of course, the

At Maidstone they danced in the High Street.

pubs throughout the county had special late-night extensions.

Despite the parties, the dancing and the rejoicing there was a certain sadness. The editor of the *Sevenoaks News* wrote: "Considering the trials through which we have passed and the burdens which have been endured, the release which VE brings might have precipitated greater hilarity. But the good news had been expected for days, which dispersed much of the spontaneous joyful reaction. What had a much greater effect was the feeling of thankful deliverance from all the dangers. Moreover there was the realisation that many of our men and women are not yet home from the various fighting fronts and that the Japanese still have to be conquered and that cessation of war is bringing with it fresh new problems. Above all we remember those who will not return."

On Wednesday May 9th many Kent units of the Civil Defence Services were stood down and on Sunday May 13th big parades were staged in every Kent town. Street parties were held throughout the week, many against the background of blitzed buildings and bomb sites. At Riverhead, scores of children were tucking into a delicious-looking fare when two fighters appeared in the sky above. The children didn't run to the shelters or fall flat on their faces. They stood and cheered and waved their flags. The response was memorable — two red and green flares and two perfect Victory rolls.

The war was over.

The highly exacting task of defusing unexploded bombs was the most dangerous job of all. This fell to the "suicide squads" as they were known in the early days of the war — the bomb disposal section of the Royal Engineers. According to Churchill most of them had "haggard faces with a blueish look and bright gleaming eyes". They spent day after day in many feet of water and mud, in danger every minute of the shaft caving in or, worst of all, the sudden sound of ticking. Here are the brave men of Folkestone with one of the "whoppers", possibly an 18 pounder, recovered on July 6th, 1940. Hundreds of men of the bomb disposal units died during the war. Those that survived needed iron nerves, steady hands and good luck.

Folkestone 'all-clear' after 3,000 warnings

THE celebrations in Kent continued. Another effigy of Hitler was burnt at Ashford, a torchlight procession attracted thousands of followers at Gravesend, a bonfire was lit on the Common at Tunbridge Wells, speeches were made outside town halls and, at Maidstone, the band of the Royal West Kent Regiment played on till the early hours. With them was an armed guard and 50 standard bearers carrying the flags of all the Allies.

Folkestone, like all coastal towns was still enduring the blackout. It was feared that enemy submarines might not have received the surrender instructions and, if they had, they might not obey them.

Tuesday May 8th, however, was still a day to be remembered. At noon, airmen from Hawkinge and Lympne appeared on the streets in pyjamas and dressing gowns and, in the afternoon, the All Clear was sounded for the very last time. The people of Folkestone went to their

thanksgiving services recalling the horrors of the last six years. They remembered the devastation and carnage left by the exploding shells, how American gunners, with their bare hands, helped to rescue those buried under tons of rubble, the long line of blitzed buildings with beds and baths still visible, the Churchill tank which impaled itself on the railings outside the Railway Bell pub, the dogfights, the doodlebugs, the summer of the blazing Messerschmitts, the mined beaches, the barbed wire, the deluge of "friendly" shells and the funeral cortèges which passed by so frequently with Union Jacks draped over the coffins.

Folkestone endured 2,914 air raid warnings and 102 shell warnings. 85 people were killed and 181 seriously injured. Every citizen was a hero but particular acts of courage were shown by policemen, William Spain and Cyril Williams, a carpenter, George Fenton and Doctor Robert Lindsay. They each won the George Medal.

Have you heard the one about the sailor and the bus conductress who danced a jig in the middle of Maidstone High Street on a Tuesday afternoon!

This is Nursery Road, High Brooms, near Tunbridge Wells — just one of scores of street parties in the Royal Borough.

The wounded, lovingly nursed back from a living hell, somehow got caught up with the euphoria of victory. Here are a few of the survivors, minus a leg, an arm or foot, preparing to take their place in a society that was a scarred replica of its pre-war existence.

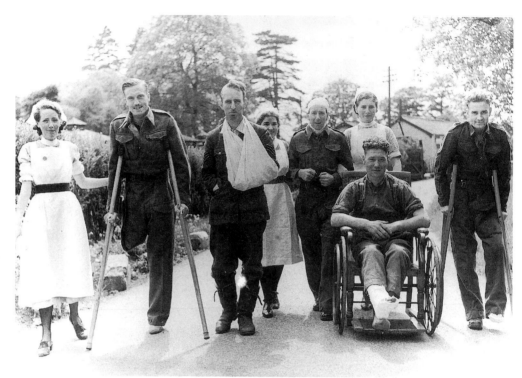

The mines had been lifted from the sands and Ramsgate beach was open again for children and donkeys.

*Hartnup Street, Maidstone welcomed "Old George" to their VJ street party on
August 31st, 1945 He certainly took a liking to the ice cream.*

Bomb drops and Japan surrenders

AS the war in the Middle East continued, British and American scientists were making history of a most deadly kind — a bomb more powerful than any the world had known. Much of the early research work had taken place at Fort Halstead, near Sevenoaks, the Government's armament research and development establishment. Physicist, Dr William Penney was the British inspiration behind a device that was to be the most controversial in history and one that cast a shadow that still hangs across the world today. The scientists' plan was to "implode segments of plutonium to form a critical mass in which neutrons would split the atomic nuclei".

Dr Penney who lived at Belgrave Road, Sheerness and had been a student at the Sheerness Technical Institute was present at the first successful test in the Mexico Desert. The weapon exploded with a force equivalent to 20,000 tonnes of TNT. It fused sand into glass, sent a mushroom cloud 40,000 feet into the sky and released enormous energy in a chain reaction. It was a bomb capable of devastating Japan, forcing them to surrender and ending the war. Dr Penney may have had doubts about using it but generally there was little dissent among the scientists. The decision lay with the politicians.

The rest is history. On August 6th, the USAAF B-29 Enola Gay dropped the atom bomb on Hiroshima killing 80,000 people and maiming more than 200,000 from blast, burns and radiation. Three days later the target was the shipbuilding port of Nagasaki and, on this occasion, Dr Penney was a British observer along with Wing Commander Leonard Cheshire. Tokyo condemned the act as "an atrocity", demanded peace talks and, on August 14th, Japan surrendered unconditionally.

By now, Churchill was no longer Prime Minister. In the General Election of July, Labour had won an overwhelming victory — even gaining six of the 16 "safe" Kent constituencies, including Dover which had been a Conservative stronghold for years. It was Clement Attlee who made the announcement just before midnight that "the last of our enemies has been laid low".

Kent plunged into heartfelt celebrations but not quite with the same enthusiasm with which they had greeted the end of the war with Germany. The Japanese surrender was seen by many as a distant affair and really an American revenge for Pearl Harbour.

The US troops in East Kent were the first to show their delight. People asleep at Folkestone were woken by an announcement from a jeep that was driven wildly through the streets. In the Thames Estuary at Gravesend a single ship started to hoot. It was followed by another, then another until the noise was deafening. For more than two hours the hooting continued — short and shrill by the tugs, deep, throaty sirens by the bigger vessels.

County Hall at Maidstone announced the news at 3pm

In October, "Monty" came to Canterbury to receive the freedom of the City. Huge crowds welcomed him and he was cheered all the way as he drove through the blitzed streets in an open car, a replica of the one he used in the Western Desert.

on Wednesday August 15th. A big crowd gathered to sing the National Anthem and to hear the speeches. Dover Castle was floodlit for the first time since 1939. In Tonbridge there were dances in the Medway Hall and on the Castle lawn and a huge procession went down the High Street into Barden Road. At Canterbury it was 'queue day' — queues for meat, grocery, fruit and, the largest of all, for fireworks. The New Zealanders in Margate were the stokers for the big bonfire which burned near the Grand Hotel. Many revellers climbed the clock tower and the hands stopped at 11.25, as evidence of their efforts. At Ramsgate, a group of sailors saw a policeman on point duty, picked him up and carried him triumphantly through the streets. The windmill at Willesborough, Ashford was floodlit and there was a fireworks display outside the Corn Exchange. More than 1,000 people gathered on the Common at Tunbridge Wells and then joined the dance band on the Pantiles.

Only one event stopped the celebrations — the King's broadcast at 9 pm in which he said: "We now have our part to play in restoring the shattered fabric of civilisation. It is to this great task that I call you now."

The people of Canterbury, blitzed by the Baedeker raids of 1942, of Folkestone and Hythe, devastated by the Calais guns, of Dartford, the county's most-bombed town, of Ashford and Tenterden, where the doodlebugs fell, of Gravesend and Sevenoaks, recipients of several rockets and the people of Dover, shelled, bombed, blasted and mined. They knew what the King meant. It was time to rebuild a shattered county and to enjoy "everlasting peace".

The people in the pictures — additional information from our readers

When we first printed Kent at War in November 1994 we invited readers to let us know if they recognised a friend or relation in any of the photographs so we could include a little more information in our next reprint. We should have known better! Our mail bag was jammed and the telephone line red hot with names and locations. It's impossible to mention all those who contacted us but here's a selection of some of the more important. The overall impression was that you all enjoyed the book. Thank you for your comments and thank you for the additional information.

Page 9: From Derek C.Harden of Worthing: "The three schoolboys in the railway carriage were contemporaries of mine from the Mathematical School at Rochester. They were being evacuated to the safety of Canterbury! They are (l to r) Boswell (in the background), Field and Len Craft. For obvious reasons we didn't stay in Canterbury long and were soon off to Wales".

Page 19 (top): From Mrs Vera Porter: "The policeman was Sidney Chambers, PC14 of Gravesend and later Sergeant. He had been awarded the OBE in 1916".

Page 21: From Ian Ellis: "The old man with the dog was R.H. Ellis, a veteran of the 1914-18 war and a stone mason by trade. He is pictured in his yard at Gillingham Cemetery. His eldest son was killed in the 1914-18 war and his youngest son, Don, became editor of the Chatham Observer."

Page 27: From Frank Wright: "I was working at Chatham Dockyard when a bomb from a Dornier just missed the *Ajax*, moored by the Upnor wall. The bomb exploded on the jetty and overturned a steam crane whose driver/operator was Mr Fever. He died from shock and injuries some months later. This was in autumn 1942. The chief designer for Short Bros was Arthur Gouge who lived at Ashley House, Rochester".

Page 31: From Tony Webb of Maidstone: "The photograph was taken in Maidstone West goods yard. Fourth from the left in the front rank is Albert Parker". Other personalities include Ernest Savage (3rd from left front rank).

Page 42: From John Haybittle: "The photographer in the foreground is my uncle R.G.V.Ottaway, at the time the Southern Railway staff photographer".

Page 46 (top): From Mrs D.Hymers: "The old gentleman was my grandad William

Ambrose Rolf of Boughton Adulph who died in 1947 aged 90. Among the children are Brenda Mills and her brothers Leonard and Peter".

Page 60 (top): From Tony Webb: "The man with the badly bleeding head is George Wise".

Page 62 (top): The Observer Corps Ops Room was in the basement at Fairlawns, 57 London Road, Maidstone.

Page 65 (top): The man who bought the drinks was Major Jackson of the 208 Heavy Ack Ack and he won the Military Cross for his Battery's achievements on that day. Among the sharpshooters was Alfred Charles Ludlow, then aged 18.

Page 70: From Mr D.W.Horne: "Two people were killed at Bilsington. My neighbour, Charles Ashdown, aged 18, was working at Staplehurst station on that day (15-9-40) when the Hurricane crashed and he was killed. His gravestone can be seen today in Pluckley churchyard".

Page 74: From Derek Harden: "It is possible that the bombers over Maidstone were trying to hit the Army barracks just across the road from Hope Street when they caught the Walls ice cream depot where my father was the manager. Empty ice cream metal cans, stored in the depot, were reduced to tiny mangled zinc objects and scattered all over the district".

Page 77: From Jean Bishop: "The little girl sitting on her mother's lap with fingers in mouth is Jean Bishop (nee Harris), aged two. She lived in Dartford with her parents but often stayed at Greenhithe. The girl next to her (on lap) is cousin Ena Harris, who still lives in Greenhithe".

Page 77: From Syd Chester: "The accordianist in the Greenhithe tunnel was known to us as 'old Ben'. He used to tune my father's piano before the war."

Page 82: From Cecilia Valentine: "My father and brother were in the Star at Swanscombe on Sunday November 10th, 1940 and were both killed. They were Frank Swaisland (junior and senior). The last words my mother and I heard from father (to his son) were — 'let's go down to the pub and have a drink and then turn in and have an early night'. Half an hour after they left there were a number of very large explosions".

Page 92: From Jack Edwards: "The house shown in the photograph is 23 Chalk Pit Hill, Chatham. By the doorway is my wife Joan (then Nisbett) and her brother Albert (on leave from the Army). Their home was more or less intact. Next door a lady was killed."

Page 98: From David Rutland: "Land

Army girl Freda Penn was a friend of my wife's (then Peggy Cheeseman) and both worked as apprentices at Sibthorpes in Calverley Road, Tunbridge Wells. She became Freda Lambert; sadly they have lost touch".

Page 99: From Dorothy Reynolds: "I was the blacksmith in the photograph (then Dorothy Stanford Beale) — the only one at the time in southern England. I was 18 and worked until 1944, when, running away from a doodlebug I injured myself and ended up in hospital. I then returned to office work.

Page 100 (bottom right): Elsie Jones (then Taylor), the first postwoman in Gravesend.

Page 104: From David Rutland: "Could the E.J.Wallis who threw a stone through the window be the senior provision hand who worked at Uridges Stores in Sevenoaks? I know he was in the Home Guard, and a church organist".

Page 108: From Geoff Kennell (historian 131 Squadron). Mr Kennell who names all the pilots writes: "The aircraft is a Spitfire Vb serial BM420 coded NX-A and named *Spirit of Kent*. It was the mount of Squadron Leader Pedley".

Page 110: From Brian Bridges: "The police officer, bottom left, is Pc Fred Coatsworth, traffic patrol officer at Canterbury. He retired as Superintendent and in 1995 was living at Penenden Heath, Maidstone".

Page 112: From Derek Harden; "The lower picture shows the yard of Batchelor's Farm opposite the Rose Inn at the junction of Cecil Road and Catherine Street, Rochester. In the top left hand corner is a young man smiling and not wearing a hat. His name was Dick Benman who went on to join the RAF".

Page 136: From Jenny Uglow: "My mother, Mrs J.L.C.Crowther of Whitstable was the Wren who saluted to Churchill, without a hat. The date was 1940 and full uniform had not yet been issued".

Page 140: From Mr W.Barrett: "The photograph of Dover Street must have been taken in 1944 or later because I notice that the local cinema advertises a film called "Up in Arms" starring Danny Kaye which was not made until 1944".

Page 141: From Mr A.Jackson: "The first accordianist in the back row I believe to be my dad's brother, Bill Jackson, who was with the BEF in France and captured about 1941 or earlier and sent to Germany with other Tommies".

Page 146: From Mr W.Barrett: "Gerry Chalk first joined the H.A.C. as a gunner, later remustering to the RAF initially as a

rear gunner."

Page 161: From Brian Bridges: "The young boy (front left) biting his nails is James Burden who then lived with his mother in Grecian Street."

Page 165: From John Robertson: "I think I am one of the pupils at Dymchurch School and another is Derek Woodland, in the front row, who lived opposite me at Lyndhurst Road. He was related to Mr E.E.Woodland who observed the first V1 crossing the coast (see page 188). Derek and his father Frank were injured when a damaged B17 crashed in our road. I think that Elizabeth Uden and Ian Jones are also in the school picture."

Page 172: From Elias Smith: "The Thunderbolt flipped as it approached, lopped the lower poles and trees and crashed. I helped to pull out the pilot. In the background is The Folly".

Page 174: From Mr R.S.Hall: "The Churchill tank (bottom picture) was a 1943 version with a 2-pounder gun. It seems that it had a broken track. Sergeant Len Wainwright, a South African is pictured (centre) but I do not recall the names of the other two. The tank belonged to No 14 Troop, C Squadron, 9th Royal Tank Regiment. The Officers' Mess was in Pitts Place, Charing. We stayed in Charing until we moved to Aldershot and onward to land in Normandy about June 20th, 1944. I was Troop Sergeant".

Page 206 (top): From Mr Kass: "Among those in the photograph are Mr Mallion, Mr Wells, Percy Geal, Peter Wells, Tommy Martin, Ethne Lockyer, Helen Godfrey, Pamela Boakes, Audrey Martin, June Chilman, Nobby Moseley and Myrtle Minton".

Page 211: From W.G.Coley: "The bus conductress dancing with the sailor is Miss Joyce Shead (or Sheed) who worked with Maidstone and District Bus Co at the time. She married in the late forties and emigrated to Australia".

Page 211: From Mr R.Kempton: "My wife has recognised her grandparents Mr and Mrs Camfield in the picture of Nursery Road, High Brooms. My wife should have been in the picture as she was living with her grandparents after her mother died. She may be under the table eating a rock cake!

Page 211: From Joan Clark: "I was born in Nursery Road and lived there for 64 years. I clearly remember the preparation for the street party and I can see my mother sitting in the front plus many friends and neighbours".

The Doodlebug map

EACH OF THESE SMALL DOTS REPRESENTS A FLYING BOMB BROUGHT DOWN INTO THE SEA

This map, printed by the *Kent Messenger* on September 15th, 1944, shows where every doodlebug had landed up to the beginning of September. This issue of the *Kent Messenger* sold out within hours of it arriving in the shops so, the following week, the newspaper published the map again and also offered it for individual sale with proceeds going to the county's Civil Defence Fund. Within days orders for 100,000 copies had been received but the strict rationing on newsprint made it impossible for the *Kent Messenger* to meet all the enquiries. Today, the "Doodlebug Map" is a treasured memento in thousands of homes throughout the county.

Where the rockets crashed in Kent

No less than 130 V2 rockets fell in Kent and the Kent boroughs which formed the London Civil Defence region. The code name for the missile was Big Ben and here are the dates and times of all incidents between September 11th, 1944 and March 25th, 1945 when the campaign ended.

September:
11th Lullingstone 09.07
12th Keston 08.52
17th Knockholt 05.11

October:
4th Eastchurch 08.15
18th Chislet 06.32
19th Borough Green 07.17
23rd Hoo 16.53
24th Queenborough 02.07
27th Swanley 10.15
27th Lewisham 23.47
31st Bexleyheath 18.11
31st Orpington 23.40

November:
1st Dartford 22.45
2nd Lewisham 10.05
3rd Lewisham 04.38
4th Sutton at Hone 17.25
5th Penshurst 01.30
6th Yalding 10.51
6th Bexleyheath 14.58
11th Cliff-at-Hoo 15.40
11th Birchington-on-Sea 19.09
11th Ide Hill 23.44
12th Stone 17.30
12th Swanscombe 23.43
13th Erith 12.49
13th Gravesend 16.38
13th Southborough 22.47
14th Orpington 06.21
14th Eltham 09.38
15th Lewisham 12.50

17th Dartford 08.27
18th Erith 16.08
19th Bromley 21.18
21st Erith 05.37
21st Erith 13.20
21st Orpington 18.02
29th Bexley 21.18
29th Gravesend 23.38

December:
3rd Bexley 21.00
6th Crayford 07.15
6th Erith 19.46
10th Erith 00.38
10th Lewisham 04.50
10th North Foreland 20.50
12th Sidcup 17.58
19th Lewisham 19.25
20th Crayford 02.59
23rd Bexley 18.49
30th Northfleet 21.34
30th Sutton at Hone 22.34

January:
2nd Beckenham 12.15
3rd Tonbridge 20.03
5th Beckenham 00.12
6th Dartford 02.15
8th Wilmington 13.14
8th Sidcup 19.44
9th Beckenham 10.50
14th Lewisham 16.14
15th Whitstable 11.15
16th Herne Bay 09.09
16th Sidcup 19.10
20th Riverhead 16.37
21st Plaxtol 02.05
28th Benenden 03.30
28th Bromley 05.07
28th Sidcup 06.51

February:
1st Chiddingstone 05.19
6th St Mary Cray 09.48
6th Crockenhill 18.05

8th Chislehurst 03.03
8th Erith 12.06
8th Chislehurst 17.40
9th Hayes 17.25
9th Chislehurst 21.34
11th Bromley 13.51
11th Lewisham 22.00
13th Erith 16.33
13th Bexley 19.15
14th Platt 00.32
14th Farningham 02.21
14th Chislehurst 14.51
15th Erith 00.55
15th Crayford 07.05
15th Shoreham 11.22
17th Aylesford 03.32
17th St Mary's Hoo 14.22
18th Dartford Heath 10.15
18th Rochester 12.01
18th Bexley 12.18
18th Erith 19.44
21st Sidcup 09.17
21st Beckenham 11.21
22nd Eynsford 14.46
23rd Sevenoaks 09.45
27th Chevening 04.43
27th Swanscombe 09.21
27th Erith 05.07

March:
1st Orpington 08.23
2nd Orpington 12.21
3rd Sevenoaks 04.49
4th Penshurst 04.52
6th Bexley 00.57
6th Sidcup 04.35
7th Sidcup 10.33
8th St Mary Cray 04.36
8th Blackheath 12.06
8th Sidcup 14.55
8th Horton Kirby 19.53
9th Marden 02.15
10th Beckenham 00.01
10th Biggin Hill 00.16
10th Bexley 10.01
11th Westerham 10.02
12th Sidcup 02.33
13th Erith 08.30
14th Sutton at Hone 23.27
16th North Foreland 02.52
17th Dartford 07.30
18th Ightham 03.40
18th Aylesford 06.30
19th Erith 10.31
20th Sidcup 08.20
22nd Hoo 03.57
22nd Dartford 23.21
26th Bromley 15.22
27th Orpington 16.54

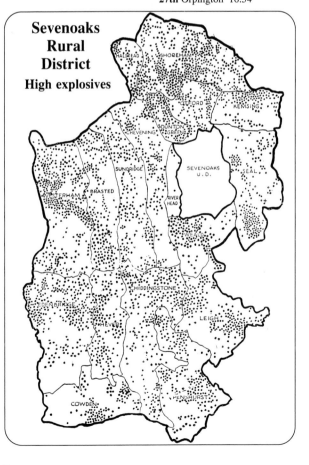

**Sevenoaks Rural District
High explosives**

THE rural districts of Dartford and Sevenoaks ended the war with the unenviable reputation as the most heavily bombed in Kent. More than 5,000 heavy explosives fell in the Dartford villages while Sevenoaks received well over 3,000. The two were the recipients of more than 200 flying bombs, scores of rockets and up to 300,000 incendiaries. The Shoreham valley which links the two authorities was known as "bomb alley" and, even today, it is estimated that many hundreds of unexploded devices lie buried beneath the farmland.

There were several reasons for the extraordinary attention shown by the Luftwaffe — the proximity of Biggin Hill and the "dummy" airfield at Lullingstone, the activity in the Thames Estuary and the regular dumping off of bombs by enemy aircraft who would not want to return to France with any left.

The map of Sevenoaks Rural shows an approximate plot of the high explosives (50 kilos or over) which fell between June 28th, 1940 and the end of August, 1944. Incendiary and anti-personnel (butterfly bombs) are not included.

Casualty figures from the serious raids

High explosive and incendiary

Almost 30,000 high explosive and 727,000 incendiary bombs were dropped on Kent. This list shows those incidents in which more than 10 civilians were killed during a single bombing raid on a town or village. The second figure refers to those seriously injured.

March 24th, 1943 (**Ashford**): 50 / 77
June 1st, 1942 (**Canterbury**): 43 / 40
June 24th, 1940 (**Ramsgate**): 31 / 11
August 16th, 1940 (**Northfleet**): 29 / 18
November 27th, 1940 (**Swanscombe**): 27 / 6
September 6th, 1940 (**Dartford**): 24 /0
September 27th, 1940 (**Maidstone**): 22 / 44
August 27th, 1940 (**Gillingham**): 20/ 22
March 2nd, 1944 (**Strood**): 18 / 8
March 23rd, 1942 (**Dover**): 16 / 6
April 3rd, 1942 (**Dover**): 16 / 18
December 14th, 1940 (**Chatham**): 15 / 20
June 12th, 1941 (**Dover**): 15 / 20
November 18th, 1941 (**Sturry**): 15 / 11
October 22nd, 1942 (**Deal**): 15 / 7
April 20th, 1941 (**Dartford**): 13 / 6
May 29th, 1941 (**Folkestone**): 13 / 4
January 21st, 1944 (**Dartford**): 13 / 13
September 12th, 1940 (**Tun Wells**): 12 / 2
April 8th, 1941 (**Rochester**): 11 / 28
October 26th, 1942 (**Ashford**): 11 / 0
June 1st, 1943 (**Margate**): 10 / 4

Shelling

Shelling of the coastal towns began on August 12th, 1940 and continued until the Calais guns were captured at the end of September, 1944. The more serious incidents, in relation to civilian casualties, were as follows:

January 20th, 1944 (**Deal**): 12 / 17
September 1st, 1944 (**Dover**): 8 / 8
September 12th, 1944 (**Dover**): 7 / 7
September 13th, 1944 (**Dover**): 7 / 17
September 14th, 1944: (**Folkestone**): 6 / 10
October 6th, 1943 (**Dover**): 6 / 8
The last month of the shelling was, in fact, the worst. Between September 1st and 26th, 1944 a total of 54 people were killed in Dover, Folkestone, Ramsgate and Hythe.

Flying bombs

Civilian deaths in Kent attributable to V1 flying bombs, totalled 152 with 1,716 injured. Of all the south-east counties, Kent had the most to endure with 1,444 crashing on land and a further 1,000 shot down in the sea. The major incidents were as follows:

June 21st, 1944 (**Charing Heath**): 44 / 28*
June 30th, 1944 (**Crockham Hill**): 30 / 9
July 30th, 1944 (**Swanscombe**): 13 / 22
August 5th, 1944 (**Snodland**) 12 / 15
August 6th, 1944 (**Dartford**): 10 / 12
March 3rd, 1945 (**Sevenoaks**): 9 / 13
August 16th, 1944 (**Newington**): 8 / 24*
November 8th, 1944 (**Rochester**): 8 / 16
July 9th, 1944 (**Dartford**): 7 / 0
June 24th, 1944 (**Smarden**): 6 / 0
August 15th, 1944 (**Hythe**): 5 / 5

*includes military fatalities

Aircraft crashes

There was civilian loss of life caused by aircraft crashing on these occasions:

August 25th. 1940 (**Dover**): 3 killed
September 1st, 1940 (**Elham**): 1 killed
Septem,ber 15th, 1940 (**Bilsington**): 1 killed
October 10th, 1940 (**Maidstone**): 9 killed
October 21st, 1940 (**Tonbridge**) 1 killed
November 21st, 1940 (**Buckland**): 2 killed
May 11th, 1941 (**Upchurch**): 3 killed
July 31st, 1941 (**Dartford**): 2 killed
October 24th, 1942 (**Cliffe**): 1 killed
July 4th, 1942 (**Strood**): 1 killed

Other action

In addition, the following type of enemy action caused loss of life.

November 18th, 1941 (**Sturry**):
15 / 11 (parachute mines)
September 6th, 1940 (**Hollingbourne)**
1 killed (shrapnel)
March 10th, 1941 (**Sheerness**):
2 / 3 (anti-aircraft shell)
March 20th. 1941 (**Hythe**):
1 killed (machine gun)
May 10th, 1941 (**Deal**):
1 killed (machine gun)
October 26th, 1942 (**Ashford**):
1 killed (machine gun)
October 31st, 1942 (**Barham**):
1 killed (machine gun)
January 26th, 1944 (**Northfleet**):
1 killed (AA shell)
July 4th, 1944 (**East Peckham**):
1 killed (shrapnel)
July 6th, 1944 (**Maidstone:**
1 killed (machine gun)
August 4th, 1944 (**Horsmonden**):
1 killed (machine gun)
August 16th, 1944 (**Appledore**):
1 killed (machine gun)
November 13th, 1944 (**Chatham**):
1 killed (mortar)

These figures come from the Civil Defence war diaries and relate to those recorded at the time of the incident. Many people may have died later from injuries received.

Photograph credits

We acknowledge with thanks the photographs supplied by the following: Rural History Centre University of Reading 6: Pilots Pals 7: John Topham Picture Agency 12, 13, 15, 16, 46 (top), 47, 48, 64, 65 (top), 66, 68 (top), 74, 79 (both), 83, 133, 147: Imperial War Museum 36, 39, 108, 116, 182: John Haybittle 42. Bexley Local Studies 45: Folkestone Library Heritage Services 210. Hulton Deutsch 58, 69: A. Webb 73: Guinness Brewing Worldwide 86: Bromley Local Studies 96, 155: Southern Railway 136. National Archives of Canada 194: Gordon Anckorn 215. Independent Books (London) 156. Other illustrations were supplied by Mrs Hazel Pelling, the Biggin Hill collection (Bob Ogley), Phyllida Warner.

There are one or two photographs for which we have tried to find the source, without success.

Civilian casualties, damage and bombs

(excluding the Kent boroughs in London Civil Defence Regions)

Local Authority	Killed	Seriously injured	Slightly injured	Property wrecked	Severely damaged	HE Bombs	Incendiary bombs (approx)	Flying bombs
Ashford area	103	162	245	184	393	974	12,645	184
Bridge-Blean	29	35	84	81	151	1,364	18,300	13
Broadstairs	7	6	48	18	163	278	300	3
Canterbury	115	140	240	808	1,047	445	10,000	1
Chatham	47	47	225	297	454	267	1,535	nil
Dartford MB	92	72	205	174	357	553	11,982	14
Dartford RD	50	80	280	120	894	5,359	200,000	76
Deal	64	55	198	172	718	173	118	nil
Dover MB	199	307	420	910	2,998	464	1,500	3
Dover RD	5	10	8	36	141	389	2,380	21
Eastry RD	20	32	57	27	65	667	1,700	8
Elham RD	15	15	57	27	203	930	6,500	64
Faversham	17	26	60	12	29	442	1,283	15
Folkestone	85	181	484	290	1,486	378	1,113	29
Gillingham	57	68	184	168	359	275	3,885	3
Gravesend	38	81	202	45	211	292	300,000	3
Herne Bay	9	21	39	12	45	104	1,090	1
Hollingbourne	10	20	38	11	170	946	1,720	81
Hythe	24	36	106	96	385	79	nil	11
Maidstone MB	60	105	182	127	210	264	1,000	6
Maidstone RD	9	16	59	22	198	689	7,000	63
Malling RD	46	62	164	36	287	1,979	11,332	97
Margate	35	40	201	268	592	584	2,489	nil
New Romney	12	32	52	61	218	718	3,823	149
Northfleet	40	47	39	35	104	362	11,000	4
Queenborough	Nil	nil	5	nil	1	52	1,000	nil
Ramsgate	84	89	139	393	418	860	283	nil
Rochester	75	86	360	276	1,221	238	14	5
Sandwich	Nil	2	8	7	107	52	1,000	nil
Sevenoaks UD	22	59	111	42	133	98	4,000	5
Sevenoaks RD	62	70	188	86	169	3,259	53,500	137
Sheppey RD	8	13	8	12	39	633	680	5
Sheerness	2	nil	18	8	4	23	150	nil
Sittingbourne	31	47	109	64	153	828	17,000	19
Southborough	Nil	1	18	nil	45	23	15	5
Strood RD	8	32	74	29	162	1,983	22,987	35
Swanscombe	62	105	141	93	367	211	5,000	10
Tenterden area	21	64	151	34	235	704	3,500	238
Tonbridge UD	9	27	101	17	232	142	1,200	11
Tonbridge RD	11	45	30	14	157	673	3,400	95
Tunbridge Wells	15	31	36	13	113	186	660	6
Whitstable	10	35	118	84	735	232	700	2
Total	1,608	2,402	5,492	5,209	16,170	29,272	727,784	1,422

ON a clear day it is possible to see the prominent cliffs of Cap Gris Nez across the Channel waters. From 1939 until the Nazis were driven into Holland, the people of East Kent saw a powerful enemy that had always intended to invade. They saw the great guns of Calais and they could watch the intensive German activity as they mounted attack after attack — fighter bombers, high explosives, parachute mines, incendiaries, calibre shells and flying bombs.

The civilian casualty figures show that more than 1,608 people in Kent were killed and nearly 2,500 seriously injured. Of these, many were to die of their wounds in the months after the war. The casualty total is more than Surrey, Sussex and Essex added together and just behind Lancashire and Warwickshire.

For Civil Defence purposes Kent was split into two parts. The Kent boroughs of Beckenham, Bromley and Erith and the urban districts of Chislehurst and Sidcup, Crayford, Orpington and Penge formed part of the London Civil Defence Region. The casualty figures for this area were 1,366 killed, 3,670 seriously wounded and 6,376 slightly hurt.

The figures show that Dover, Canterbury and Ashford suffered the most fatalities while Dartford Rural was easily the most bombed borough in Kent — more than 5,000 high explosives and approximately 200,000 incendiary bombs. Not far behind was Sevenoaks Rural which, apart from high explosives and incendiaries, received 137 flying bombs. The highest single death toll from a single raid was 50 at Ashford in 1943.

Swale Rural District casualties are included in the figures for Faversham. Other Swale figures are divided between Faversham and Sittingbourne. It is important to stress that the casualty list above refers to all known civilian incidents. Military figures are not included.

Kent men who won the Victoria Cross

Twelve men — soldiers, sailors and airmen — who were born or who were living in Kent during the war won the Victoria Cross for conspicuous acts of bravery. Six of the medals were awarded posthumously. The VC is the world's most coveted medal for bravery. It is cast in bronze from the cannons captured at Sevastopol in the Crimea War.

John Pennington Harman
Lance Corporal, 4th Bn, The Queen's Own Royal West Kent Regiment.
Born: Beckenham 20.2.1914

On 8th/9th April, 1944 at Kohima, India Lance-Cpl Harman was commanding a section of a forward platoon where the enemy had established a machine gun post. He went forward by himself and threw a grenade, annihilating the enemy post.. Early next morning he charged a party of Japanese with fixed bayonet, shooting four and bayonetting one. He was fatally wounded.

Thomas William Gould
Petty Officer, Royal Navy
Born: Dover 28.12.1914

On 16th February, 1942, north of Crete the HM Submarine Thrasher, was attacked and later, after surfacing, two unexploded bombs were discovered in the gun casing. The First Lieutenant and Petty Officer Gould removed the first but the second was lying in a very confined space and Gould lremoved it bylying on his back with the bomb in his arms while the Lieutenant dragged him along by the shoulders. It was 40 minutes before they got the bomb clear and dropped it over the side.

Roderick Alastair Brook Learoyd
Flight Lieutenant (later Wing Commander) 49 Squadron RAF
Born: Folkestone 5.2.1913 (See also p. 84)

On 12th August, 1940 Flight Lieutenant Learoyd was one of the pilots briefed to bomb the Dortmund-Ems canal in Germany. He took his plane into the target at only 150 feet, in the full glare of the searchlights and flak barrage all round him. Although the aircraft was very badly damaged the bombs were dropped and he managed to get back to England, without further damage or injury to his crew.

Robert Anthony Maurice Palmer
Squadron Leader 109 Squadron RAF Volunteer Reserve
Born: Gillingham 7.7.1920

On 23rd December, 1944 over Cologne, Palmer was leading a formation of Lancaster bombers to attack the marshalling yards in daylight. He came under heavy anti-aircraft fire but managed to keep the badly damaged aircraft on a straight course and released his bombs. The Lancaster was last seen spiralling to earth in flames.

Thomas Frank Durrant
Sergeant Royal Corps Engineers and No 1 Commando
Born: Green Street Green, Orpington 17.10.1918

On 27th March, 1942 at St Nazaire, France Sergeant Durrant was in charge of a Lewis gun on HM Motor Launch 306 which came under heavy fire during the raid. Although he had no protection and was wounded in several places he continued firing until the launch was boarded and those who were still alive were taken prisoner. He died of his wounds the next day.

William Philip Sidney (later Viscount de L'Isle, Penshurst, Tonbridge)
T/Major 5th Bn Grenadier Guards
Born: Chelsea 23.5.1909

During the period 7th/8th February, 1944 at the Anzio beachhead Italy, Major Sidney led successful attacks against the enemy, engaging them with his tommy gun at point-blank range. Although injured and weak from loss of blood, he continued to encourage and inspire his men.

Augustus Charles Newman
Lt Colonel The Essex Regiment, attd No 2 Commando
Born: Chigwell, Essex 19.8.1904, lived and died at Sandwich 26.4.1972, buried at Barham.

On 27th March 1942 in the attack on St Nazaire, France, Newman was one of the first ashore, leading his men and directing operations quite regardless of his own safety. He and his men were eventually overwhelmed and taken prisoner.

Lionel Ernest Queripel
Captain The Royal Sussex Regiment attd 10th Parachute Bn
Born: 13.7.1920 Lived in Tunbridge Wells. (See also page 192)

On 19th September, 1944 at Arnhem, Holland Captain Queripel displayed the highest standard of gallantry during the whole of a period of nine hours of bitter and confused fighting. Under heavy fire he carried a wounded sergeant to the regimental aid post and was himself wounded in the face. Later, he insisted, despite the protests of his men in remaining behind to cover their withdrawal, armed only with his pistol and a few hand grenades. This was the last occasion on which he was seen.

Richard Been Stannard
Lieutenant (later Captain) Royal Naval Reserve
Born: Blyth, Northumberland 21.8.1902 died Sidney, Australia 22.7.1977 Lived in Bexleyheath

From 28th April to 2nd May, 1940 at Namsos, Norway HMS Arab survived 31 bombing attacks in five days. On one occasion during this period Lt Stannard and two of his crew tackled for two hours a fire on the jetty caused by a bomb igniting ammunition. Part of the jetty was saved, which proved invaluable at the subsequent evacuation. Later feats included the destruction of a Nazi bomber whose pilot, thinking that he had HMS Arab at hismercy ordered that she be steered into captivity.

Henry Eric Harden
Lance Corporal Royal Army Medical Corps attd 45 Royal Marine Commando
Born: Northfleet 23.2.1912 (See also page 192)

On 23rd January, 1945 at Brachterbeek, Holland, three Marines of the leading section of the Royal Commando Troop fell wounded. Lance Corporal Harden at once ran across the 100 yards of open ground, gave first aid and, although slightly wounded, formed a rescue party to remove the men, one by one, to safety. He was killed rescuing the third man.

John Henry Cound Brunt
T/Captain The Sherwood Foresters (Notts & Derbys Regt) attd 6th Bn The Lincolnshire Regiment
Born: Shropshire 6.12.1922 Lived at Paddock Wood.

On 9th December, 1944 near Faenza, Italy, the house round which Captain Brunt's platoon was dug in was destroyed by mortar fire. The captain moved to an alternative position and continued to hold the enemy although heavily outnumbered. Firing a Bren gun he killed 14 and then fired a Piat and 2m mortar left by the casualties. This aggressive defence enabled him to re-occupy his previous position and get his wounded away. Later he showed similar aggressive and inspiring leadership which caused the final withdrawal of the enemy.

Eugene Kingsmill Esmonde
Lieutenant Commander Royal Navy 825 Squadron Fleet Air Arm
Born: Yorkshire 1.3.1909. Memorial Woodlands Cemetery, Gillingham. (See also p. 116)

On 12th February, 1942 in the Straits of Dover, Lieutenant Commander Esmonde led his squadron of six Swordfish to the attack of two German battle cruisers and the cruiser Prinz Eugen. , entering the Straits under a strong escort. Although his plane sustained a direct hit he still continued the run-in towards his target until it burst into flames and he crashed into the sea. None of the six aircraft returned.

George Cross — the roll of honour

During World War II there were instances when it was not easy to decide whether a Victoria Cross or George Cross was the more appropriate award. The GC was intended to be an award for outstanding civilian bravery but as many people in the armed services were unavoidably engaged in non-military work they became eligible for recommendation for the GC equally with civilians. Here are the recipients of the award who lived in Kent.

Leonard Henry Harrison — Civil Armament Instructor, Air Ministry. Lived at Bexleyheath.

On 11th February 1940 he defused bombs aboard the steamship *Kildare*. This was the first action for which a George Cross was awarded.

Richard Frank Jolly — Commander, Royal Navy. Memorial St Peter's Churchyard, Boughton Monchelsea.

Commander Jolly was on the bridge of *HMS Mohawk* off the East Coast soon after the outbreak of war when she was attacked. Although severly wounded he commanded the ship to safety then collapsed and died.

Alfred Miles — Able Seaman, Royal Navy. On 1st December, 1940 while freeing another seaman caught by a wire aboard *HMS Saltash* in Grimsby, Miles lost his own hand.

Wilson Hodgson Charlton — A/Flight Lieutenant, later Squadron Leader, RAF.

Lived at Petts Wood. During September and October 1940 Charlton was employed on Special Duty for bomb disposal and dealt with over 200 unexploded bombs with undaunted and unfailing coolness.

Sidney George Rogerson — A/Staff Sergeant Royal Army Ordnance Corps.

Lived at Ramsgate. On 2nd January, 1946 amid explosions at an ammunition depot in Savernake Forest, Wiltshire he worked all through the night moving railway wagons to prevent more of them catching fire.

Anthony Henry Tollemache — Flying Officer (later Squadron Leader) 600 Squadron Auxiliary Air Force.

On 11th March 1940 at Manston, Kent his aircraft crash-landed and burst into flames. Tollemache was thrown clear but went back into the blazing aircraft to rescue a passenger. He suffered injuries which nearly cost him his life.

Eric Laurence Moxey — A/Squadron Leader RAF Volunteer Reserve. Memorial, Churchyard of St Peter & St Paul, Cudham.

On 27th August, 1940 while trying to defuse an unexploded bomb at Biggin Hill, it exploded and he was killed. He had already risked his life many times in rendering bombs safe.

Rt Hon Earl of Suffolk & Berkshire, Charles Henry George Howard Research Officer, Ministry of Supply.

On 12th May 1941 Lord Suffolk, while in charge of a Scientific Research Experimental Unit was killed by a seemingly harmless unexploded bomb being examined by him and his assistants on Erith Marshes.

John Herbert Babington — T/Sub-Lieutenant (later Lieutenant Commander) Royal Navy Volunteer Reserve.

Babington volunteered to deal with a very dangerous bomb in Chatham dockyard in the autumn of 1940. knowing that this type had recently killed an RAF officer trying to deal with it. Lowered into a 16ft pit he made three unsuccessful attempts to remove the fuse.

Daphne Joan Pearson — Corporal WAAF medical orderly, of Detling.

Knowing a bomb could be about to explode on a crashed aircraft, Pearson risked her own life by dragging a wounded airman from the cockpit to safety. She was awarded the EGM, later exchanged for the George Cross. See page 85.

Sources

In writing this book I have referred to a variety of pamphlets, newspaper articles, miscellaneous documents, war diaries, ARP reports and official files. I have also referred to a number of published and unpublished books including the following:

Front Line County, Andrew Rootes
Hellfire Corner, Roy Humphreys
Scrapbook of British Forces Newspapers (HMSO)
Kent Unconquered, H.R. Pratt Boorman
Military Airfields (Vol 9), Chris Ashworth
The World at War (Illustrated London News)
Men of the Battle of Britain, Kenneth Wynn
Fear Nothing (501 Squadron), David Watkins
Battle over Kent, A. Webb
Polish Wings in the West, Bohdan Arct
Undaunted (The story of Bromley), Graham Reeves
The Chatham Dockyard Story, Philip MacDougal
A History of Short Brothers of Rochester

Born Leader, Alan Cooper
Target Folkestone, Roy Humphreys
Most Secret War, R.V.Jones
Tumult in the Clouds, James Goodson
Battle of Britain, Richard Hough and Denis Richards
RAF Biggin Hill, Graham Wallace
Though the Streets Burn, Catherine Williamson
Operation Sealion, Peter Fleming
How We Lived Then, Norman Longmate
The Blitz (Volumes 1,2 and 3), After the Battle
The Secrets of D Day, Gilles Perrault
Roof Over Britain, HMSO
Chronicle of the Second World War, Longman
The Battle of Britain, Now and Then, After the Battle.
The following publications: Kent Messenger, Kentish Express, Kent and Sussex Courier, Isle of Thanet Gazette, East Kent Mercury, Folkestone Herald, Dover Express, Kentish Times, Dartford and Gravesend Reporter, Sevenoaks News, Kentish Gazette, The Register of the Victoria Cross and George Cross, This England.

INDEX

This list contains places and people but does not include the statistical information on pages 216 and 217.

About the author

Bob Ogley's family moved to a flat in Sevenoaks High Street in 1938 during the same week that Chamberlain returned from Munich "waving his piece of paper". Before papering the sitting room, the decorators wrote across the wall: "There nearly was a war" — a comment that was uncovered many years later!

Bob was born in July 1939 — too young to remember the excitement a year later when incendiary bombs destroyed an adjacent row of cottages, set the High Street on fire and forced the Ogley family to flee their home in the middle of the night, dodge the burning debris and seek refuge in a basement room in another part of the town.

He certainly remembers the doodlebugs and especially a walk with his mother in the countryside in the summer of 1944 when she pushed him violently into a ditch, pointed to the sky and said: "Here comes Hitler on his motorbike". He also remembers taking to the police station a "live" incendiary which his brother had carefully buried as a souvenir.

In later years Bob Ogley became editor of the *Sevenoaks Chronicle* where he took a great interest in local history. His life took a dramatic turn in 1987 when he wrote and published a book on the great storm which was entitled *In The Wake of the Hurricane*, after being rejected by a publisher. The book went into the national bestseller list and was followed by a national edition which reached number two in the country. Through these two books and regional editions which followed Bob, and his partner Fern Flynn, have raised more than £60,000 for environmental charities.

Since 1989, when he left the newspaper after 20 years as editor, Bob has written *Biggin On The Bump*, a history of the RAF fighter station which raised £15,000 in author's royalties for the RAF Benevolent Fund and *Doodlebugs and Rockets* — already in its second reprint. He has also published *Flying Bombs over England* — a lost manuscript which he discovered in the Public Record Office. This was written by the late novelist H.E.Bates and then embargoed by the censor under the "30-year rule".

Recently Bob has teamed up with Ian Currie and Mark Davison to research, write and publish the illustrated history of the weather in Kent, Sussex, Essex, Norfolk, Suffolk, Hampshire and the Isle of Wight, and Berkshire. His latest book is *Surrey at War*.

As well as his writing and work with Froglets Publications, Bob has discovered a supplementary career as a speaker to clubs and organisations.

Froglets Books in print

In The Wake of The Hurricane (National Edition)
ISBN 0 9513019 1 8..£8.95

Surrey in The Hurricane
ISBN 0 9513019 2 6..£7.50

London's Hurricane
(Paperback) ISBN 0 9513019 3 4................................£7.95
(Hardback) ISBN 0 9513019 8 5.................................£11.95

Eye on The Hurricane (Eastern Counties)
(Paperback) ISBN 0 9513019 6 9................................£7.95
(Hardback) ISBN 0 9513019 7 7.................................£11.95

Biggin On The Bump
(The most famous fighter station in the world).
ISBN 1 872337 05 8..£9.99
ISBN 1 872337 10 4..£16.99

The Sussex Weather Book
ISBN 1 872337 30 9..£10.99

The Kent Weather Book
ISBN   1 872337 35 X..£9.95

The Norfolk and Suffolk Weather Book
Paperback ISBN 1 872337 99 6...................................£9.95
Hardback ISBN 1 872337 98 8................................£16.95

The Hampshire and Isle of Wight Weather Book
ISBN 1 872337 20 1..£9.95

The Berkshire Weather Book
ISBN 1 872337 48 1..£9.95

Doodlebugs and Rockets (The Battle of the Flying Bombs)
(Hardback) ISBN 1 872337 22 8...............................£16.95
(Paperback) ISBN 1 872337 21 X.............................£10.99

Flying Bombs over England (by H.E.Bates)
(Hardback) ISBN 1 872337 04 X.............................£16.95

Westerham and Crockham Hill in the War
by Helen Long
ISBN 1 872337 40 6..£8.95

Underriver: Samuel Palmer's Golden Valley
by Griselda Barton and Michael Tong
ISBN 1 872337 45 7..£9.95

Tales of Old Tonbridge
by Frank Chapman
ISBN 1 872337 55 4...£8.95

Surrey at War by Bob Ogley
Hardback ISBN 1 872337 70 8...................................£16.99
Paperback ISBN 1 872337 65 1..................................£10.99

If you wish to order any of the books listed on this page, please contact Froglets Publications on 01959 562972.